EUROPEAN GLORY

Eyewitness accounts of United's 1968 and 1999 European Triumphs

Edited by
Barney Chilton
Martin Day, Phil Holt & Phil Williams

First published in 1999 by
Juma
44 Wellington Street,
Sheffield, S1 4HD
Tel: 0114 272 0915
Fax: 0114 278 6550
email: MLacey5816@aol.com

AN UNOFFICIAL PUBLICATION
INTENDED FOR ADULT READERSHIP

ISBN 1 872204 65 1

The views expressed in each chapter of EUROPEAN GLORY are those of the individual contributors, and don't necessarily represent the views of either the Editors or any of the other contributors. All writers submitted their work independently of each other, and each chapter should be viewed as a separate piece of work.

You can contact any of the authors featured in EUROPEAN GLORY at:
P.O.Box 384, London, WC1 N 3RJ

Cover photographs:
1999 - Paul Windridge, Jason Taylor, Mario Georgiou and Roger Brierley,
1968 - Red News.

Other photographs by: Kenneth M. Ramsay, Teresa McDonald, Jason Taylor, Lyndon Lomax, Roger Brierley, Alison Watt, Emma Dodd, Rob Ferrari, Mario Georgiou, Paul Windridge, Barney Chilton, Nigel Appleton and Jim Connolly. Ticket stubs: Peter Hargreaves and Barney Chilton. Programmes: Barney Chilton.

SUBSCRIBE TO RED NEWS, the first ever United fanzine - £15 for 10 issues!
Red News, P.O.Box 384, London, WC1 N 3RJ

Introduction

Photo: Kenneth Ramsay

Welcome to EUROPEAN GLORY, a book whose aim is to celebrate, pay tribute, and capture just some of the many emotions on the night of perhaps the greatest climax to a football match ever. That it happened on the 26th May 1999 in a European Cup Final, with our team Manchester United involved - the pinnacle of many of our United supporting lives - just makes it that much sweeter.

Those present will never forget those magical moments, where they were, where their seat was, who they were with, etc, and this book is dedicated to all those present, in spirit if not in body, in Barcelona that night. You may remember some of the contributors in EUROPEAN GLORY from our previous book on European travel with United, IF THE REDS SHOULD PLAY IN ROME OR MANDALAY. Consider this its older brother with a few new excellent writing 'faces'.

Wherever it be the season's successful culmination provided by perhaps one of the greatest football sides ever or destiny or both, the fate-filled finale in the Nou Camp was unbelievable. As genuine and dedicated Manchester United supporters we wanted to bring together various United fans so that they could capture what that night meant to each one of them. Any fear that there may be some repetition in the stories couldn't have been further from the truth. The 2-1 win over Barcelona may have been of equal joy to the massive travelling army lucky enough to be at the Nou Camp stadium, but to each one it meant something contrasting and amazing as you'll find out later in the book. It didn't mean more or less to each other, but the triumph gave forth to varied emotions and this book describes some remarkable tales. There were many scenes, exploits and sensations when the referee blew the whistle that night and I am delighted that EUROPEAN GLORY captures just some of the amazing experiences.

As with IF THE REDS there are many diverse people and backgrounds represented within these pages as contributors, and to all of them I would like to thank them for their time and effort (and again blame me for any mistakes and thanks to JC and TM for the delightful proofreading duties) as well as Martin Lacey the publisher, for all he has ever done. The whole point was not to censor and allow a free reign with each contributor so that they could tell their own personal and compelling story. There may be many you relate to, some you say 'that sounds like me' or others you disagree with but the point was to provide representation for at least some of the many different people, backgrounds and cultures that attend Old Trafford each game. Like taking a snap shot of a row of seats in the ground, the people within these pages are a random selection taken from the crowd, all sharing a cosmopolitan belief in a shared passion that is the remarkable and amazing, Manchester United. It's not meant to be a sociological or political work but a truthful representation of different people and what it meant to each one of them to win the European Cup. Each tale is amazing and emotion packed.

It's remarkable to think how far we've come in such a short space of time - regaining that most holiest of grails just eight years after being re-admitted back to Europe after a five year absence. It's been some amazing journey and with each year so - give or take just the odd season - it has just got better and better. I'd say winning the treble just about tops the lot! The craic following United has

remained at its unbelievable peak and the pleasure that Manchester United gives to so many people is again felt within these pages. As the saying goes 'there is nothing on earth like being a Red', and so with a three trophy haul in just under two weeks in May 1999 we sit proudly at a peak last sat on 31 years ago. There to stay hopefully.

We wanted to capture the emotions of that 1968 period as well for EUROPEAN GLORY as in United's future we always must remember the amazing past. But for two mighty managers we wouldn't be watching the glorious club that we currently do and the supporters' represented here, whether they have been a member of the Red Army for just a few years or for several generations all share the same lifetime dedication to the cause.

The fanzine movement at long last gave 'normal' supporters their opportunity to have their say, showing that not only were they as clued up with the goings on within football as the opportunists within the tabloid industry but unlike many within the latter they could actually string a decent sentence together. The articles enclosed may vary from tears to joy, from comedy to the sublime, from the absurd to down right disgusting but each is intelligently written.

I hope that the book entertains you as much as it did me whilst putting it together. May 26th 1999 meant something to everyone, and everything to someone, and the joys of European travel that are provided on a European away football trip were further re-affirmed. Hopefully there will be plenty more great days to come, and maybe even the odd additional astonishing and miracle making ending thrown in as well!

We'll all be looking back on that night and our place within it for years and years to come. Even now I can remember it all as it comes flooding back. Moments like that are few and far between in life, the outpouring of fervour shown on the terraces when that second goal went in is something I'll never forget, or want to. Reading each contributors build up to the remarkable finale and the mind is transferred back to the terraces within the Nou Camp, and that is all I wanted to achieve.

I hope you enjoy EUROPEAN GLORY and the memories provided from a selection of United fans who witnessed the unbelievable success and saw Manchester United reach the promised land once again. BC

CONTENTS

I. ACHIEVING BUSBY'S DREAM - '68 GLORY

ACHIEVING BUSBY'S DREAM - '68 GLORY

Manchester United 4 - Benfica 1 (a.e.t.)
European Cup Final
May 29th 1968, Wembley Stadium
Stepney, Brennan, Dunne, Crerand, Foulkes, Stiles, Best, Kidd, Charlton, Sadler, Aston.
Scorers: Charlton (2), Best and Kidd
Attendance: 100,000

YOU CAN STICK YOUR MALTESERS...
Howard Coomber

Howard was born in Manchester in 1955 and the first United match he attended was the 1964 European Cup Winners Cup Quarter-Final against Sporting Lisbon. He has not missed a European home tie since then, nor an away one (Wrexham excepted) since 1976.

As soon as Celtic won the 1967 European Cup final, every Red was absolutely convinced that it was to be ours in 1968. The attitude was almost as though we would win it by divine right and, as the campaign progressed, it seemed that it was so easy. Looking back with the detachment of time, it was, in reality, a struggle. Apart from the first round, we scraped through by one goal each time and there were moments when United got the benefit of a dodgy decision or two which could, if they had gone the other way, made all the difference.

The fact is that we should have won it in 1966. We had hammered Benfica 5-1 in Lisbon in the quarter-finals. Benfica had won all their previous 18 home European games, all but two by three goals or more yet United had demolished them only to inexplicably cock it up in the Semi-Final (without an injured George Best) by losing to Yugoslav no-hopers Partizan Belgrade 2-1 on aggregate, with a particularly disastrous display in the away leg.

When the draw for the first round of the 1967/68 competition was drawn, we were to play Floriana. At first, my schoolmates and I thought it was a toughy against Fiorentina until we heard they were not from Italy but Malta. It transpired that UEFA had little more knowledge of who it was than we did as they had messed up by putting the Maltese Cup-Winners Cup representatives in the Champions Cup draw and vice versa. It took a couple of days for them to decide not to re-draw both competitions and that we were to play the real champions of Malta, namely Hibernian.

The standard of Maltese football was then, as now, at the bottom end of European ratings but, in those days, the gulf between top and bottom was much wider than it is today. Hibernian were the equivalent of the likes of Yeovil Town but they were not without their characters. They were managed by a priest who wore his robes on the bench at matches and one of their players, Francis Mifsud, went missing for two days in London en route to Manchester and only just turned up in time to play - a Euro away performance which went some way to encouraging the European careers of the likes of Drunken Dave!

On paper, no-one would have been surprised if we had won 10-0 but, in one Albert Mizzi, they had a goalkeeper who was being sought by Arsenal and Atletico Madrid and who knew how to marshal a defence. The crowd at Old Trafford was around 48,000 which, in that season when we averaged over 57,000, seemed disappointingly poor to a naïve twelve year-old like me. The Stretford End invented songs about packets of Maltesers to relieve the boredom of such a one-sided match.

United had almost constant pressure but struggled to find the net against a team who could only hope to keep the score down. Two goals each from Denis Law and David Sadler gave us a comfortable, but not spectacular, 4-0 win.

I was, of course, too young to attend Euro aways and, in those days of poor TV coverage, had to be satisfied, for the second leg, with newspaper reports which concentrated on the huge United support in Malta and their disappointment at seeing United at well below their best. Tony Dunne and George Best both hit the post but United, with a long season ahead of them, were happy to play out a goalless draw, something of a moral victory in the eyes of Hibernian.

I have since visited the ground in Malta where the match was played and, although much of it has now been pulled down and the capacity considerably reduced since 1967, it has a colonial grandeur about it with a raised paved area in front of a clubhouse which resembles a cricket pavilion where, no doubt, club directors and dignitaries would have sat to watch the match. The matchball is on display in the Manchester United Supporters' Club in Malta, a club which I would recommend as a must to visit for any Red holidaying in Malta.

In the second round, we drew FK Sarajevo of Yugoslavia. Following United's demise at the hands of Partizan two years earlier, we should have been wary of this lot. They were not a well-known club but could, with more luck, have knocked us out. Sarajevo had no airport at the time and the team reached it by flying to Dubrovnik and taking a coach over bumpy mountain roads.

By all reports, the match was a bruising affair with Pat Crerand later being quoted as saying that Jack Crompton, the United trainer, had been on the pitch so often that half the crowd must have thought he was playing. The Yugoslav national captain, Musemic, thought he had scored in the first half when Alex Stepney stopped his shot after the ball had appeared to have crossed the line. In the circumstances, United were happy to hold on to another goalless draw.

After the dispute over the Musemic shot and the general bad-temper of the first match, the scene was set for a fiery evening at Old Trafford. United set out to try to destroy Sarajevo from the off with waves of attack orchestrated by Pat Crerand controlling the midfield. Johnny Aston scored early on after Sarajevo keeper Mustic made a superb flying save from George Best only to knock the ball into Aston's path.

United's onslaught continued into the second half with Kidd and Best, twice, hitting the post. Then, the tensions, which had been simmering beneath the surface since the first leg, boiled over. Mustic and Best had an altercation and Mustic appeared to complain that Best had hit him but the officials missed the incident. In revenge, Prljaca clobbered Best and was sent off amid Sarajevo protests about the injustice of the punishment for one offence but not the other.

To wind up the Yugoslavs up completely, Best then scored to make it 2-0 after a build-up which saw the ball go so close to the bye-line that Sarajevo claimed a goal-

would allow. He played for Gornik. So did Hubert Kostka, regarded as a challenger to Gordon Banks as the world's top goalkeeper. It was his penalty save in Kiev which had got them through the previous round.

Manchester's sizeable Polish community crossed the city from their Cheetham Hill clubhouse to turn out in force for the first leg, displaying a huge Polish flag in the United Road Paddock. This was Gornik's first match after the winter break and it is quite possible that this tipped the tie in United's favour. Another first-half onslaught from United hit a brick wall. At the other end, Lubanski failed to connect cleanly when in the clear, allowing Stepney to save an apparently simple chance.

The 1968 semi-final v. Real Madrid at Old Trafford

kick. I distinctly remember that the Sarajevo team, bar one player, walked off the pitch in protest and disappeared down the tunnel. It took about ten minutes for the referee, amongst others, to persuade them to finish the match. It was not unknown in those days for this type of protest to take place and, in the following season's Semi-Final in Milan, the United team appeared to be about to make a similar protest before Matt Busby went on to the pitch to persuade the players to continue.

As far as Sarajevo were concerned, they came back on to play like demons and quickly pulled a goal back. This was the first season of the away-goals rule and another one would have put us out. United held on but only just. So to the quarter-final. Gornik Zabrze of Poland were to be the opponents after the continental mid-winter break. This was a tough one. Celtic, the holders, had gone out at the first stage to Dynamo Kiev. Kiev, in turn had lost to Gornik. Wlodek Lubanski was the up-and-coming teenage world star, as near an equivalent to today's Ronaldo allowing for the lower profile of players in those days

On the hour, Crerand put Best through. In characteristic fashion, Georgie bamboozled the defence and Florenski, attempting a last-ditch tackle to stop him, put the ball into the corner of his own net. It was always Matt Busby's philosophy that a two goal lead was necessary when travelling to an away second leg, especially against a team of this calibre. Time was running out when Jimmy Ryan mis-hit a shot which fell to Brian Kidd . Ryan's mis-hit confused the defenders trying to block the shot and, when Kidd hit a slow, low shot as the ball reached him, the Poles were throwing themselves back the other way and the ball somehow evaded a maze of legs to creep in the corner past the unsighted Kostka. Busby had his two-goal lead.

British reports were unanimous that the second leg in Chorzow should not have been played. The pitch was covered in snow and the match played in a blizzard. Despite the weather, a 100,000 crowd turned out. In the circumstances, it was astonishing that United went through. Busby tried to get the game postponed but Italian referee

Concetto Lo Bello, who often seemed to be suspected, at least by the British press, of being corrupt, insisted the game went ahead. Mr. Lo Bello was further slated when he penalised Stepney, for nothing according to the press but for time-wasting to the non-xenophobic observer, when he rolled the ball out of the penalty area before kicking it clear. Lubanski scored from the free-kick.

So defensive were United's tactics that striker David Herd, just back from a year out with a broken leg, played deep enough to clear the ball off the line when Lepner thought he had scored. The press reports described United's tactics as deep defence interspersed with taking a breather with clearances to Best leaving him, flitting through the snowflakes, to get on with taking on the Gornik defence alone. Again, United had held on under intense late pressure.

The Semi-Final against Real Madrid happened to be on my thirteenth birthday. My parental present had been a new red-and-white scarf which I had gone out to buy during my dinner break from school. For weeks beforehand the Stretford End's favourite song had been "We'll get rid of Real Madrid, hallelujah." When Real came on the pitch, the traditional exchange of pennants between captains saw the Spaniards produce a flowery number which prompted the crowd to adopt the then hit record "San Francisco" by Scott McKenzie - you know the one: "When you're going to San Francisco, be sure to wear some flowers in your hair."

A few hundred Real fans, dotted about in the Cantilever stand around where H and J stands are now, made themselves known with a mass of white handkerchiefs and a collection of magnificent banners. I went round there after the match to try to get a banner as a souvenir but was unsuccessful. In response, the Stretford End chanted "Hands Off Gibraltar" and "Franco out, Busby in," Franco being the Fascist dictator still ruling Spain at that time. It was nothing personal or political against Franco when British Prime Minister Harold Wilson had visited Old Trafford for a match earlier in the season it had been "Wilson out, Busby in."

Real Madrid were no longer the outstanding team they had been when they had won the European Cup for its first five years between 1956 and 1960. Only one player, the now ageing winger Gento, survived from that team but they had still won the competition for the sixth time two years earlier when they had beaten Partizan Belgrade in the final.

Our hearts were in our mouths when Real had the ball in the net early on but the linesman, belatedly it seemed, signalled for an infringement. United played well with Johnny Aston causing them problems down the left. Crerand hit the post and Best scored with an excellent volley before half-time. We could not break through again and, although a one goal lead was a precarious margin to defend before a 130,000 crowd at the Bernabeu, there was confidence that our forwards had attacked well enough to suggest we could score again in Madrid.

By the time of the second leg, the League season had finished. United had lost three of the four games remaining following the home leg against Real and had thus conceded the Championship to, of all clubs, Manchester City.

The first half in Madrid was a disaster. Amancio, the star Real striker of the era, had missed the first leg through suspension but he made up for it now. He set up

Pirri for the first goal. Then Pirri put Gento through for the second when Shay Brennan should have intercepted the pass. A mis-hit clearance by Zoco from a Tony Dunne cross went into his own net which at least was a Real error to make up for Brennan's but Amancio made it 3-1 showing his famous skills with an individual goal.

At half-time, it was Busby's job to pick the Reds up to try to save the tie. It is well-documented that he did so by pointing out that they were only one down on aggregate and telling the team to forget his pre-match instructions to play a containing game and, instead, go out and enjoy themselves by playing attacking football. Sadler moved up front and got the breakthrough when he got amongst the Real defenders to head home a Crerand cross.

As this was the first, experimental, year of the away goals rule, that rule only applied in the early rounds so United were now on course for a third, deciding, game scheduled for neutral Lisbon. Bill Foulkes, famously ignoring the bench's screaming at him to get back in defence, ran forward at a throw-in disrupting the Real defence when two players went to pick him up. It gave Best the space to get to the bye-line and cross for Foulkes to side-foot home on the volley.

That was it. The papers next day were full of how Foulkes had survived Munich ten years earlier, how Bobby Charlton collapsed in tears on the pitch at the final whistle and how Nobby Stiles had been hit on the head by a bottle and didn't care because United were in the final.

I listened to that Madrid game on the radio with my father. It wasn't live on TV and anyone who has seen footage from the game will know that coverage in those days was so appalling that the highlights, shown late at night, did not include a clear picture of the winning goal as the sole camera failed to pick up Foulkes' shot. The film shows Best about to cross the ball followed by an indistinguishable picture, possibly of a spectator's back, and then the ball in the net.

If the Madrid game has been well-documented, the story of the final has received saturation coverage so I will not go into too much detail here. Benfica, like Real, were a famous club past their peak. It was Benfica who had been the first team other than Real to win the European Cup in 1961 and had confirmed their new supremacy by beating Real themselves in the 1962 final before losing the 1963 final (at Wembley) to AC Milan.

Apart from Eusebio, then at his peak, they had an ageing team whose European victories had rather belied their week-by-week domestic form. At Wembley with the crowd and, unlike today, virtually the whole nation behind them to the point of euphoria and with the psychological advantage of that 5-1 win in Lisbon two years before, United were expected to win comfortably.

It was believed also, correctly as it turned out, that the balance of European club football domination was in the process of moving from the Latin countries to northern Europe. After eleven years of European champions from southern Europe, Celtic had broken through and United were to be next. In the following eleven years, the European Cup was to be won only once by a Latin team.

The atmosphere was one of a wall of noise for United but the team struggled to break through as Benfica made it difficult for them. Stiles and Eusebio had one of their several epic man-to man battles with Nobby succeeding, one way or another, most of the time but Eusebio deadly dangerous when he did get the better of his man. Lo Bello officiated again and allowed Stiles to get away with some dodgy tackles and then only had a word with him when Eusebio feigned injury to get some sympathy from the ref.

A rare header from Charlton in the second half broke the deadlock and that looked to be enough. Sadler, who had supplied the cross for the goal, missed a sitter which would have tied it up. Against the run of play, Torres, the giant centre-forward headed down for Jaime Graca to unexpectedly equalise 10 minutes from time. Having escaped from apparent defeat, Benfica had their tails in the air and Stepney saved the Reds with, not one as is legend but two, world-class saves from Eusebio in the dying minutes.

Having believed they had won, United were dejected at having nearly lost, as well as exhausted. As in Madrid, Busby had to pick them up by telling them to keep attacking. Nobby Stiles reckoned he was encouraged when he looked at the Benfica team and surmised they looked even more knackered than he was.

It was over in no time when Stepney's long kick was headed on by Kidd to Best, who took it wide of 'keeper Henrique, went past him and slotted the ball into the net. Within five minutes, Kidd himself, on his nineteenth birthday, had two attempts to head home, succeeding the second time before Charlton made it 4-1 from an acute angle.

It only remained for Bobby to collect the cup before handing it straight to Matt, for Nobby to do another Wembley jig and the press to reminisce about Munich, making much of the point that relatives of those who had died had attended the final at United's invitation. Ten years of agony were over.

DREAMS OF EUROPE - MAN AND BOY
Peter Hargreaves

Peter is an old fart who has been watching Manchester United since 1954. He is in that period of his life known as the 'middle age crisis' and he would suggest to anybody not yet there to avoid it at all costs. He is married to Cathy, a Welsh lass, who has, to his great astonishment, become a Red fanatic too. They have no children, though they do have three cats who are the same thing. The youngest is Eric named after Cathy's favourite footballer, Eric Catona. Peter's dad, with whom he has been going to Old Trafford all his life, is his best mate and his mum has totally supported them, as they have supported the Reds. In his time watching his beloved Reds there have been many high points and a few low ones; the article you may be about to read describes the two highest points in his time as a spectator and thus of his life.

This story actually begins on the evening of Wednesday the 6th of February 1957. My dad had got a ticket for the night's match but had not been able to get one for me; or at least that's what he told me. In reality he had decided that the crowd was going to be so large that it wouldn't be safe for me. This match, remember, was being played at Maine Road and although we lived only fifty yards from the main entrance, it was a ground not as 'familiar' to us as Old Trafford; as such he was reluctant to let me go. We had our 'own' place at Old Trafford, on the popular side near the back. There the crush barriers had a middle rail and I could sit on the top, with my feet on the middle one and my dad would stand behind me to stop me from being pushed off. We stood (I sat!) there for about five years, until I was 'grown up'! Anyway over tea, that night, he promised that he would give me a full account of the match as soon as he got in; but, to be honest, I was really disappointed that I couldn't go.

During tea, when he managed to get my attention (I was in a serious 'sulk'!), he told me that he wasn't so sure that our young lads would be capable of overhauling these Spanish champions after their brilliant 5-3 win in Bilbao. So even dad wasn't sure that we were going to do it and that was unusual for him. I think in retrospect that he, too, was upset because he knew how much I wanted to go and he was trying to lessen the blow by suggesting that I wouldn't be missing much - how wrong he was if that was the case! Anyway at about 7.00 o'clock off he went, wearing 'our' red and white scarf (I 'retired' our scarf on the way home from Rotterdam and it is now framed for posterity) and he did not look too confident.

By this time, of course, the floodlights were on and our house was lit up as if it were daytime. I really couldn't settle and all my mum's efforts to engage me in conversation came to nought. At 7.30 I heard the roar and that was it! I went out into the backyard and locked myself in the 'lav'! I sat there for the whole game, listening, every sense withdrawn into the one - my hearing.

When you live next door to a football ground you become accustomed to the noise of the crowd, attuned to such an extent that you can 'see' exactly what is happening by sound alone. Every nuance of the crowd noise tells you whether they are defending, attacking, whether it a near-miss or a bad miss! And, of course, when it's a GOAL! So it was that I knew the score and at the final whistle there came a roar so loud that it shook our house!

So it was all over and I 'knew' that we had won 3-0 (or 6-5 on aggregate). I ran straight through the house pausing only for a second to tell my mum that we'd won (I think she thought I sneaked over the back wall and gone in at three-quarter time, but I hadn't). I ran straight to the front door and stood there in silence as all the supporters walked past. It was strange because, where only minutes earlier there had been absolute pandemonium, there was now a weird calm. Later in life I too would know this feeling of total and absolute tiredness, having been completely drained of adrenaline. One thing that happened that night which took me completely by surprise was that a man, a complete stranger, stopped and without saying anything just gave me sixpence and 'ruffled' my hair. Now sixpence was a lot of money to me at that time and he just gave it to me, just like that, never said a word, wonderful. I guess he just wanted to share the moment of celebration with someone and as I was the chosen one, the sixpence gift was all that he could think of.

Then my dad came round the corner and I ran the twenty or so yards to meet him. I was full of it and he never said a word! We got in and he sat down and never spoke. You know it took me ages to realise that he'd lost his voice. I mean he'd shouted so much that his vocal chords had packed in. It has happened once since, but more of that occasion later. So in fact, by the 'letter of the law' he didn't keep his promise for he wasn't able to tell me what had happened! But strangely his silence said more than any words could ever have done. The knowledge of what had happened, of what he'd gone through to bring about how he was, brought it into complete focus. If I hadn't been before, at that moment I became a totally committed Red.

My story moves on exactly twelve months to the day, when an event occurred which changed my life for ever. From that day forwards I felt sadness almost every day. As I grew up it eased just a little, but only a little. Maturity told me that only one thing could ever begin to ease the hurt, to bring some small relief from the pain that I had inside me and that 'thing' was to WIN the European Cup.

Ten years pass and I go from boy to man. I leave school, I start work. I begin to shave and do those things that 'men do'! With work comes a little bit of money and facility, facility amongst other things to follow United abroad. My first game was to Madrid and I made a mess of it to be honest. Showing off with the lads I got drunk and that, on top of the flu, made me feel very bad. The match, indeed the whole occasion, remains a blur to this day and that is a source of great disappointment to me. But we WON; at half-time I wouldn't have given much for our chances, but we scraped through.

Almost immediately we'd got to get tickets for the Final from somewhere. The time period from that night in Madrid to the night in Wembley was only two weeks! At that time neither dad nor myself had our season tickets so, like the vast majority of the others, it was panic time to make sure that we'd got enough (programme) tokens for the tickets. There are still some programmes in my collection missing their token (ie with the corner of a page cut off), but I just couldn't think of replacing them.

Dad and I queued all night and I remember Wilf McGuinness talking to us early doors, as we queued. He was full of it, like a little lad, marvellous. We got our tickets (they cost ten bob - fifty pence!) and I can say with absolute honesty that nothing, no amount of money, could have tempted me to part with that ticket.

Then dad and I got a big, but very pleasant surprise. Mum came home from work (she worked in the city centre) and she'd been up to London Road station and booked for us to go on the train to Wembley. But not only were we going on the train but we were having a meal both ways! Unbelievable, fantastic. Now all the lads had to do was to win the game. Easy, easy!

I worked on the morning of the match and met my dad at London Road. The journey down was quite uneventful and we spent the time reading the papers and talking about the match. It is my recollection that not one person suggested, even by implication, that we were going to lose. Don't forget that Benfica were a team boasting nearly all international players, including one of the all-time greats, Eusebio, and we knew by now that the King (the true 'King', Denis - for the youngsters!) wasn't going to play. Now that might seem a strange thing to say because Denis had missed the Madrid match and the last few games of the season, but somehow we all hoped and prayed that he would make some sort of miraculous recovery. I didn't know at the time that Denis had already gone into hospital for a knee operation.

So we arrived at Wembley and it was strange because there was a lot of blue and white around; indeed I bought a blue and white scarf for just that one match (I still have it amongst my treasured possessions, even though it's only been to ONE game!). It was really eerie to see blue and white whilst at the same time thinking 'Red'. When we got into the ground we found that we were standing at the players entrance end, above and to the left of the tunnel; a pretty good view, with no posts in the way (so initial prayers answered).

Of the game itself, I remember only isolated incidents. Bobby's goal, a header and most unusual; my dad losing his glasses as we went mad, then finding them on the floor and being able to bend them back into some sort of shape (second prayer answered). Then all I wanted was the final whistle. It had been a poor match and all I wanted was to get it over with and see us get the cup. Then disaster struck, they scored. But there were no doubts that we'd still win. I can remember this as clear as if it happened only yesterday, I had NO doubt that we would win; neither, I'm sure, did anyone else. Having said that when Eusebio went through with only Alex to beat I saw my whole life flash before my eyes. What a save and what a reaction from Eusebio. How many people noticed that he applauded Alex for the save - what a great man! Extra time. Alex hoofed one upfield, an 'ale-house ball', it went to George...and it WAS all over. We played like men possessed from that moment on. Benfica could have brought all their supporters on to the pitch but we'd still have won.

The final whistle and I cried, oh God how I cried. I cried like I had never done before or since. I cannot describe how I felt, I just can't, it's impossible. But I know that what I saw before me wasn't the cup, or Bobby, or Matt, or my dad, or anyone there. What I saw were the boys of '58 and I KNOW as sure as I'm writing this right now that they WERE there with us.

My dad couldn't speak, not one sound. In fact he went for nearly a week before his voice returned properly. He's a very tough man is my dad and he doesn't show much emotion, but that night I know that, quietly, he cried too, though he's never admitted it and we've never talked about it.

As we walked around the ground and back to the station a Benfica supporter came up to me and gave me a small medal, a commemorative medal from Lisbon. It was a wonderful gesture of sportsmanship, from a representative of a very gracious people. I still have it and it is one of my most important and treasured mementoes.

We got on the train and they had run out of beer. Can you believe that? Not a bottle to be had. I can't remember what we had to drink, but we did have something. The pain in my throat was terrible, how my dad felt I really couldn't imagine.

We arrived back at London Road in the small hours of the morning and my mum had come to meet us. She'd got one of my aunts to drive her in and they were both waiting at the barrier. It was quite right too. Because, although over all those years she'd rarely been with us to the match, mum was as much a part of Manchester United as we were. Before we went home, to a cup of nectar (my mum's tea), I bought EVERY morning newspaper at the station; I still have them all.

It was a day the like of which I will not, I don't think, experience again. For me it was the healing of a wound that had been hurting inside me for a very long time; for very nearly half of my life. I know that I'm not alone in feeling that.

Thirty-one years later...

On the way home to my mum's from the airport early on Thursday morning we found a newspaper shop which was open and so, with a cup of my mum's elixir, I sat down at the dining room table to read all the morning papers and to make sure that I really wasn't dreaming!

I had decided to stay over at my mum and dad's on the Tuesday night as this meant I would not disturb Cathy, my wife, early doors Wednesday and would have an extra hour in bed (was I glad for that extra hour by four o'clock Thursday morning!). It was a bit like old times when I got to my mum's as she had sorted my old bedroom out and I had clean jim-jams, toothbrush and the like (my mum is still convinced that I am only ten years old!) - but it was nice! Like a ten year-old I was wide awake when my dad brought me a cuppa at 05:00 on Wednesday morning; I had been asleep, but only for a couple of hours I think.

When we got to the airport it was already pretty busy. Checking-in was completed with the usual efficiency. For those of you who have never been on a European away trip with the Club let me tell you they are very well organised. Barry Moorhouse (who runs the whole thing) is the unsung HERO of Manchester United. You rarely hear this lad's name mentioned and yet without him and his staff we would never get to see these away matches. Then we were through into the international departure lounge and the butterflies in my stomach taxied for take-off!

By noon we were in sunny Spain - and sunny it was. It was sweltering and I knew immediately that my decision to leave my vest off was justified. As an aside let me tell you that on the Thursday before the Cup Final I had been forced to take to my bed with a really bad dose of the flu. I really felt awful and Cathy said (in complete innocence - honest!) "If you don't feel like going to Wembley, don't worry I'll go with your dad"!!! 'Don't feel like going?' - I'd have crawled on my hands and knees to get there - and to Barcelona, if necessary.

We decided to go straight to the ground so that (much later on) we would be able to find our way back to the coach; the area around the ground was absolutely heaving, even at lunch time. The police (already out in force) would not let us go near the stadium, informing us that we could not approach until 17:00. This did not bother us unduly as I had already been able to buy my programmes. So it was really time to go and find a nice (quiet!) bar for something to eat and a few drinks.

We started off down the main road and it was just wall to wall Reds, singing and drinking, so we decided to turn off the main road and investigate the hinterland. This proved to be a good decision for within ten minutes (and after a few turns) we found a quiet bar with tables outside and we were sorted. We stayed there for most of the afternoon and it was whilst we were there that I 'discovered' why I really wanted Manchester United to win the match. Daft as it seems dad and myself were (fairly) relaxed about things as we had seen the Reds win the European Cup before. Now that might seem crass but I think that it did make a difference. Some young lads joined us and I was absolutely intrigued to hear what one lad had to say.

It was obvious that his dad was about my age and that he had been in attendance at Wembley on that never to be forgotten night in May 1968. This young lad had been on the receiving end of his dad's "You've never seen us win

the 'BIG ONE'" taunts for years, and it really did mean a lot to him. I had not really thought of it from that perspective until that moment and suddenly it dawned on me how much it was going to mean to all these young (and, perhaps, some not so young) people to be able to look me and my dad (and that lad's dad) in the eye and say "We've seen it TOO"!. It was a good moment for me and in a way gave an even greater emphasis to the events which were going to unfold before us.

After a couple of hours in the tremendously enjoyable company of these lads, another group of lads arrived and they, quite obviously, had had a fair amount to drink. Let me say straight away that they were no problem, but they were intent on having a right good sing. Fair play, that was their right and good luck to them, but it was just a bit too noisy for us and so we took our leave.

On the way down to the bar we had walked along the main road and discovered that they had benches along the 'central reservation' (a nicely shaded and grassed area). So it was to these seats that we repaired for the last couple of hours. It was great to sit there and watch the world go by. All the Reds in great voice and so full of expectation. "Blimey", I thought, "I hope these people aren't sad at the end of the night". And a few Germans, quieter than our lads (as you'd expect perhaps), but looking pretty confident nevertheless. Anyway we sat in the sun, had a short nap, read and then re-read the match programme, talked with a few Reds we knew and generally enjoyed the most splendid and relaxing few hours.

At about 18:00 we decided to make our move to the ground; I'm glad we decided to go that early. When we had been at the ground at lunch time we had noticed the police setting up a 'road block' - a filter if you will, and we just knew that this was going to cause a problem as the kick-off approached and the tension grew. When we got to the checkpoint it was already quite busy and people were finding it difficult to funnel from the edges into the middle of the road. Anyway we got through without mishap and then went through the two sets of turnstiles and into the ground. To be fair to the stewards at the outer gate they were apologetic for having to trouble us to empty our (big) bags and one said "I'm really sorry, sir" to my dad; that was nice.

I had never been to the Nou Camp before and it was with great anticipation and no little excitement that we actually entered the ground itself. It is impressive, of that there is no doubt, but somehow it seemed smaller than I had imagined. Maybe that was because we were on the lower tier, or maybe I had built it up in my mind, but whatever it is a great stadium and I was not disappointed.

First job after taking a large breath was to have the obligatory photographs taken. Because I had had a bad experience of camera 'theft' at another European away game, many years before, I had taken a disposable camera with me and, as always, I was praying that the pictures would come out. Dad and myself in the Nou Camp - that really is a photograph to treasure for ever.

By this time we were both hungry. The next bit should embarrass me, but it doesn't! I am your typical, lazy Brit and have a complete inability to master foreign languages. The beer we identified without a problem. Food however was a different story. 'Jam and cheese' rolls it said. "Jam and cheese, eh? Well that's different - we'll have two of those". Later it occurred to me that Jose is pronounced Hose! So you now know what was in the butties!

I don't intend to deal with the match in great detail. Other, that is, than to say that I thought that it was one of the greatest demonstrations of grit and determination that I have ever seen by any Manchester United team; possibly the greatest.

As the clock ticked over to show 45 I felt dad reach down and move his bag onto his seat. "Blimey" I thought, "he knows we've lost". Nothing was said, but I hang on my dad's every move and that really did shake me. Then we scored. Then we scored again. It was crazy. If I never see another game of football in my life then that two minute period will do for me. In 1979 we went through similar sorts of emotions only for it all to end up pear shaped. This time it was absolute delirium. I can't describe how it felt for I am not clever enough with words. It just felt very, very good.

We watched the presentation, saw the boys come over to our end and then made our move. We didn't want to go but felt it was the right thing to do. We can't rush these days, particularly when we've been on the go all day. As it happens when we got to the first turnstiles the police refused to let us out; no reason was given. As we were moving back into the seats there was a shout from somewhere and they all ran off and we were sorted and on our way.

When we got out of the stadium I was just staggered how many Reds there were outside. My heart ached for them. They had been so close and yet so far - it must have been a heartbreaker and I couldn't have done it. There were many, many thousands of them and they were dancing and singing and all was well with the world. No trouble at all.

As people got back to the coach the atmosphere was quite surreal. People were physically dazed and almost incapable of cohesive thought and speech. What we had witnessed was beyond anybody's comprehension and it showed. All I heard was "Unbelievable" and so it was.

As we sat on the coach just outside the airport it became 00:01 Thursday and I thus achieved the grand old age of FIFTY! It was the birthday present to end all birthday presents. On my fiftieth birthday I was sat next to my dad, on a coach in Barcelona, Spain, having just seen Manchester United complete the TREBLE. I ask you - how much better can it get?

We had to endure a three hour delay at the airport but everybody was really patient. They had so many people to get home and I thought that, all things considered, they did a wonderful job. The journey home was pretty quiet but oh, so satisfying. Then there was my mum and she had a cuppa waiting for us.

Thirty-one years? It seemed like thirty-one minutes!

EUROPEAN CHAMPIONS
Ray Evans

Ray 'Cat' Evans has been going for as long as the steam train that carried him to the '68 final. He has followed United for over 35 years and in that time has seen many highs and lows. He is one of a fortunate number to have seen both European Cup Final triumphs. What follows are his brief observations from both finals, 31 years

apart. Some things it appears never change, the massive support Utd enjoy and the way in which we party!

29th May 1968. The day has arrived at long last. My first major final watching the Reds since my first game in 1964. The previous night had been spent working an 8 hour night shift (yes, I did actually work in those days!). Finishing at 6am on the day of the game there was just enough time to go home, have a quick shower and change in time to catch the early morning train from Flint to London.

With no sleep the previous day I had hoped for a quiet journey down to the smoke, and my hopes were raised when arriving at the station there was just - at a rough estimation - well, just me. Where were all the local Reds who for weeks had planned to make the journey? Armchair supporters I thought to myself.

Anyway there I was, on Flint Station all clad in denim jeans and jacket (some may say I still wear them, eh!), my red and white scarf (wow) and my E for B and Georgie Best badge. My ticket from the local supporters' club by way of the programme token scheme, safely tucked away in the top pocket.

My first setback came with the arrival of the train. Then the order of the day were corridor laden compartment trains which to my dismay looked absolutely packed full of the North West Coast Reds. If you travelled by train in those days from Flint to London it had all the attraction of a Tuesday night mini-bus trip to Norwich nowadays - a 4 and-a-half hour journey. I managed to squeeze in amongst fellow Reds but alas no sleep was forthcoming (20 hours now without). At last the train chugged into London Euston (well done Casey Jones was the cry down the train). Euston is already well populated with Reds, banners and flags are well in view with the then fashion of scarves on wrists and even a few rattles in evidence.

After having my train ticket checked (about £3 return) it's a mass exodus down into the underground. First call was the West End and, surprise, surprise, into the West End to taste the local ale. I can now admit I was underage (yeah, yeah, I was 17 years old at one time before anyone says anything....) so with that in mind and the big occasion drawing nearer it was a pretty sedate afternoon (about 8 pints, I think). Time moved quickly with thoughts of the match and it was soon 6pm, time had arrived to move on to what was to be - I didn't know at the time - the first of many visits to Wembley.

Believe it or not, arriving at Wembley Stadium in those days after taking in the Wembley Way was like a different world! There were thousands of happy Reds and only pockets of Benfica supporters. 30 years ago, Old Trafford wasn't the Mecca it is nowadays, so I have to admit Wembley Stadium then was a different class. After a half hour queue I was finally inside the stadium, standing in the opposite end to the tunnel (they were the proper days for atmosphere). Time moves on quickly and then to a tremendous roar (must be 80,000 Reds inside), the team appears. I have never been in an atmosphere like this, even a 63,000 full-house at Old Trafford has nothing on this.

The game fluctuates, United scoring first with Benfica equalising and looking the stronger towards the end of normal time (have I any fingernails left!). Into extra-time we go, with the noise level of the crowd getting unbelievably louder and louder. Georgie scores, Kiddo scores another, this on his 19th birthday, and, as the song goes, Bobby obliged by making it four. Benfica are beaten, United are Champions of Europe. Tears are flowing both on and off the pitch, it is incredibly emotional.

Bobby lifts the Cup to a deafening noise of "Busby, Busby", "Champions of Europe", and as the song of the sixties at that time went - to slightly altered lyrics: "Ob-la di, Ob-la-da, Man United, European Champions" to the well known song by the legendary group, 'The Marmalade'. 'Hi ho, Hi ho, Trafalgar Square we go' was the departing Wembley theme tune from the ecstatic Reds, so I knew where I was heading (not that I had anywhere planned as the first train home was not until 7.30am the following morning), If you think there are some crazy Reds nowadays, Trafalgar Square that night and morning was a sight to behold with thousands of Reds plied with whisky, vodka, anything alcoholic, soaked to the skin with regular dips in the fountains. I manage a few complimentary drinks of vodka, as I look on in amazement (remember that I'm only a 17 year old youngster).

Once more the time passes by amazingly fast, so along comes the time to head back to Euston with sleep and food in that order urgently required. I grab a quick snack just off the station and now sleep becomes a major priority. Euston is fairly quiet with most Reds probably in their hotels or, more likely, still in Trafalgar Square.

I board the train which thankfully is straight through to Flint and although it's still 4 hours I have no intentions of being awake ("is it a fortnight since I last slept?") during any part of the journey. There is just a scattering of Reds on this train so I booked my alarm call with a couple of the lads for Chester Station (otherwise I'll end up in Holyhead). Everything almost goes to plan as I wake up in Crewe Station (three hours kip is better than none). I must still be running on adrenaline as I reach Flint Station early afternoon and I seemed to be wide awake and buzzing again. A quick bus ride to Holywell and with the public houses in those days closing at 3pm it is just time for a few quick celebratory ones in the Black Horse.

All in all, a fantastic two days with very little sleep, moderate food intake, but adequate beer consumption, but most importantly, we came home with the European Cup. Now where have I heard those words spoken recently?

So, on Tuesday 25th May 1999, the time has arrived for my second (yes, I repeat second!), European Cup Final. Getting somewhat of a veteran for these occasions it's an early start once again, being picked up by mini-bus, on route to Stansted for the journey to Carcassone in the South of France. It's a pretty sedate journey, perhaps everyone is a bit apprehensive of what was to be the biggest occasion in their football lives to-date. We arrived in good time for the flight and thought, for a change, we'd indulge in a few beverages before boarding in case we suffered any air sickness...

The journey soon passes and we arrive in what us British would call tropical 70 degrees weather (phew). We had booked the car rental beforehand so it's all systems go for the 200 miles journey to Barcelona. Perhaps we speak too soon about the weather as halfway there it pisses down - that's more what we're used to. There is nothing more annoying than actually spotting the location you are looking for but not being able to get to it. This was one of those occasions - we could see our hotel from the motorway but to cut a long story short what should have been an equally short half-a-mile took nearly two hours. Enough said about one way systems (were we back in Derby town centre?).

The hotel is reached at 10pm, so it's bags down, check in and arrange what's left of the night. Most of the 14 lads arrange to go into central Barcelona but I opt for the hotel bar (must be feeling my age). I am actually in bed before 1.30am, very, very early for us European away travellers I must say. I am awoken at 8am with what is no surprise, Alan Gosling arriving home. So out of bed for me and straight into his for Mr.Gosling. He murmurs something along the lines of 'wake me up before 1pm' before he crashes out.

So the big day has arrived. The first drink is in the Port Olympica down by the waterfront and in an impressive scene. Most of us have now met up, including the late arrivals from Salou who have had BR type train difficulties. A quick visit to the famous La Ramblas for the last few alcoholic beverages before the trip by metro to the Nou Camp - coming off of the metro more sweaty and black than after a shift down the coal-mines.

The Nou Camp now beckons us with thousands of ticketless Reds all lined along the scenic route to the ground. Big rumours are rife that there are forgeries circulating for about £10 which have been laser-copied en masse, which is not a bad gamble for the unlucky people without one. After queuing for ten minutes we finally get into the stadium. This is my third visit to the Nou Camp and it is still an impressive sight. The atmosphere is electric in the ground with the Reds really outnumbering the Germans by at least two to one.

We all know what unfolded during the match, but to go from agony to ecstacy in such a short space of time must be the understatement of the century.

So we are European Champions for the second time (getting a bit monotonous for me!), and to cap it all we've made the whole of Britain a very happy place by completing the treble. I THINK NOT (ha, ha, Scousers, Cockneys, Geordies and all you other ABUs). The only drawback about the incredible celebrations after the game was that we all got split up due to metro difficulties. Getting a taxi to put it mildly was nearly impossible due to the numbers of people around and it was a very long night with myself, Chally and Dai eventually walking the 5 or 6 miles to La Ramblas, albeit visiting nearly every bar on route, all of which were packed with Reds. La Ramblas is eventually reached at 7am with thousands present either singing or sleeping. It's Trafalgar Square all over again and a great night and morning had by all with plenty of stories told on the way back to Carcassone.We arrive back in Britain on Thursday at 8pm - knackered, hungry and, believe it or not, ready for an ale stop. So I arrive home at 1.30am, ready for work (I think not) at 8am.

What can you say about this historic season but that it can't get any better than this - can it? Whatever, I'm off now ready for a few weeks gloating at our Scouse compatriots...

P.S. There is a rumour that we're entering the boat race next year...

MY EUROPEAN DREAM COMES TRUE
Paul Windridge

On the night of the 20th April 1966 I stood high up on the Stretford End right side and suffered with the rest as United went crashing out of the European Cup at the hands of Partizan Belgrade. I'll never forget the faces of the crowd as we left that night, to say that we were all utterly destroyed would be an understatement of monumental proportions.

That year I had managed to save enough money to be able to afford the trip to the Final had we got there, but by the time we did the following year all that money was gone and so were my hopes of getting to Wembley. By that time I was a poor art student in Nottingham and after all avenues of ticket exploration had been closed I resolved to watch the match on the old black and white TV in my digs. By this time I had learnt the meaning of irony.

My good friend Ray who was at the same college had managed to procure a ticket from his uncle in Manchester who as I remember was something to do with United at the time. But it was the only one that arrived in the envelope even though he had asked for a couple more. I was gutted, United were playing 100 miles down the road in the biggest game ever and I couldn't find the wherewithal to get there.

In hindsight I should have just gone. I should have done what I always did and stood at the side of the road and hitched down to London and taken a chance but the news was that tickets were being sold for exorbitant prices and there would be no way I could afford one.

It turned out that had I taken the initiative I would have got one for a fiver. I had just a fiver that would have to last me for over a week, but I'd gladly have spent it for the opportunity to have been at that game and sod the food.

I learned from that experience the hard way and have never made the same mistake again and have actively encouraged others to follow their dream and take a chance. You have to be there to give yourself a chance.

On the night of the Final my landlady and landlord had gone out to the pub as per usual which left me and the only other person who lived there to watch the game in their front room. My viewing companion that night was one Lionel Rudkin from Sleaford Lincolnshire whose only claim to fame was the spottiest back you have ever seen in your life. So spotty in fact that it was one big exploding crater, in truth his face wasn't much better. What a fate, but I had no choice, it was well before the days of pub TV's and big screens.

As the match developed I became more and more agitated, I've never been a good watcher on TV and by the time extra time came around I was a nervous wreck and could barely keep still. But after a couple of minutes I was leaping all over the furniture and screaming my head off while Lionel Rudkin sat there completely bemused trying to encourage me to "calm down" while he cracked open another crater.

Oh how I longed to be at Wembley.

At the end of the game and the end of the transmission everything returned to normal in the small terraced house in Nottingham, well it did for Rudkin anyway. But I couldn't stand being in the same room as him no longer and wandered out of the house.

The streets were completely empty and so were the roads. I was in a daze, a strange contradictory state of half euphoria and half depression. I didn't want to be where I was, I wanted to be pissed in the Trafalgar Square fountain along with the rest of the Red Army. But there I was, wandering the streets of Nottingham completely alone - a walking paradox. I have no idea where I went or how long I walked but by the time I returned the house was in darkness.

In the years since that night I have longed for the time when I could experience the European Cup Final first hand - to actually be there and to rid myself of the ghosts of '68. On May 26th 1999 in Barcelona my dream finally came true.

The 1968 semi-final v. Real Madrid at Old Trafford

2. FROM SIR MATT TO SIR ALEX –

THE LONG AND WINDING ROAD

FROM SIR MATT TO SIR ALEX - THE LONG AND WINDING ROAD

Howard Coomber

The morning after Manchester United won the 1968 European Cup, manager Matt Busby was quoted thus: "When I awaken, I am sure I shall shake myself and wonder if it was not all a dream. Then I will realise that the dream had a wonderful end and it is, indeed, the end of a long and wonderful dream. But then I have to tell myself that it is not the end. It must only be a part of the beginning."

No doubt, he said these words in the euphoria of victory, probably after a glass or three of celebratory champagne but, when he had found time to consider these sentiments, he must have known that the European Cup victory was, indeed, the end of his glory years at Old Trafford. He must have known that he was planning to announce his own retirement and that the team he had put together to win the European Cup would soon have to break up without replacements of similar ability being available.

Three of the winning team, Shay Brennan, Bill Foulkes and Bobby Charlton were over thirty. Another three, Tony Dunne, Pat Crerand and Denis Law were approaching thirty and it would have been clear to Busby that some of the youngsters coming through, such as Francis Burns, John Fitzpatrick, Johnny Aston, Alan Gowling and Jimmy Ryan, were not of the calibre to bring about a repeat of the European Cup success.

What not even Busby could have known was that even those youngsters who did show great promise at that time, namely David Sadler and Brian Kidd, would fail to consistently reproduce their early promise and that Denis Law would never again be free of injury for a sustained period and would only occasionally sparkle as he had done before. Even Nobby Stiles would be deemed no longer up to the required standard when Busby himself, having temporarily returned to the manager's chair in the second half of the 1970/71 season, transferred him to second division Middlesbrough. Busby could also not have foreseen that the coming years would see the club spiral to unimaginable depths of crisis and scandal.

A young fan at the time, I had been brought up with a successful United and had no inkling that there could be any other kind so it came as a shock when the 1968/69 season saw us struggle in the League and when, in January 1969, the great man announced he was to retire from football management at the end of the season.

Busby had called Manchester United an institution, meaning that its' standing was more than that of a mere football club but as an organisation people looked up to for certain standards of sportsmanship, ambition, entertainment and even propriety. Under Busby, United had gone from, in 1945, a near-bankrupt club with a bomb-damaged ground to the most famous sports club in the world.

The nurturing of young talent, the entertaining football, the loss of a youthful and exciting team at Munich in 1958 and the re-creation of the formula after the disaster made up an irresistible story. Add to it the happy ending of the 1968 success and we have the plot of a top fantasy film or novel, yet it was true and it was almost entirely Busby's work. This cocktail of triumph and tragedy had created an aura around Matt Busby and Manchester United - a mystique, which not only drew in fans from far and wide but which generated a mass loyalty unrivalled in the world of sport.

At the time of Busby's retirement, journalist Tom Tyrell wrote a book aimed at young fans called "Manchester United - The Religion." He named his second book "The Red Devils- Disciples." He had taken these titles from graffiti he had seen daubed in the vicinity of Old Trafford. They summed up the zeal of the United supporters, whose way of life had been consumed by a mission to win the European Cup, not for the glory of it, but to properly honour those who had died at Munich in pursuit of that trophy. To qualify for the European Cup, we had first to win the League Championship. So, the Championship took on an importance with a dimension above and beyond its usual significance and became the only domestic trophy that mattered to Manchester United.

Over the three decades since the 1968 European Cup victory, the fans have continued to keep the faith even through terrible times for the club, recording the top average attendance in all but three of the 31 seasons between the two United European Cup successes. Relegation, lower division opposition, turmoil, scandal, attempts to ban us from away grounds, atrocious football, none of these have deterred us. When Dave Sexton was sacked as manager in 1981, a factor in his dismissal was the directors' concern that attendances had dropped to a home average of a mere 45,000. Eat your hearts out, Geordies.

I once had a girlfriend who questioned my sanity when I travelled to Birkenhead twice in a week for a meaningless friendly against Tranmere Rovers. The match on the Monday night was postponed because of the weather and was re-arranged for the Wednesday, hence the two trips. It had meant two afternoons off work and two nights out of bed for a match of no consequence in which the team had barely tried and United had lost 2-0. My response to the young lady's criticism was, given that players and officials of Manchester United had died on a freezing airport runway, the least I can do is get off my arse and get on a train. That is the philosophy by which I have lived my life.

Over the years, it has been a matter of pride for penniless fans to ensure they got to games by hitching the length of the country even when they knew a poor performance and defeat was the likely outcome. For matches just over the Pennines at Halifax and Huddersfield, I recall large numbers meeting at midnight on Friday night in central Manchester and walking over the hills to the game.

Given that Manchester United players and officials had died on a freezing airport runway, the least they could do was get off their arses and get on their feet.

Anyway, to rejoin the main plot, the media circus spent the first few months of 1969 speculating on Busby's replacement. Those paying proper attention had been given a strong hint in the United announcement of Busby's retirement which had stated that the replacement was to be a younger man. Bobby Charlton was a favourite as was Wilf McGuinness and it was McGuinness who got the job, albeit with the title coach rather than manager, from 1 June 1969. Busby stayed on as General Manager, taken as a euphemism for mentor to the new coach.

McGuinness was a contemporary of Charlton and had been in the team in the 1950s. He had broken his leg in 1959 and, despite several attempted comebacks over the years, he had come to accept he would never fully recover and age was now catching up with him. He had not wasted those years, however, and had gained valuable experience coaching with both United and England youths.

In the meantime, the League season had been, by United standards, a failure. At Christmas, we had been in the bottom half of the table and the final position was eleventh. We had lost the World Club Championship match, 2-1 over two legs, in dubious circumstances to Estudiantes of Argentina. The saving grace was the defence of the European Cup where United defied League form to come within a referee's dodgy decision or two of a place in the final.

The first round was a doddle against Waterford of Ireland. We won 3-1 away and 7-1 at home with Denis Law creating a European Cup record by scoring seven goals, including two hat-tricks, over the two legs. Anderlecht of Belgium were next and, despite a 3-0 home win in the first leg, United struggled in Brussels. An early Carlo Sartori goal proved invaluable as Anderlecht stormed back to win 3-1 on the night. The quarter-finals against Rapid Vienna saw a comfortable home win, again 3-0, defended in a goalless away leg which United could well have won by the same score had chances been taken.

So, to the infamous Semi-Final against AC Milan. The first leg in Milan was shown, in black and white, on large screens set up on the Old Trafford pitch. Initially, United had made this all-ticket but the late kick-off, dictated by Italian custom as well as the time difference, deterred many and just 23,000 turned up. United held out until 15 minutes from the end when Milan's Sormani, appeared to knock the ball on with his hand before scoring. Milan scored again before the end from an equally dodgy free-kick. Fitzpatrick was then sent off for kicking Milan's Hamrim, at which the United team threatened to walk off in protest but were persuaded to stay on the field by Busby.

At Old Trafford, Milan came to defend their two-goal lead in depth. It was well into the second-half before we were able to break through when Charlton received a pass from George Best and pulled one back. Milan rocked under the subsequent pressure and Law scored an equaliser. Or at least we thought he had. All I remember, as a lad of 14 in the Stretford End, was that my view was blocked by everyone in front of me leaping up to celebrate a goal and, when the furore had died enough for me to see the pitch, I saw a Milan defender playing the ball when I expected to see the players lining up for the kick-off. Film of the match shows the ball cleared by a defender from behind the line but the referee and linesman were unsighted. So the goal was not given. It was to be our last European Cup-tie for a quarter of a century.

To be fair to Milan, it is doubtful whether the result would have stood had United won. Their goalkeeper had been felled by a missile thrown from the Stretford End at the start of the second half and had taken five minutes or so to recover. Milan would have appealed on the grounds that this affected the result and future cases show they would, most likely, have been successful. To illustrate the point, in the 1971/2 European Cup, an Internazionale player was felled by a missile against Borussia Moenchengladbach. Moenchengladbach had gone on to win 7-1 but Inter's appeal led to a rematch at a neutral venue and a 0-0 draw. Inter went on to the final that year. The UEFA representative on whose advice that rematch was ordered happened to be one Sir Matt Busby.

Back in 1969, Milan comfortably beat Ajax 4-1 in the Madrid final. Ajax had not yet become the power they were to be in the early 1970s and had had the luck of the draw, avoiding United and Milan to play Spartak Trnava (who? I hear you cry - exactly) in the Semi-Final. Had we got past Milan, we would surely have been European Champions for the second year in a row.

With Wilf McGuinness now in charge of the team, 1969/70 season started badly when United lost three of the first four games. McGuinness dropped Brennan and Foulkes who were clearly past their best but the sensation was that he also dropped Law and Charlton. It made no difference. The fifth match was a 3-0 defeat at Everton. The form of George Best helped us to eighth position by the end of the season. That was considered unacceptable to all connected to United and was tantamount to a crisis. How naïve we were. It had been a decent year compared to what was in store for us, both on and off the pitch.

McGuinness was promoted to team manager by the start of 1970/71 but things got worse. By Christmas, United were in the bottom five and had lost 4-1 at home to City. McGuinness's chance for success lay in the League Cup, where United had been drawn to play Aston Villa, then in the Third Division, in the Semi-Finals. I remember the mood on the train to Villa on the night of the second leg was one of despondency in the expectation that we were in for the final humiliation even though we were up against a Third Division side. Confidence had stooped that low. We lost 3-2 on aggregate.

McGuinness was sacked between Christmas and New Year and Busby took over temporarily to the end of the season. Performances improved and we rose to finish eighth, again. The demise under McGuinness has been subject to much speculation. Maybe there was a conflict between McGuinness having been friends and teammates with older players such as Brennan, Foulkes and, especially Charlton, and his now being their boss. Maybe they resented this, maybe he could not cope with supervising his erstwhile pals. Another factor involved in McGuinness's dismissal was that, as United struggled, City had been winning trophies, which had taken everyone, not least City's own fans, by surprise. McGuinness's record was not that bad. He had taken us to the 1970 F.A.Cup Semi-Final when we had lost by the only goal in three games against Leeds and to two League Cup Semi-

Finals; in 1969/70,when we had unluckily lost 4-3 on aggregate to City and in 1970/71, the year of the aforementioned Villa debacle.

It appears that the club, in particular Busby, had wanted to keep the managerial appointments within the United family and create a dynasty, similar to that we have seen over the years at Liverpool, where the tricks of the trade are passed on from one generation of club insiders to the next. Given more time, it might have worked. Certainly, the fans had remained loyal to McGuinness and had continued to believe he, with Busby's help and advice, would soon get the club back to Championship-winning ways.

The half-season of Busby's temporary tenure was awash with the usual media speculation as to who the next manager would be, including a strong rumour that a verbal agreement had been made with Jock Stein but it was Frank O'Farrell who was appointed. He was given a five-year contract, which was a reckless deal for the directors to agree to before they had seen the man work at close hand.

O'Farrell had had some success at Leicester, getting them to the 1969 F.A.Cup Final and, later back into the First division. His reign at United began, at the start of 1971/2 season, with a false dawn. He gained praise from the press for his supposed tactical genius in moving winger Willie Morgan and gangly striker Alan Gowling into midfield as United swept to the top of the table. We went to West Ham on New Year's Day with a five-point lead - it was only two points for a win in those days. United were back on the top, all was well after all and we would surely challenge for the European Cup again in 1973.

But at Upton Park, we lost 3-0 and won only two more matches before the end of the season, finishing eighth yet again. After that match at West Ham, George Best went missing for a week. It was not the first time and the reasons have been well-publicised - drinking and womanising. When Best returned, he was fined and ordered to move to live into his former lodgings. At the end of the season, he announced his retirement from football and then moved again to stay with Pat Crerand in time to start the following (1972/3) season.

O'Farrell had signed Martin Buchan from Aberdeen in February 1972 but United were bottom of the table by October. Ted MacDougall, who had scored prolifically in the third division for Bournemouth, was brought in for a record £200,000 but could not re-produce any scoring rate worth speaking of at Old Trafford. Much-travelled Welsh striker Wyn Davies arrived from City with similar results. Just before Christmas, United lost a relegation clash at Crystal Palace by 5-0 and O'Farrell was out. After some legal wrangling, he picked up his three-and-a- half years of contracted, but unearned, wages. What a mess!

Again, speculation as to what had gone on was rife. It is said O'Farrell could not communicate with his players, that some of the players, notably Best, Law and Charlton, had fallen out with each other and that Busby and/or the directors took over certain matters, especially dealing with Best, which O'Farrell felt were his responsibility.

Certainly, the Best scenario had taken over at the expense of everything else and had greatly upset the fans. We had worshipped him and felt he was letting us, and the club, down at our time of greatest need. I had a friend who had attended every match, home or away, for

years but it got to the point where he felt so let down that he would boycott a game if Best was playing. He would travel to the match and, if Best was in the team, would head for home without entering the ground. It was not possible to ascertain, before travelling, if Best would play because he was so unreliable at this time that no-one knew whether he could even fulfil a promise to turn up.

Within days of the Selhurst Park hammering, Best had retired again. Tommy Docherty had resigned as manager of Scotland and was in the manager's chair at Old Trafford. Apart from a spell at Chelsea in the 1960s, when he had had a flamboyant team, his career had been roller-coaster. He had taken a series of clubs, in a series of divisions, to relegation although he had usually brought them back up again. He also had a reputation for unguarded outspokenness, not at all in the United/Busby tradition.

He launched into the transfer market bringing in the aged George Graham (past it) from Arsenal, Alex Forsyth from Partick Thistle, Lou Macari (instant hero) from Celtic and Jim Holton from Shrewsbury, all Scotsmen. With the Scots already at Old Trafford (Buchan, Law and Morgan), he turned United into "Scotland United," which became a favourite chant. It became fashionable for Reds to wear tartan as well as red-and-white and the Scotland team which lost the Scottish F.A. centenary match 5-1 to England at Hampden Park included five United players (it was a surprise that it was only five) although the blame for the Scots' defeat lay with City's Willie Donachie, who scored an own goal!

Docherty kept United up that year with a team that improved just enough to claw together the necessary points. In the summer, Charlton announced his retirement and Law was given a free transfer to City. It is typical of the stories surrounding Docherty that he had allegedly promised Law a job for life, in one capacity or another, at Old Trafford and then sold him without telling him. Law has been quoted as saying that he knew nothing of his transfer until he saw the newspapers.

After the relegation scare, we thought the worse was over but it was not. Best came out of retirement and played 12 games before being dropped and retiring again, on this occasion for the last time as a United player. Inexplicably, the team played defensively. This was the season when goalkeeper Alex Stepney was joint-top scorer (with two penalties) at one stage. Whilst Holton and Buchan were effective in the middle of the defence, their very different styles complementing each other superbly, the full-backs, Forsyth and Stewart Houston, another Scottish Docherty signing, were better going forward than they were when defending. In midfield we had Mick Martin, whose abilities were concisely summed up by the regular advice from the crowd to "Hit him with your shovel, Mick." I recall the game at Derby that season when we set out playing for a draw, conceded two early goals and had not the players or tactics to attack to try to recover the deficit.

I still believed, contrary to all the evidence, that we would beat the drop until a vital relegation clash at Birmingham in early March. We lost an awful, scrappy match 1-0 and, at that point, I became resigned to relegation. At the end of March we went to Chelsea expecting another debacle. Without warning, Docherty changed tactics and United astounded us with 3-1 win in an attacking performance not seen since O'Farrell's false dawn of 1971.

Playing like that, United won four and drew two of the next six games before losing at Everton on a vital Tuesday night. That sent us into the famous last game at home to City. As is well-known, Law reluctantly scored the only goal for City near the end. For the record, that did not send us down. The other results - Birmingham and Southampton both winning - went against us and we would still have been relegated had we won. As for the much-publicised pitch invasion before the final whistle, my recollection is that it was not an attempt to annul the result but a spur-of-the-moment emotional reaction. We had spent six years stumbling from one unthinkable set-back to another but had never dreamed United could possibly be relegated. The pitch invasion was a manifestation of mass shock.

The 1974/5 season in Division Two was great fun. We would go to all these little towns and football clubs and take them over. At places like York, Orient, Oxford and Cardiff, we outnumbered the home fans by two or three to one. Playing attacking football as we had in those last few games of the previous season, we topped the table virtually from the start and waltzed through the season in style. The year in Division Two helped the new United attacking style to develop against less strong opposition. Docherty became a hero, especially amongst the tartan-clad young fans and we had every confidence we could challenge for the First division title next year.

For the second season in a row, we started as we had left off, producing superb attacking football and were in with a shout of the League and F.A. Cup double by the time we met Derby in the F.A. Cup Semi-Final. It was a great day at Hillsborough with a 2-0 win before a euphoric, overwhelmingly United crowd, but it was to be the last good performance of the season. The F.A. Cup Final seemed to be on the players' minds and a 3-0 defeat at Ipswich finished our title hopes.

The Cup Final was a shambles. Second Division Southampton were tipped by the so-called experts on the grounds of experience but our football, as played throughout the season would surely see us win comfortably. The "experts" had said much the same about our chances against Derby in the Semi but we had blown them away. On the day, we didn't play. Gordon Hill, the two-goal hero against Derby was so poor he was substituted. A late, possibly offside, goal saw us lose 1-0. Southampton had never won anything before and have won nothing since. Manchester City won the League Cup that season - the last thing they have won too - but we had, at any rate, qualified for Europe for the first time since the Milan defeat in 1969.

In the UEFA Cup, we beat Ajax 2-1 on aggregate - a prestigious win as they had been European Champions for three years in a row in 1971-3 - before going out 3-1 on aggregate to a strong and experienced Juventus team. It was neither a surprise nor a disgrace to lose to Juventus and all Reds remained upbeat about our chances of further success. In the League, the flowing football continued but we were not in the challenging position we had been the previous year. Our success came in the F.A. Cup, where we appeared to be on a mission to make up for the disappointment of losing the previous year's final. Another Hillsborough Semi-Final, this time against Leeds, saw the Leeds fans corralled into one corner of what was supposed to be their own end and United win more easily

than the 2-1 scoreline suggests.

The Final was against Liverpool, who had won the League and had a European Cup Final against Borussia Moenchengladbach to come. We outfought Liverpool, who perhaps had the European game on their minds, to beat them 2-1 and thus deprive them of their treble as, four days later, they became the second English club to win the European Cup. This was a foretaste of things to come. United were to spend the next 15 years or so as mere spoilers to Liverpool's dominance.

We would regularly beat them when we played them, chase them without coming close to catching them in the League and deprive them of the odd trophy by beating them in a league game or cup-tie but we were merely a thorn in their side as they swept title after title before them. At Anfield recently (season 1998/9), Liverpool fans were ecstatic at having taken points from us as we chased the Championship and young United fans expressed bemused contempt that the Scousers should celebrate so vehemently when the point gained by Liverpool was of no use to them. It's not so long ago that the boot was on the other foot and we were leaping with delight at having done just the same to Liverpool.

The day after that 1977 Cup Final win, the Sunday newspapers carried a story that Docherty was having an affair with Mary Brown, wife of the club physiotherapist, Laurie Brown. Docherty then told the board he was leaving his wife to live with Mrs. Brown. Apparently, the couple, unknown to anyone at the club, least of all Laurie, had been having an affair for about three years. Initially, the club reaction was that it was a private matter and would not effect Docherty's position. As I recall, the reaction of fans was that the club should be loyal to the wronged party, Laurie Brown. The outcome was that Docherty was sacked, the club citing financial irregularities including allegations that Docherty had accepted personal payment for having allowed George Best to guest for a non-league club and had touted Cup Final tickets.

Docherty was a contradiction personified. For more than a year after his arrival, the team played just about the most appalling football that ever emanated from a United team. Overnight, he turned that round and, for three years, we played football as entertaining and attractive as United have ever played. The young fans loved him, in particular for the delightful football but also because his public image was one of a jack-the-lad, a loveable rogue.

The Docherty stories are legend. It is said he would ensure Laurie had plenty of work to attend to at the club - even sending the physiotherapist on football scouting missions(!) - so he and Mary could get together. It is reported that hardly any of his players have a good word to say for him. His method of dealing with players' advertising deals brought bitter criticism and it is alleged he would criticise and insult players in front of each other, in public and to supporters, and that he would try to force players out of the club by devious means.

As well as the Denis Law transfer, there was the Willie Morgan transfer. Morgan returned from the 1974 World Cup with an eye problem so, according to Morgan, Docherty told him to rest at home instead of joining the team on a pre-season tour. The press, quoting Docherty as their source, reported that Morgan had refused to go on the tour. The outcome was that Morgan was transferred to Burnley, whence he had originally come.

Later, **Morgan** told a Granada TV interviewer that Docherty was "about the worst manager there has ever been." Docherty sued Morgan and Granada for libel. When the case eventually came to court, Morgan had a number of United players ready to give evidence but Docherty admitted, under cross-examination, that he had lied in the witness box so Morgan's witnesses were not needed. Docherty ended up having to pay over £50,000 in costs and wound up on a criminal charge of perjury but was acquitted. What a shambles!

The new manager was Dave Sexton, who had previously managed Chelsea and Queen's Park Rangers. He was known as a master tactician and players were to comment that they saw more blackboards than football fields during his reign. He was known to be friendly with Busby, not least as both were staunch Roman Catholics. I suppose we should be grateful that, after years of crises and scandal, Sexton's reign was relatively uneventful.

Sexton's first season (1977/78) saw him sign Joe Jordan and Gordon McQueen, both from Leeds. They were top players and became great favourites of the fans. After Docherty's attacking policy though, Sexton's negative tactics failed to excite the crowds and we appeared to be going nowhere. In his second season, we somehow reached the F.A. Cup Final, beating Liverpool in a Semi-Final replay thus preventing them from winning the double.

I had not bothered to save my tokens through the season as I adjudged we were crap and they would not be needed so I had to scramble around for Semi-Final tickets and got into the Final by the traditional method, that of bribing the gateman. We lost the Final 3-2 to Arsenal. It was the one where we got two extremely late goals to come back from two down only to be caught out still celebrating when we should have been defending, thus allowing an even later Arsenal winner.

The next season, 1979/80, we chased Liverpool for the title without ever looking like catching them and finally conceded defeat, losing 2-0 at Leeds in our last game. Liverpool clinched it that day and still had a game to play. It was the only time we finished as high as second in the twenty years between 1968 and 1988 but Sexton could not repeat it the next year.

Sexton's football was unattractive to watch and can be summed up by the last seven games of 1980/81, all of which we won 1-0. Until I checked this, I thought it was only five monotonous 1-0 wins so I must have fallen asleep at the other two. Sexton was dismissed at the end of the season. He must be the only manager sacked after seven consecutive wins but the fans were bored with the style of football and the directors were concerned that attendances had fallen.

So to his replacement, Big Ron Atkinson, whom United prised away from West Bromwich Albion. Atkinson quickly brought in Bryan Robson and Remi Moses from his former club. I have always thought Atkinson would make a good international manager as, wherever he has been, he has put together a decent team finding the players he wants and fitting them around each other as if in a jigsaw. As an international manager, he would be able to do this without the restrictions of availability and cost. He put a team together alright, but he paid scant attention at Old Trafford to the overall set-up. He appeared to take lit-

tle interest in the junior teams, preferring to buy from outside rather than finding and nurturing youngsters.

Nevertheless, he improved the first team. The F.A. Cup was won in 1983 at the end of his second season and again in 1985. We chased Liverpool for the 1983/4 title but faded near the end, finishing fourth. We also reached the Semi-Final of the European Cup-Winners Cup losing 3-2 on aggregate to a late goal away to Juventus, having played the home leg with a number of regulars missing through injury. That was the campaign when we famously beat Barcelona 3-0 at home in the Quarter-Finals to overhaul a 2-0 first-leg defeat.

Everton had re-emerged under Howard Kendall to challenge Liverpool and the 1985 F.A. Cup win prevented the Blue Scousers from winning a League and F.A. Cup double, not to mention a treble as Everton also won the European Cup-Winners Cup that year.

In 1985/86, United began the season in outstanding style, winning the first ten games but failed to maintain the early pace. A series of injuries, not least to Robson, allowed Liverpool to peg back the lead and pull clear in the closing weeks of the season. We finished fourth. We seemed to have developed the habit of finishing fourth in a two-horse race! After our flying start, it was hugely disappointing to fail, once again, to take the title. Atkinson had had five full seasons and had chased, but not caught, Liverpool. Everton had managed to do so, at least for part of this period.

It was during the Atkinson years that the club directors went off at a tangent which gave all the wrong signals to the fans, leaving them despairing as to whether those running the club had a clue what Manchester United was supposed to be about. In 1984, United bought the ailing Warrington Vikings basketball club, re-named it Manchester United and turned it, for a modest investment in football terms, into the top basketball team in the country.

As far as the fans were concerned, this raised huge questions over the directors' commitment to the success of Manchester United Football Club. The supporters were fanatically committed to the ambition of winning the League Championship but the directors had gone off on a diversion. The fans perceived that Chairman Martin Edwards and his pals had not the bottle for the main event so they were choosing, instead, to amuse themselves at some sideshow.

Two examples of the incidents that annoyed us spring to mind. One first game of the season, the programme did not contain the football fixtures - surely a must in the first programme of the season - but included the basketball fixture list instead. And, in a later United Review, Martin Edwards was pictured shaking hands with his Spanish counterpart at a Real Madrid versus Manchester United European match - at basketball, would you believe. So, while we were banned from European football as a result of the 1985 Heysel disaster, here was the chairman gallivanting off on what was seen as a beano to Real Madrid on a mission of irrelevance. United bailed out of basketball in 1988 when they had failed, over four years or so, to make it pay.

Four months into the 1987/8 season, Atkinson was replaced by Alex Ferguson. The official version is that the Ferguson deal was sorted out quickly in a few days before the official announcement was made. This surely cannot be true. I, an ordinary fan, had heard from two sources, one emanating from within United's coaching staff and one from Frank Stapleton, then with United, via his old friends at Arsenal, that Ferguson was to be manager several months before it came about. If I knew, then surely the players knew and so must have Atkinson. In the early part of 1986/7 season, Atkinson appeared to be going through the motions. The performances were lacklustre to say the least.

Ferguson had been amazingly successful at Aberdeen, where he had created a young team to break the Old Firm monopoly and had even won the European Cup-Winners Cup. He had his own ideas and, at United, soon began to purge players he deemed indisciplined, in particular some with a reputation for drinking. Initially, he made himself unpopular with the fans as this failed to improve results and those involved (for example Norman Whiteside and Paul McGrath) were revered players. Supporters in the know believed that Robson was being allowed to get away with that for which others were being pushed out. When Ferguson dropped Mark Hughes from the team, it was the last straw for a considerable proportion of the crowd who staged an open protest, many sitting on the terraces.

In Ferguson's second season, United again chased Liverpool and finished a poor second. By New Year, 1990, Ferguson had failed to transform the team. United fans and, indeed the club as a whole had, by now, got themselves into a cycle often seen in football. It goes: new manager comes in, fails to achieve what is required, gets sacked, new manager comes in, fails to achieve, gets sacked, new manager and so on ad infinitum. The manager gets the blame for matters often outside his control or which have persisted since his predecessors' periods of office but, nevertheless, everyone feels much better when he is dismissed. The mindset is that the scapegoat is gone, it was all his fault so it can't be ours and now we can start afresh. In most cases, though, a managerial dismissal does not solve the problems in the club and the cycle just starts all over yet again. Manchester City have expanded this syndrome over the years so that, in their case, it does not only apply to managers but to chairmen as well!

So, whatever the official version may be, only an idiot does not believe Ferguson was in danger of dismissal when United, unexpectedly, won a third round F.A. Cup tie at Nottingham Forest in January, 1990. The football began to improve and we went on to win the Cup. That gave Ferguson the breathing space to come to terms with the club he had taken on and to make the changes he wanted. The following season, we were the first English club allowed to compete in Europe following Heysel and won the European Cup-Winners-Cup beating Barcelona 2-1 in the Rotterdam Final.

The following season, we were neck-and-neck with Leeds in the race for the title and always seemed to have the edge. In a remarkable coincidence, we drew them away in both Cups - the draws were even made the same day - and beat them both times but as the season came to its climax we hit injury problems. Gary Pallister continued to play with a back injury as we had no adequate replacement and, when we lost to an already relegated West Ham three games from the end of the season, I knew the chance had gone again. We lost at Liverpool to hand the title to a Cantona-inspired Leeds. Along with relegation in 1974, that was my most devastating moment following United.

At Barcelona airport, the day after winning the 1999 European Cup (and this new trophy known in the media as the Unique Treble), I was discussing that 1991/2 season with fellow long-term Red, Steve from Romford. He agreed with me that, having dreamed of the Championship all those years and having lived in hope against hope, time and again, of trying to prevent Liverpool's points' leads disappearing over the horizon, we had finally got ourselves into prime position to clinch it and we had then gone and blown it. It had seemed then that it was just destined never to be.

Of course, the resilience and determination of Alex Ferguson proved us wrong and thank God for him.

This time, the team is young enough for it, indeed, to be "a part of the beginning."

3. EUROPEAN SONGS

EUROPEAN SONGS

THE OLD TRAFFORD CLASSICS THAT CELEBRATED THE TRIUMPHS

FROM THE TERRACES OF THE STRETFORD END TO THE STADIUM OF LIGHT...

Thanks to Howard for many of the words, and to the many songsters who came up with these great words to songs that never should be forgotten...

"Some speak of Man City and Bury as well, Of Oldham Athletic I've often heard tell, But the team to remember, The team to recall, Is Manchester United, The best team of all...We went down to Wembley one fine day in May, With a host of supporters so loyal and gay, And when it was over and when it was done, We defeated Benfica by four goals to one. The first was by Bobby, he outjumped the rest, The second was scored by wee Georgie Best, The crowd they all chanted but I never did *(or no wonder they did)*, When the third goal was scored by young Brian Kidd. The crowd they all chanted for more and for more, So Bobby obliged by making it four, The team to remember, the team to recall are Manchester United, the best team of all"

Tune: '*Days to remember all my life*'. "I'm thinking of those goals, Those four great goals, On Wembley's turf they gave us, I can't forget those goals, I can't forget a single one believe me, Goals I'll remember all my life, Goals that were scored from left to right, We won the Cup (We won the Cup), We got pissed up (We got pissed up), We're in Europe believe me..."

"We are the people, Who sing of victory, Of games that's brought us glory, From Newcastle to Torquay, Where sixty thousand voices, Roar us on to victory, We will follow United,
(Chorus) Hello' Hello' We Are The Busby Boys, Hello' Hello' We Are The Busby Boys,
And if you are a City fan, Surrender or you'll die, We will follow United, Whether we're across the sea, Or whether we're at home, It matters not we follow to all corners of the globe, We wear the colours proudly, The black, the white, the Red, We will follow United, (Chorus) And now we're back in Europe, The feelings f**king great, We'll try to emulate that team, Of 1968, We'll win the Cup, Have no fear, And then we'll drink your beer, And we will follow United..."

"For we are the great supporters, Man United is our team, And as you all know, Into Europe we will go, In the colours of the team supreme, So we're all off to Europe in the Red (in the Red), Denis Law will dazzle in the sun, Where the goals are scored, The crowd all roar, Especially the Stretford End, Well we are the Champions as you all know, Denis Law and Busby are grand, We'll win the European Cup this year, We're the best team in the land, So all you City fans remember this, We are the greatest

side, And as Law goes up, To receive that Cup, You'll be sure to hear us cry: We are the Champions! Champions of Europe! We are the Champions! Champions of Europe, (etc)..."

"Who's that team we call United, Who's that team we all adore, They're the boys in Red and White, And they fight with all their might, And we're out to show the world how we can score. Bring on Sunderland and Arsenal, Bring on the Spaniards by the score, Barcelona, Real Madrid, they will make a gallant bid, But they'll only know the reason why we roar..."

(When City were in the European Cup (I know...hard to believe) in 1969 Malcolm Allison comically told the media that: "City would conquer Europe". They were superbly knocked out in the 1st Round by Fenerbahce and thus this verse was added)

"Who's that knocking on the window, Who's that knocking on the door, It's Joe Mercer and his mates, With a turkey on their plates, Cos they can't get into Europe anymore. So here's the health unto United, Play the game and play it fine, At the end of every game, We'll immortalise the name, Of the boys who wear the famous Red & White"

"If you ever walk down Warwick Road near Salford, And maybe if it's on a Saturday, You must buy a ticket for the Cantilever, And watch the World Club Champions as they play, For we've beaten all the Russians and the Ities, And we've hammered Real Madrid, the pride of Spain, For we are the toast of Europe and all Asia, And Manchester United is our name. If we're going to be Champs in the hereafter, And something tells me that we're going to be, We will have to beat those mighty men from Ajax, To bring the Cup back home across the sea, And then we'll be the Champions of Europe, And every team we meet will say the same, We had no chance against those World-Wide Champions, And Manchester United is our name"

"Bent it, curled it, even hit the post, Denis Irwin must be Pele's ghost. *(Chorus) = With a red scarf on me arm - I went to Rotterdam* - Sparky, 1-2, that'll do for me, piece of silver, perched upon my knee. (Repeat chorus) Planed it, Boat it, even crossed the sea, 30,000 came along with me. (Repeat chorus) Barca, Barca, came from Catalan, One big flag but not a lot of fans" (Repeat chorus)"

"Bobby gets the ball upon the centre-spot, He knocks it out to to Georgie on the wing, Georgie beats his man and then puts in a cross for Denis Law, And it's a goal, And he's the King...Ob-la-di Ob-la-da, Man United, European Champions..." *Tune: 'Ob-la-di, Ob-la-da'*

"Who put the ball in the Germans' net, who put the ball in the Germans' net, who put the ball in the Germans' net - Ole Gunnar Solskjaer!"

"Forty-one years ago, Our team lay in the snow, Battered and bloodied and some lost their lives, But some of them survived. Charlton and Matt Busby went down to Wem-ber-lee. We beat Benfica and we won the Cup, All those years ago"

"It was on a fine and a sunny day in a week that had

seen no rain, When all roads led to Wembley, a European night again, They poured down from King Cotton*, they came from far and wide, There were a hundred thousand in the ground and thousands more outside, Deansgate was closed like Sunday, the streets were silent, Still For the Reds who chose to stay at home were either dead or ill, But those who went to Wembley will remember till they die, How Benfica were defeated and how the pubs ran dry, Aye, the beer flowed at Wembley, piped down from Tommy Ducks** And the hands that held the glasses high were strong from cotton and muck, And the air was filled with singing and grown men were seen to cry, Not only when we won but when the pubs ran dry, When dawned the morning after on empty factories, We were still at Wembley, bloodshot absentees. But we all had our excuses, each of them the same, Suffering from red fever, contracted at the game, And all the little babies down in Salford from now on, Will be christened Matt or Georgie, Bobby, Brian, Pat or John. And a hundred years from now, They'll all still sing the songs, Of the day the Wembley scoreboard read "United 4, Benfica 1." And when I'm old and my hair's turned grey and they put me in a chair. I can tell my great-grandchildren that I was there, And they'll ask to hear the story of the twenty-ninth of May, When we all went down to Wembley to see United play"

*King Cotton is an old nickname for Manchester and its surrounding areas. **Tommy Ducks was a famous old Manchester pub near St.Peter's Square, now sadly (and, apparently, illegally as it was a listed building) demolished and replaced by a mock-Georgian development.*

BARCELONA DAZE
by Seamus

"It was on a fine and sunny day, In a week that'd seen no rain, All roads led to Barcelona, Champions' Final night in Spain, They travelled from all England, They came from far and wide, There were 90,000 in the ground, And loads of Reds outside, Old Trafford was deserted, The streets were silent, still, For Reds who chose to stay at home, Were either dead or ill, Matt Busby, T'was his birthday, And now the Reds entered the fray, We were playing Bayern Munich, A German team all dressed in grey, The Germans hit the post, They even hit the bar!, With Peter Schmeichel still in goal, They won't get very far!, When Dave put in the cross, We sang loud and searched our soul, And up popped Teddy Sheringham, To score that vital goal, The Germans were distraught, They could hardly toe the line, When Ole struck that ball, For that second fatal time, They got the trophy ready, For the Germans to collect, But they hadn't catered for, Ted and Ole to connect, The air was filled with singing, Grown men stood there and cried, Not only when we won: When Munich's ribbons were untied, This year it's Man United's, Last year t'was Real Madrid, We never thought we'd lose, We nearly bloody did!, When dawned the morning after, On empty German factories, Their fans were still in Barcelona, Weary, bloodshot absentees, They all had their excuses, Each one of them, the same, Suffering from red fever, Contracted at the game, And all the little babies, Down in Barca' from this eve, Will be christened Ted and Ole, Ryan, Denis, Jaap and Steve, And all those at the Nou Camp, Will remember till they die, How Bayern Munich were defeat-

ed, And how the Ramblas Bars ran dry, In a hundred years from now, Supporters' stories - they will still, Tell of the time the scoreboard read, Bayern one, United nil, And when they ask to hear the history, Of the final we did play, I'll say "We beat the Germans, Bayern Munich, On the twenty-sixth of May"

THE BARCELONA TREBLE
© by Andrew Lindsay

"We went down to Barca one fine day in May, United were playing in the Nou Camp that day, And when it was over and when it was done, We'd beat Bayern Munich by two goals to one, We'd just won the double for a record third time, The reds were already on cloud number nine, But this was the game where we just could not fail: To be Kings of all Europe our Holiest Grail, Paul Scholes was suspended along with Roy Keane: Playmaker and captain absent from the team, So the captain's armband went to Peter the Dane, The world's greatest keeper in his last ever game, Bayern took the lead with a dubious free-kick, Dispatched to the net with the craftiest flick, A tough uphill struggle began right away, Manchester United were chasing the game, They worked and they tried but they got no reward, Despite valiant effort they just could not score, So on came the substitutes, Ole and Ted, The last anxious throw of the dice for the Reds, A corner was won and up came the Great Dane, The Bayern fans whistled for the end of the game, But the ball fell to Teddy who slotted it home, The determination had finally shown, The ninetieth minute had shown on the clock, When Ole popped up, to win us the lot: Munich were defeated on what would have been, The ninetieth birthday of Sir Matt Busby, United's two goals came in injury time, Confirming the best football team of all time: From the jaws of defeat, a victory was snatched, And Fergie's United will never be matched"

"They all laughed when Arsenal won the Double, and when we signed Jaap Stam, They all laughed when we signed the Trinidadian, They all laughed when Schmeichel said he's leaving, Oh how they laughed and how...But ho, ho, ho - who's had the last laugh now!"

A STORM IN HEAVEN
Pete Boyle

Peter Boyle is a 29 year old part-time DJ famous for many things as diverse as poetry, songwriting and swigging unlimited bottles of Low C (in an attempt to reduce his vegetarian waistline). The loving father of four has that many pop star mates that, rumour has it, he sometimes forgets what band each are in. To celebrate Fergie's contribution to Utd, Pete is recording a CD with the help of some of his 'high ranking' pals and although he knows that Keith Fane will never play it, he isn't concerned in the slightest.

Many reds have doubted God's allegiance to our beloved team over the years but surely now he has proved himself. The heartache of losing to the dirties in the THEN important League Cup Final in '83 and Anfield '92 are almost erased. May 11th '96, I said to friends could never and never will be bettered, how wrong I was.

At this point I will uncharacteristically give credit where due to Arsenal. Their double of '98 was done in fine style and unlike Leeds, Villa, Blackburn and Newcastle, their challenge to us will be around for more than one season. On the back of that and the forgettable Charity Shield, it was evident they would be the team we would have to beat.

As ever, opposing fans gave Beckham even more (yawn yawn) stick for his World Cup exploits but, as ever, us reds were one step ahead. It was so satisfying to see the nation in uproar over our 'ironic' Argentina chants, disgrace? Not credit! Yes! After a stuttering start, we hit form and apart from our annual no show at Hillsborough we were looking quite good and a certain Dwight Yorke was making 50,000 reds eat humble pie.

Just Who Is the 5 o' Clock Hero?

I approached the cup game with the dirties in my usual paranoid state of mind. "They're due a win" I said to the lads (as I said every time we played City), no worries they replied. So nervous was I that I rang a United legend whom I'm privileged to know socially and asked him if we would win. In typical fashion he gave me a five minute analysis of the teams and convinced me that we would win, or did he? For 88 minutes my pre-match fears were looking justified but, for once, I was actually coming to terms with it. It had to happen one day, I told myself as those witty scousers hounded us with very original (not) songs about Becks and his fiancée. Then 'WHAM BAM THANK YOU MAM' this was it, this was going to be a season to remember. Gary Neville and Becks have UNITED tattooed on their hearts and the epitome of this was their celebrations after Ole's goal. I proudly and subsequently updated an old Lou Macari Chant for Ole but little did I know that too may need to be re-written come May.

Suddenly the press were predicting the impossible, The Treble. I took no notice knowing how fickle these people were and how they would love us to finish with nothing. Then one of the most important results of the season was announced and what an upset it was. Long standing Utd Fan Rupert Murdoch was prevented from making us even better. This was the moment that reminded me that my IMUSA subscription was due again and how proud I was to renew my membership.

You've Got a Lot to Answer For

The neutrals of the nation rubbed their hands with glee when we were paired with Arsenal in the FA Cup Semi-Final. David Elleray was auditioning for the part of George Courtney in the Quentin Tarantino thriller based on Bruce Grobbelar's assault on Gordon McQueen provisionally titled 'Whose legs are they anyway!' Into the replay after Keane's goal that never was. 'What goes around, comes around' proved to be the most accurate of all clichés. We all know what happened next and boy were we on course.

After the never to be forgotten night in Turin the League and FA Cup were returned to their rightful home and now onto the one we had all waited for and what a place to end our search if we could pull off one last masterstroke.

It's the End of The World As We Know It (And I Feel Fine)

Being the surprise recipient of an unexpected windfall, well £105 to be honest, I gambled with fate but convinced myself I wasn't alone. February 3rd 1999 was the day this smug bastard booked his flight to Barcelona for the grand total of £98. Still recovering from sunstroke from Wembley and self-inflicted over indulgence with pop stars I arrived in sunny Spain in need of a bed instead of a beer. Monday night in Barca (was alas a drunken sing song and courtesy of the Governor and his Chorlton mates (Oh hello!) I bunked into a room that made a Copenhagen cell seem like the Hilton.

Lots of Reds and Germans alike stayed on the coast at various 'Costas' and 'Bays', we were slap bang in the middle of Barca and loving every minute. Reds of all generations were present as the beer and songs flowed through the night. Not surprisingly, LA RAMBLAS was again a focal point for the Mass red army party of parties. Sunburnt, hoarse and totally exhausted and the match wasn't until the next day.

Match day and, of course, Busby's birthday. Winning the FA Cup on his birthday in '83 was sweet but this would be unbeatable. Thousands of Reds on the day trips joined the intoxicated but vibrant Red sea as we headed to the fantastic stadium. Fittingly Mani and John Squire were both here. THIS IS THE ONE, INDEED.

Never have I witnessed a game of such importance go so quickly. A nervous start and all mine and all Red's worst fears were addressed. Despite starting numerous songs and chants of encouragement I, and the ultra-cool pop star sat behind me, began to accept it wasn't going to happen. I certainly wasn't nervous anymore. Just immensely proud of what those Red shirts had achieved already.

The Drugs Don't Work

For years to come, people will try in vain to explain how the next bit happened. To do it in the FA Cup against Liverpool was a one off, this is the European Cup Final and Roy of the Rovers was only make-believe. When those goals were scored in quick succession, I wasn't even sure who I was watching, Manchester United or Melchester Rovers. Meanwhile, me and Mr Ashcroft had gone from being complete strangers to Bosom Buddies in just over 90 minutes, I am a lucky man. Goodbye Big Pete, arise Sir Alex, Thank you once again Manchester United.

4. THE ROUTE TO BARCA

Brøndby IF
vs
Manchester
United

ZONE	RÆKKE	SÆDE
Gul	09	Nr. 60

ESTADI FC BARCELONA, 26 MAY 1999, 20:45

GOL NORD 3 GR

CHAMPIONS
LEAGUE

MANCHES

FC BAYE

MANCHESTER UNITED FC

013361

DATA:25-11-1998

FC BARCELONA

FILA: 0001 ASIENTO/SE

lympiastadion
München

z Nordkurve
— incl. 16% MWSt.

| F¹ | 15 |

NORD

ACCE

PORTA

PR U:10000

ICE St. CERMELSKA

UNITED

20:45

CHAMPIONS
LEAGUE

MAN

ENTRANCE	BLOCK	ROW	SEAT
	1 C		15

✱ 003298

300,- Sk

rona Software B.V.

Date: 05-11-1997

Kick-off time: 20:45

 nstile: 01-06

idium open: 18:00

45.00

CLUB CARD

UEFA Champions League
Quart de Finale - Aller
Mercredi 4 mars 1998
20 h.45

A.S.
MONACO

MAN
UNI

MECZ II RUNDY WSTĘPNEJ LIGI MISTRZÓW (UEFA)

ŁKS Ptak - Manchester United

środa - 26 sierpnia '98
godzina 21.05
Stadion ŁKS Al. Unii 2

ampions League

yenoord -

nchester Ut

Posiadacz niniejszego biletu oświadcza, iż znana mu jest treść „Regulaminu stadionu ŁKS". Regulaminu tego zobowiązuje się przestrzegać, a w przypadku przekroczenia jego przepisów przyjmuje
do wiadomości, iż mogą być wobec niego zastosowane sankcje regulaminem tym przewidziane.

№ 0000416   CENA: 50 zł   TRYBUNA
sektor XIII-XIV

LOUIS II - MONACO

CATEGORIE	RANG	
NC	00	

0060

00

F

iateur, doit être présente à l

ns League

UEFA CHAMPIONS L

Man. United
TORINO 10 DICEMBRE 1997 ore 20,45

3º TRIBUNA
EST 3 OSPITI

JUVENTUS-MANCHESTER UNITED
10.12.97
Settore

FOR MANCHESTER SUPPORT

JUVENTUS

MANCHESTER UNIT

STADIO DELLE ALPI

THE ROUTE TO BARCA

TALES FROM A SLOVAKIAN OUTPOST
Phil Williams

Kosice 0 - Manchester United 3
European Cup Champions League, 1st group match
September 17th 1997
Schmeichel, Neville G, Irwin, Berg, Pallister, Keane,
Beckham, Butt, Cole, Scholes, Poborsky.
Sub used: McClair.
Scorers: Irwin, Berg and Cole.
Attendance: 9,950

However hard it was, it was time to forget the brutally disappointing semi-final defeat against those other Germans, Borussia Dortmund and set our thoughts and sights on yet another European campaign. This time we were without Eric Cantona - what would that do to the club - and the season's tours started with a trip into the relative unknown of Slovakia. This was part of the old Czech Republic until Slovakia had split and they became two independent countries - yet shared the same old money. Having previously not travelled to this part of the world before we were looking forward to this particular trip with interest.

When the draw had been made back in August '97 it threw up a mixed bag for the travelling Reds. Another trip to Juventus, a trip to Rotterdam (and that meant Amsterdam) to play Feyenoord - and the final itself to be played at Ajax's ground - and the final team drawn was one place I'd never heard of, Kosice. As usual the maps are out at the time of the draw and the phone soon starts buzzing. This time it took a very detailed atlas to work out where this place was, revealing that Kosice (pronounced Kozeetay) was approximately 400 miles east of Prague, near to the Ukrainian border. Bearing in mind the limited available time before we were due to play there it wasn't going to be an easy trip to sort out.

This was an understatement, as sorting out the best available option became a nightmare. It's difficult to believe how many times your plans can change in the space of a week but believe me, I must have been on about 20 different trips all told, via various modes of transport, starting and finishing at various times. There were about a dozen of us intending to travel, no matter what it took to get there. Quite a few of the usual suspects had opted out of this one as the flesh pot trip to Amsterdam for the Feyenoord match was far more tempting and much cheaper.

Originally we were going to fly to Prague on the Monday, get an overnight train to Kosice and return to Prague early on the Thursday morning. This sounded great and we provisionally booked the flight for just over £200. The train times and fare were checked - no problem - it means in total, with hotels and match ticket, that it would work out at around £280. A reasonable sum for such a journey.

Just by chance we knew somebody who was working in Prague and asked him to book our train tickets. When he went to the train station he found out that due to flooding in Eastern Europe the timetable had changed and in order to get back to Prague in time for the flight back home we would have to leave Kosice during the half-time interval!

As that idea had been ruined we had to quickly cancel the flights and the next idea was via Budapest or any other close European city, but none of these options turned out to be practical. We then heard there was a charter flight from Manchester - direct - staying for 2 nights costing £300-£350. Things were looking up only to find out when the price was finalised that it was over £400. The charter was then moved to Stanstead for £350 - didn't fancy that much so we then tried to fly to Prague and get a flight on from there to Kosice, only for Czech airlines to lose the plot and that option was out. It was then

Charter flight to Kosice

the charter from Birmingham (now for £350) only to find it had moved back to bloody Stanstead! Sod it! Let's book it and go and be done with it. After all the messing about I was just glad to be actually going.

As usual when United play anywhere abroad the rumours that circulate before a match are incredible. This trip for the few hundred going was no different. Unusually most of them were true this time and here's just a few:

Their ground is a cesspit under reconstruction and they are borrowing their rivals' ground, it only holds 9,500 and Utd are only getting 500 tickets - TRUE.

It's only 20p a pint and £1.50 for a steak dinner - TRUE.

The airport is only big enough for an airfix model plane to land at as the runway is only 10 yards long and it needs a great pilot to navigate to land - NOT FAR FROM THE TRUTH!

The mafia run a lot of the drinking establishments - AGAIN NOT FAR FROM THE TRUTH!

The flight was due to leave Stanstead at 10am Tuesday and with such an early flight it means a 4am start from home to make sure we arrived in time for our customary pre-flight drink. When we arrived the bar was packed, not with Reds but Leicester City fans flying off to Madrid for their UEFA Cup tie. You could tell they were inexperienced European travellers as who would set off for their first game in Europe for over 36 years on the actual day of the game! Mind you, judging by the nightmare that happened to some of their fans who travelled by coach they took the best option!

After a couple of beers everyone was nicely relaxed and ready for the flight only to hear the horrific news - the flight is dry. Heaven forbid, get to that Duty Free Emporium quickly. The flight passed by in a mere 2 hours 10 minutes - who said it was in the back and beyond? We landed at the TINPOT airport at around 2pm on a gloriously sunny afternoon. Passport control was just a bloke at the bottom of the plane's steps with a stamp and an ink pad - very high tech. The airport was tiny (a bit like Old Trafford metro station) and as it happened the players and officials landed just before us - they heading off to their awaiting coach while the 83 of us battled for the 5 taxis on offer outside the airport. The players looked at us with the expected caution and bafflement although they did acknowledge that we were there to support them, well all expect Sir Bobby who did his best to ignore our presence completely.

Eventually four of us managed to secure a much needed taxi and headed off in search of our hotel. The scenery was spectacular and this did genuinely seem like a lovely city to visit. The Hotel Hutnik could find no trace of our booking even though it had been confirmed by phone that morning. After an hour sampling the local loony juice in the hotel bar the receptionist informed us that she had managed to book us into another hotel a couple of miles away. Off we trotted to the Hotel Ferro Centrum, which was decent if not a little pricey for Slovakia at £13 a night. The odd thing here was that you could only book for one

A good thing steak is cheap in Slovakia!

night at a time and then you had to re-book the next morning if you wanted to stay the following night. Even stranger the receptionist told us they were already full for the Wednesday - how could they be if you could only book on the day. All will be revealed later.

It was a pleasant evening in what was a great city, and everything was set for a top night, especially when we realised just how cheap the beer was (ranging from 20p to 50p a pint), and a good choice of Amstel or Pilsner Urquell. After a few drinks an excellent 3 course meal for eight of us came to only £32 - being the generous buggers that we are we gave the waiter £40 and told him to keep the change. We believe he may have since retired!

The plan for the night was the usual. Drink and yet more drink and this place looked like it could more than adequately cope with our needs.

We met up with a few of the Ramsgate lads, one of whom (John!) was already worse for wear and this showed as he fell down a hole in the middle of the main street which was being re-built - nice one John. To an even cheaper bar down the road we bump into Terry McDermott's doppelganger, who persuaded us to try some of the local brew, which was named Slivovitch. This surely was also the local petrol as it had the distinct effect on all of us as we became rather boisterous and within minutes the local constabulary converged on this little bar with large wolves to quieten us down. Needless to say we decided to depart.

Four of us hailed a taxi to take us to the next port of call - Evelyns - yet he drove for miles until we reached a place which he was enthusiastically calling a "private club". We were in the middle of nowhere and stupidly got out, for the driver to amazingly then open the back door of the club with his own keys and let us in. The door locked behind us and lo and behold we were in a high class brothel, full of Russian minky and not what we wanted...honest! It seemed that the option was to pay an obscene amount of money for a shag or be shagged by some Ukranian gorillas behind the bar. Thankfully they must have felt sorry for us as the taxi driver eventually took us out of this den and to the club we actually wanted. Yet this was another bloody brothel yet this time we couldn't even get in as they had some very distinguished guests from United who didn't want to be disturbed - I wonder who they were? We all knew but I am not at liberty to divulge this information but let's just say that he's been seen in this sort of place before on Euro away trips.

After this detour without a drink we decided to head to the Jazz Club, a rocking disco bar full of local youth and a group of slightly older drunken Reds trying to mingle the best they could, difficult when nobody speaks a word of English! Bearing in mind this was a club, it was a massive 40p a pint - scandalous.

We stayed until closing as this was the place to be, although it appeared all the action was happening elsewhere. There had been trouble in the place we were heading to - The Hacienda. Apparently one of our lads had a disagreement with one of the dodgy looking Ukranian mafiaso in the bar and as Gary and Danny both tried to help they were hit over the heads with a stool and a bottle. These Ukrainians apparently have a massive 'say' in the running of many things in Kosice - being so close to home - and were as dodgy as hell. Just a month later one was shot dead in the very same club. So perhaps it was a

Fraternising with the Kosice fans

and headed off to the Hacienda Club only to meet up with bloodstained Gary in need of urgent medical attention. Off trundles Dai to spend three hours in hospital, and all night without a sniff of alcohol.

We move on and frequented a fair few quality bars and end up in a 20p a pint watering hole with local moonshine - if you dared - at 10p a shot. We vegetated here with Kevin buying everyone (locals as well) a moonshine or two (50 drinks for about a tenner!) which unfortunately took its toll on some and their stomachs. There was a tremendous atmosphere brewing - and good banter with the few Kosice fans, the only sign in a quiet build up to possibly the biggest game in their history.

Onto another bar where the drinking got heavier and the singing got louder, a party in full swing. One particular absentee was Barney - so completely wasted in a bar that was hidden behind a bookcase the night before that he was now sleeping to try and regain what small senses he has left in time for kick-off.

With an 8.45pm start we decided 8pm would be a suitable time to get a cab to the ground as it was only about a 10 minute ride away on the outskirts of town. It said a lot that this was the improved Kosice stadium - it was a tip with cables running all around the terraces - and the usual communication problems with the police. They indicated to us that the away entrance was the exact opposite direction to where they actually were.

We eventually managed to get in - well most of us anyway. Lee did an impression whilst trying to get in of a man who'd just been shot, falling flat on his face as the police looked on suitably unimpressed as he couldn't even find his ticket when he got back up. He picked one out of his wallet but it was a Spurs away ticket! A quick clip around the ear and the ticket was found and to his relief they let him through.

We then had a two mile walk round the ground to find the Utd section - the locals looking at us as if we'd just landed from another planet and in Lee's case he still was on another planet! When we finally got in the Utd end he again dropped like a sack and landed head first in the front row and perfectly landed in a seat where he sat prone for the rest of the game.

The atmosphere in the ground at kick-off was hardly electric but wasn't bad considering it was an open ended ground and the crowd was a long way from the pitch. The team started tentatively but settled once Denis had scored the opener. There wasn't a great deal more action on the first half but we stepped up a gear in the second. We ran out comfortable 3-0 winners with Coley finally managing to notch one. The highlight of the match was not so much the good away scoreline but the carnival in the Utd end (about 600 strong) in the second half led by Peter Boyle. Firstly getting the local army involved: "You're the best armed soldiers we've ever seen" sort of thing and then becoming a Brian McClair concert as he came on as sub with classics such as "Brian McClair, walking down the wing", 'Twelve Brian McClair's', 'Ooh Ahh Brian McClair" to name but a few - he looked absolutely baffled by it all.

bit stupid to still try and get in there after the club had been cleared of United fans by the police - needless to say the large looking gentleman at the top of the stairs put a block, literally, on that idea. Outside one Red had just been mugged of everything he had and was not happy.

By this time it was nearly 3.30am and perhaps time to call it a day. On our way back to the hotel we passed the UEFA hotel, the Slovan, and duly checked if the bar was still open. Alas not, but in the foyer there was a large Champions League team board. In the rightful place at the top of the board was the Utd team crest. At the bottom, where it belonged, was the Newcastle badge. This was duly dispatched in the gutter outside.

Due to the early (relatively) night I managed to get up bright and early and make it for 8am breakfast - I shouldn't have bothered. After catching up on the stories from last night (Danny using a steak to heal his eye wound from last night - telling the local Doctor that he had got the cut from an "apple peeler slipping out of my hands", yeah right!) we try and re-book the hotel for another night only to be told by one receptionist that it is full and by another that it'll be worth trying at 11am - all very strange. So at the hour we turn up to be told there is room in the inn and most of our group were given the same rooms we'd just left. But all is revealed when we discover that the Ukrainians also control some of the hotels and sell to the highest bidder before 11am and thereafter to anyone - hence our success.

To the bar. We order the first drink of the day only for 5 minutes later another tray to arrive courtesy of the chef! Six more Slimovitch's arrive - no! - and this generous hospitality did us no favours so early in the day I can assure you. It was here that more stories are caught up on and we have time to count the stitches in the back of Gary's head! One of the funniest stories concerned Dai, who due to a medical condition could not touch alcohol on the trip - poor bugger. Having spent just £2 all night on soft drinks he followed his more inebriated companions who walked into a house of ill repute, one of whom promptly fell over and smashed a plant pot. This deeply upset the local heavies as they demanded £100 to replace it or none of them would see the match. Dai duly paid his £20 share

Yet at this stage we have to spare a thought for Steve the Greek, or should I call him Steve the Sleep. After the heavy pre-match session he managed to fall asleep in a park (as you do) and only wake up in darkness, all this whilst impressively standing up. He headed to the ground, which in fact turned to be the loud noise coming from a bar showing the match and ended up coming into the ground just as we were all on our way out. All the way from Athens and he missed the game. That takes some beating. However things were to get worse for him. He intended on his way back to stop off in Budapest and take in Vasas Budapest against Real Betis in a ECWC game. But the match was in Spain - and he was destined to not see any football this trip.

After passing Steve on his way into the ground we pass Mick on the street verge taking a piss. He is immediately set upon by the local police. "Penalty" they shout. "Ok, who's in goal" was Mick's response - and it obviously did not go down well as he was fined 1,000 Slovokian dibble dobbles and insisted that he take the receipt. When he said he didn't want one - why would he need it? - the response was a baton across the body.

We headed back into town and eventually head back to the Jazz Bar only to find it a lot quieter with an actual jazz band on. By 2.30am it was time to move on again, but the only places still open were the dens of ill repute - the price to pay I suppose for a drink in life.

By this stage Nige and Lee were completely blitzed, both finding the use of their legs more and more difficult to manage and Lee finding the floor an inviting place to rest. The beer had run out with a few Reds already inside and it was vodka or nothing. A stripper was reluctant to take off her clothes in front of Mick so in a gesture of Anglo-Slovak relations he did it for her and stripped himself down to some awful y-fronts. He was having a bad night as Taylor and Phil had been spiking his drinks. Not as you'd expect though. Instead of putting the vodka in with his ordering of tonic, they were just buying tonic water. Thus they were surprised when Mick kept grimacing with every sip saying that: "Phew, that's got a nasty kick to it". When told the truth the next morning he replied no wonder he felt so good! Also there and up for a top night was Dave Watson - pogo dance and all - who was to die so tragically the next year. Missed and not forgotten.

We eventually returned home with the birds (of the feathered variety!) just waking up at 6am! Breakfast was missed and I managed a massive 3 hours sleep before returning to the bar - well, there's nothing like a hair of the dog! Unfortunately the hospitality from yesterday was still apparent as the barmaid insisted we drink some 4-star petrol to go with the beer! I ended up blowing the rest of my Slovak money on 6 bottles of spirits and still having change out of a tenner!

There was just about time to return to the TINPOT airport for our 12.30 flight and have a look at a duty free shop smaller than my bathroom and with as much choice of aftershave! The departure lounge was a subdued place with many of the 90 intrepid travellers (7 couldn't be arsed with the train back and got on our flight) nursing major hangovers and not even Mr.Boyle could muster a song.

After a lengthy drive north it was straight to bed at 9pm - and did I need sleep. And then to work...

This was yet another classic couple of days in a distant outpost of Europe (yes, it was only a couple of days) and all this with a nice quiet trip to Amsterdam just six weeks away!

THEY DIDN'T LIKE THAT SONG
Peter Shaw

Feyenoord 1 - Manchester United 3
European Cup Champions League, 3rd group match
November 5th 1997, Stadion Feijenoord
Schmeichel, Neville G, Irwin, Berg, Pallister, Beckham, Scholes, Butt Cole, Sheringham, Giggs.
Subs used: Neville, P, Poborsky & Solskjaer.
Scorer: Cole (3).
Attendance: 45,000

Pete, late thirties and K Stand regular, made only one Euro away during the 97/98 season. As soon as he heard the draw he translated the words 'Feyenoord' quickly into 'Amsterdam' and decided that was 'the one', as he travelled with ten of his mates to that famous den of iniquity. It's a major miracle that he actually returned home as the 'atmosphere' in the Dam is Pete's idea of utopia. Indeed, he can often be seen in a haze of smoke in Castlefield on a Saturday night. As he so rightly puts it: "my disgusting behaviour". He has, like so many, supported United all his life and vowed to run down Deansgate naked if we were to ever win the European Cup. We wait - not - with baited breath...

Looking back it's becoming increasingly hard to recall many of the Euro aways that I've been fortunate enough to get to. I haven't been to that many - always try to make the vital ones though - but perhaps it's the norm for most people for them to drift into some forgotten oblivion where the bars visited, drinks drunk and the rest of the sordid activity of the trip merge into one. Was that bar in Amsterdam or Barcelona? Did that happen on the Tuesday night in Budapest or after the game in Milan? Whatever, if ever there is a certainty it's that you get home, knackered and ready to sleep for a year, and know that - lack of memory not withstanding, you've had a blinding trip. Even though they are all the same!

And so the four days in Amsterdam will rank as one of the best ever. But I'll be buggered if I could really tell you that much about it. Perhaps that's the same for most people - certainly judging by the continual stream of off their heads Reds walking aimlessly (or maybe not!) at about 3am each morning in the red light district. Yeah there's more to Amsterdam than the square mile or so of debauchery but even so whatever the game (going back to those early 80s tournaments over there when United decamped and made it our own) you can guarantee that the old hardcore Red faces will be out in force for any trip to Holland and the red light will be the only place visited for most. Cheap dive of a hotel there, drink there, puff there, collapse there.

This one was to be no different - and a great time was had doing the predictable things - a great laugh doing the stuff that we've always done. Nothing better than getting shredded with your Utd mates, a legal piece of grass next to you watching the hours tick by and the local nutters act as if every inhabitant who stays in the red light too long has now become a right old loony tune. And that includes us! I think the term is to vegetate and that's what many of us did - some ticketless too cabbaged even to move from the den to try any efforts to get in the ground or into Rotterdam for that matter.

If I could remember much I'd try - random memories come up of attempting to throw a busted sofa with two mates in it into the canal and of ending up in some local bar full of totty and then to be given the mike at the end of the night after singing Utd songs during the live band and trying to teach them the words to the Calypso. But other than the usual (you can fill in the gaps by now) it all spins forward to the day of the game. And yet more garbage about alcohol bans in Rotterdam and 'stringent' ticket checks.

Talk about faces. The United contingent meeting up for the 'arranged' near Central Station was like the 70s and 80s. All the bars were mobbed nearby, waiting for THE train. Obviously with Feyenoord's reputation, so United had taken the 'call'. On my part it wasn't a good idea to reenact a literal interpretation of the Chemical Brothers' new album - I think I passed the Mir space station whilst on the train and for the rest of the day I watched the violent goings on as if it were all a dream. Perhaps it was. As we arrived in Rotterdam and followed the group so all the plans seemed to be going exactly as the talk in the nights leading up to the game had suggested.

It was later on that we were to hear that Dutch 'friends' from rival clubs had aided the Utd firm with information and it was a surreal scene which I hadn't witnessed on this scale in over a decade as the old bill lost it as the firm moved on. The head count was unparalleled for a European away fixture. You couldn't make this up and people wouldn't believe you anyway. It's a secret sort of world, two sets knowing what is going to happen and both wanting it to happen. It was mental, their fans couldn't even get out of their bars at first and before the game was to have even kicked off the local news channel was showing 'rampaging United fans in central Rotterdam'. One well known Red even reached page 3 of the Sun.

I remember thinking that there were more local shoppers watching it all than there'd been when it first went off minutes earlier and one of our mob didn't do his future trip piss-taking status that good when he picked up a flower bed to launch ('stupid young boy') - as everything and anything I recall was being used - and it was chained to the front of the shop.

Eventually some buses were found which encouraged a belated Dutch revival as we were herded (tickets or not) into the ground, and the trouble took a new turn. There were just a few stewards, cozzers and suits protecting the doorways between the two ends. It doesn't take Einstein to work out what happened next. United made their move. Everything not stuck to the floor was being used to throw with (even concrete from the walls) and it said it all about how mental it got when some Utd fans in their end were met by the Dutch who had an array of baseball bats! One lad I know well from years gone by said that if either lot had properly got through it would have been bedlam. And I thought it already had been! The police had to shut the turnstiles as they lost the plot - whilst I was still flying high, well past my used by date and still thinking that this

was some vivid dream. It all really had to be seen to be believed. Gone away my arse!

On the pitch things were going just as unbelievable. Cole finally showed his top flight talent and bagged a hat-trick to begin to dispel the doubters after Kosice and the Utd end in the lower tier had much fun during a running verbal battle between the fairly flimsy perspex shields buffeting the two sets of fans only yards apart. That lad from Ramsgate was slaughtering them with abuse and every once in a while the Dutch would make a run at the perspex which baffled and creased up all the United fans.

But the result was a top one. Finally we were beginning to go away and not just score but win! If it took a few more years for us to reach utopia these were the games where we were plying our trade and starting on the road to success. It was hostile at the start but United coped with it and began showing a maturity - along with Andy Cole - that was to progress with each game up until the Nou Camp in May.

As they realised that any hopes of them making a game for it were disappearing they began singing a right load of old crap which led to the United fans singing the name of a certain rival team to theirs. To say that they didn't like it is a tad of an understatement and one of the funniest things I've ever seen. They went barmy. Their players were obviously taking it just as badly as an truly career threatening horrendous tackle on Irwin led to only a yellow card and the comical sight of Fergie dragging the team away from swapping shirts as he also tried to re-enact the downstairs Utd scenes by nearly getting in a scrap with their manager.

All in all it gave a lot to talk about as we waited after the game and listened to the sound of sirens trying to shove their fans away from the ground as we were kept in for eons and delayed from reaching the Den as we waited for trains back. Whilst I don't condone the trouble and all that all those involved said it was the maddest it had been for years and the sight of hundreds of United fans heading off that day from Amsterdam was mental.

Back to the Dam, and back to a very unhappy police force. It was like being back at school and sent to detention. Because we'd misbehaved there were no drinkies for us tonight. Yeah, right. So that wasn't a strip club drinking den that we found ourselves in until 7am and they weren't plant leaves that I started eating at 5am thinking they were God knows what.

Back home eventually and back to the family. What was it like? "Oh, alright".

NOT QUITE THE ITALIAN JOB
Wayne Iball
Juventus 1 - Manchester United 0
European Cup Champions League, 6th group match
December 10th 1997, Stadio Delle Alpi
Schmeichel, Neville G, Neville P, Berg, Johnsen, Pallister, Beckham, Poborsky, Solskjaer, Sheringham, Giggs.
Subs used: Cole and Mcclair.
Attendance: 47,786

Wayne is 35, made his first visit to Old Trafford in 1967 and hasn't missed a home game since 1976. Like so many other Reds, he longed for the day he would see United lift the European Cup. However, unlike the many armchair supporters and Statto type historians associated with another North West club which have previously won the European Cup, he lives in the present and for the future. He now longs for the day (hopefully in the year 2002) when United have won the European Cup five times, and such small-time armchair types might have realised just how futile and pointless their pathetic attempts at one-upmanship are.

When the draw was made and the fixtures announced for the initial group stage of the competition, most people (myself included) would have thought that Juventus vs United in the final game would be the group decider. It might well also have sealed the fate of one of the two clubs following the latest episode in the annual "tinkering with the format" exercise conducted by U.E.F.A. "Greed is Good" ought to be the motto of this cash crazy outfit and their rag-tag bunch of multi-national sponsors. Their latest little experiment was to expand the Champions League group phase from 16 to 24 teams. This meant that there would be 6 groups of 4 teams fighting for the 8 quarter-final places. Therefore, unlike the previous season when all group winners and runners-up progressed to the quarter-final, only the 6 group winners and 2 best runners-up would qualify.

At the time it looked somewhat ominous, as we had hardly set Europe alight in qualifying for the knock-out stage the previous season. We qualified despite suffering three defeats, and still needed Juventus to avoid losing at home to Fenerbahce in the final game to ensure that we scraped through as runners-up. With this record, it seemed as though we would need to actually win the group to progress, as one of the runners-up would be a long shot. How different the script would turn out to be!

Following the penultimate set of fixtures when United had comfortably seen off Kosice at Old Trafford and Juventus had lost away to Feyenoord, our qualification as group winners had been secured. It was Juventus who now had to win the final game and rely on other results going their way to enable them to scrape through.

Whilst the marathon mini-bus trip to Turin the previous September had been both memorable and enjoyable, it was also quite exhausting. With this in mind, it was decided to look for cheap flight options this time around. As luck would have it, the Daily Mirror was running a promotion through August and early September for cheap flights to various destinations, including Nice. It seemed worth looking into, and proved well worthwhile when I was able to book eight flights from Liverpool to Nice for just over £40 each. Unfortunately, the budget airlines seem to have caught on to this, and now tend to exclude from such promotions any dates when United are playing in Europe. I wasn't too keen on flying from Self-Pity City, but at that price it was just about bearable!

We made the short journey to the airport on the Tuesday morning by taxi, as understandably no-one was too keen on taking their car there to be left as easy pickings for the local light-fingered entrepreneurs. As the taxi pulled up at the "terminal" the only real clue that we were actually at an airport was a sign indicating as much. The terminal building resembled a down-market low budget industrial unit. The usual formalities were completed, including the obligatory pre-flight drinks, and as we eventually boarded it struck me just how much the whole set up resembled Toytown - even Mickey Mouse would have been embarrassed.

During the flight a few of the Manchester lads sang a jokey reference to the airport having the free-est duty-free in the land. No doubt it was out of character and more a case of "when in Rome" and all that. The flight to Nice was short and relatively uneventful, and in no time at all we had arrived in a city which is a complete contrast to the one we had departed from. Nice is nice, Liverpool isn't - enough said!

It was a short bus ride to our hotel, the Hotel Westminster right on the promenade. It was to be a quick half-hour turnaround and we met in the bar and had a couple of rather expensive beers whilst organising the essentials for the following mornings train trip to Turin. The owner of the little shop round the corner must have thought Christmas had arrived early when we practically cleared him out of his stock of Kronenberg which was attractively priced at about the equivalent of 30p a bottle. Our hotel staff were also very obliging in allowing us to store our supplies in their fridge for the evening.

We headed off into town and eventually sorted our train tickets out after a few bar stops along the way. Our theory that we probably wouldn't have much time to spare in the morning turned out to be spot on. We did the usual bar crawl afterwards and had a relatively quiet night until one of the lads took exception to a shaven-headed Feyenoord fan who hated United - these ABUs are everywhere, but I suppose jealousy is a powerful emotion which tends to afflict those with weaker minds and spirits. The bonehead was dealt with and seemingly had just about enough intelligence to disappear into the night. The bar didn't stay open that much longer, although we did manage a couple more while the group were finishing their set. We staggered back to the hotel and eventually arrived back at about 3am after one or two wrong turns.

An early breakfast had been arranged at our ever accommodating hotel and more than one or two of the party sat bleary-eyed sipping their black coffee at the ridiculously early time of 6.45am. It was a bit of a rush to make the train so we had to improvise and take our croissants in a doggie-bag together with ample jam butter and the odd butter knife or two. The train left on time at 7.25am and in under an hour we arrived at Breil-Sur-Roya, our first change not far from the Italian border. Our connection was waiting, and we changed without too much bother and headed for Cuneo, our second connecting station. This was farcical in the extreme.

We had about an hour to wait at Cuneo and were greeted as the train pulled in by what was probably all of the local constabulary, which was pretty much one for every two Reds on the train. They were insistent that no-one was to leave the station, even though there were no facilities there whatsoever. So there we were, about 100 miles from Turin and still being treated like lepers by the local plod. It's priceless really that after more than ten years, United fans are still made to suffer for the actions of so-called fans of another club (although they'd probably say it wasn't them - it was the Chelsea fans and the National Front). Just as well that we still had some of our supplies of Kronenberg to keep our spirits up.

We eventually arrived at Torino Porta Nuova at about

12.45 and took taxis to our hotel. Thankfully it turned out to be a decent one, unlike the former brothel that we'd stayed in the previous year which also had some very questionable electrical handiwork. It had to be another quick turnaround and it was back into town to the area near the station where we'd had a decent pre-match drink last time. We squeezed a pizza in between bars just to soak up some of our excesses. There wasn't quite the same buzz around, which was probably due to the fact that we'd already qualified, but at the ground the Reds were there in the usual good numbers and seemed to be up for it. The Italians certainly were and made it a cracking atmosphere, even though they must have known that their chances were slim. United's approach to the game was at the time a little bit mystifying. Yes we had already qualified as group winners, but the performance seemed to be one of going through the motions. We created very little and had rode our luck through much of the game, with Schmeichel keeping us in the game with a string of outstanding saves. The game entered the final ten minutes and it seemed as though we might just hold on for the draw which would have eliminated Juve.

Then, in the 83rd minute, up popped Inzaghi with a goal that gave the Italians hope. It might still not have been enough though as their main rivals for the second best runners-up spot, Rosenborg, were winning at Olympiakos. Then when it seemed as though it was all over for them there was a massive roar from the crowd as though they had scored again themselves. The scoreboard had flashed up the news they had wanted from Greece, Olympiakos had equalised. I wondered at the time if we might pay the price later in the competition for not finishing Juve off when we had the opportunity. The sudden and dramatic change in fortune for the Italians was incredible and was summed up the following morning in one of their papers with the one word headline - "Miracolo".

Even though we were through, I reflected that just like the two recent visits to Galatasaray, we had failed to score in either of our two recent visits to Turin. It seemed as though we just couldn't put the ball in the net in certain types of European away fixtures in hostile environments. How that was to change the following season, when we scored at least once in every European game and even produced a "miracolo" or two of our own, including of course our remarkable comeback in Turin.

We had the customary 45 minute lock-in of course, followed by an even longer delay waiting for the buses to leave to take us back to the city. By the time we got back into the centre, the bars that remained open were few and far between, though we did manage a few more beers before heading back to the hotel at about 2am. The travel and drink had taken its toll and another early morning train departure awaited. There were some pretty rough looking hangovers being suffered by one and all as we trudged through the station and initially boarded the wrong train before sorting ourselves out. The train was a direct one back to Nice thankfully and most people seemed to be trying to sleep it off despite the train being quite full. We arrived back in Nice around dinner-time and headed for McDonalds as we were pretty hungry by then. Considering it was early December, the weather in Nice was surprisingly warm, but very welcome following the freezing cold in Turin. We passed a few hours away drinking near the station and taking in the sun, before heading back to the airport.

The flight back to Self-Pity City was on time, which is more than can be said for the taxi we'd booked a return with. It's annoying enough waiting anywhere for a taxi, but staying in that God forsaken hole for an hour longer than is necessary is particularly galling. I suppose you have to put up with a certain amount of unpleasantness to fully appreciate the special moments that come along from time to time.

A YEAR CAN BE A LONG TIME IN FOOTBALL...
Kerry Davies
Monaco 0 - Manchester United 0
European Cup Quarter Final, 1st leg
March 4th 1999, Louis II Stadium
Schmeichel, Neville G, Irwin, P.Neville, Johnsen, Berg, Beckham, Butt, Cole, Sheringham, Scholes.
Sub used: McClair.
Attendance: 15,000

Kerry Davies is 22 years old and has supported Manchester United all his life. Following in his parents footsteps, and quite bizarrely, an undying love for Gary Bailey ensured that no other team ever came close. He regularly travels to matches home and away all over Europe and can be seen at every game with several copies of the latest Red News held aloft in his right hand! He can also be seen barging through rows of people with a box of said fanzines to get to his seat 5 minutes after kick off. A 6 month sabbatical has been forced upon him by his new job while he is away in America, but he assures us that he will be back as soon as he possibly can...

The very mention of a Euro Away these days is enough to bring a shiver to ones spine - the prospect of several days on the piss, coupled with seeing the mighty Reds in action with a few thousand other likeminded souls is enough to get anyone going. What with the advent of firms like Go, Easyjet and STA, it has never been easier to hop on a plane and jet away to just about anywhere in Europe (good job too when paired against the likes of Kosice!). However, it wasn't always like this - way back when the Holy Trinity of Best, Law and Charlton graced the pitch, following your team away in Europe was virtually unheard of, and it tended to be the hardiest of hardy souls that made these trips. It just so happens that my dear mother was one of these dedicated few, so I asked her to recall a few of her adventures in that very best of years, 1968:

"I worked for British European Airways (now British Airways) so I got cheap travel, 90% off the fare. Some truly intrepid fans did practically trek across the desert on a camel to get there, and I did feel a twinge of guilt as I stepped off the Trident aircraft. The first game I went to was in Dublin against Waterford. I remember we stayed with Sean Bowe, an Irish man who worked on the railways in Ireland and went to every single game by train and he was kind enough to put us up. The players used to stay at the Shelbourne in Dublin then - I remember seeing Georgie Best with his latest girlfriend.

Parking lot at Monaco (home supporters only)...

I did manage to get quite a few autographs (which my son now has) and I remember Franny Burns saying a lot of the players could do each other's autographs quite well so I am not sure of the authenticity of mine. I remember taking a big stuffed red and white striped snake to every game and, in my innocence, not understanding the jokes made about me.

Then I remember the semi-final in Madrid against Real Madrid in the Bernebeu Stadium. Madrid a lovely elegant city with lots of trees and one of our party trying to order chicken in Spanish and being served squid and chips! The Spanish fans barracking the players coach and Paddy Crerand putting his fingers up to them and saying "Muchos bollockos". Man Utd being behind in the first half and then Bill Foulkes running through from the back to score and all the Spanish fans suddenly going quiet and all the United fans cheering like mad from different parts of the stadium (some things never change!). Meeting Brian Kidd and offering him a radish to eat, which not unnaturally he declined. One of the boys I had gone with running on to the pitch hugging Bobby Charlton and his photograph appearing on the front page of all the papers.

My boss at the Airport managed to get me a seat in the stand for the final at Wembley and was amused when I turned from a quiet, well behaved secretary into a booing hissing witch when Eusebio did a particularly nasty foul and United being crowned Champions of Europe."

Having been regaled with these and other tales about following the Reds away in Europe from an early age, it seemed only natural for me to follow in my mother's footsteps and start travelling abroad myself. And that is how I caught the bug - after my first experience of European travel with United I was hooked, and vowed to make as many trips as I possibly could.

A number of reasons had seen my 1997/98 European away count lie at a dismal one, the Feyenoord trip that November. Aching to get back into it all, I eagerly awaited the draw once we had safely made it through the initial group stage. The draw for the quarter final saw us paired with Monaco, the

French champions. On paper at least, it appeared that we had drawn the weakest of the seven sides left in the competition, and everyone seemed generally pleased with how things had turned out.

With finances the way they were and the very real prospect of at least a semi final in the offing, I opted for the cheapest method of travel to the game - the dreaded coach! With virtually a days worth of travel ahead of us we set off on our long journey early Monday evening. After eventually managing to co-ordinate ourselves and the coach into the same car park, we were on our way. The coach was full of familiar faces and a good deal of alcohol, so prospects for an enjoyable journey looked good. After demolishing a bottle of vodka in what seemed like minutes, the journey down to Dover passed quickly, and we soon found ourselves encamped in the bar on the ferry. Here we met another load of Reds on a similar trip, and had a good craic despite the somewhat choppy conditions (or was it just the vodka?!). The rest of the journey for myself was spent in a sleepy haze so in next to no time we were pulling into Nice, our base - and a fairly stunning one - for the trip. The hotel was duly checked into, although my plan to share a room with one of the females on the trip was thwarted by a pre-set rooming arrangement! Instead I shared a room with the spitting image of Barry Manilow who I now see in every city I go to!

After taking care of the three S's it was down to the bar to get the evenings drinking underway. A few drinks

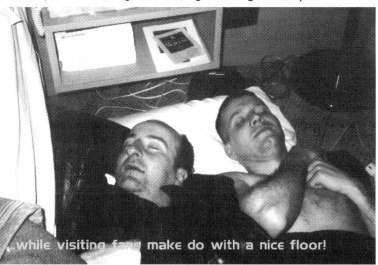

...while visiting fans make do with a nice floor!

Monaco's space-age stadium

in the bar and we made our way to find a few of our travelling companions who had flown out the day before. By the time Richard had found their hotel (no, its JUST round the corner lads, no really...) we weren't really surprised to find they had already gone out, so we set off to find the others in Wayne's Bar, a popular spot from the Monday night, but this had been shut down by the police. Luckily, they were nearby (the bar next door in fact) and we soon found ourselves caught up in one of those mammoth Euro Away drinking sessions that we all know so much about.

We made our way to the Oxford Bar just round the corner where we were greeted with the sight of one Red running around the bar and nearby streets with a statue's head in his hands while a somewhat irate barman looked on! After a while we moved on round the corner to the almost obligatory Irish bar in Europe. This was another smallish bar, but it had Sky Sports on, so we stayed around hoping to be amused by yet another City defeat, but alas this was not to be (but I'm sure a victory against the mighty Huddersfield made up for the fact that we were sunning ourselves in the South of France!). We decided to move off and find somewhere a little more lively, as we had more than lubricated our throats by now, and fancied a bit of singing. A short stroll up the road, and the unmistakable sound of drunken Reds in full flow was duly heard and tracked down to William's Bar. Some Reds had befriended a French soldier by the bar, and one of them had his rather silly looking hat perched on his head as he led the singing in the corner. I happened to mention that if possible, I fancied a slightly larger beer than the half-pints we had been drinking so far, and was shortly presented with one of the largest goblets of beer I had ever seen! Cheers!

We headed off in search of more and came across another bar with the added bonus (?) of a live band. The guitarist was the double of Karel Poborsky, and he was serenaded with songs for the rest of the night, looking distinctly bemused! An epic version of Sympathy for the Devil was aired, swapping the 'oooh ooohs' for 'Karel Poborsky' (it did seem to work, honest...) which had the whole pub singing along to an even more dumbstruck looking band! Well, it seemed epic at the time anyway. Eventually we were forced out into the streets where we bumped into the Red News lot who knew about a 'definite late bar' just round the corner. After about an hour of wandering around it was obvious that the only drink to be

had was the duty free on offer back at the hotel so a few of us headed back to destroy a bottle of peach schnapps - perhaps that explained why two of us were trying to photocopy various parts of our anatomy on a machine that was quite obvious to everybody apart from us, switched off! At that stage it was well and truly time for bed.

I woke at around 10 o'clock, and found that my 2 Nurofen and rehydration capsule had not had their desired effects - my hangover was as bad as ever. I had arranged to meet some others early on so we could go up to Monaco early and try and get tickets as several in our party were short. We made our way to the station and started what I hoped was a very long journey to Monaco, but my sleep was cut short after only 20 or 30 minutes! A quick McDonalds later (I like to sample the local cuisine) and we headed to the main looking square which was already filling with Reds. What with it being both near the ground and the supermarket we settled in for the day, and started the pre-match drinking.

With no tickets floating around in the square we thought the best bet would be to see what was on offer near the ground, but with so many looking, hopes were not too high. The going rate was about £100 so after politely telling the touts where they could put their tickets, we decided to have a look around. Round the back of the ground we found an open door, headed in, and managed to get up onto the third floor where there was a load of offices! Nobody seemed to be paying us any undue attention, so we went about exploring hoping to find a big door marked 'tickets for the game'. Surprisingly enough we were out of luck, so tried asking around in the offices. The secretaries were more than a little surprised to see us, but assured us they had no tickets, so we headed back the square and decided to get drunk and worry about it later!

We met a few lads we drank with in the Dog who were also ticketless, and they were firmly behind our decision so it was off to the supermarket. What with us being in Monte Carlo we thought it rude not to try and blend in with the locals, so we got a load of Champagne in and set about our mission! It was soon getting near enough to kick off to warrant going back to the ground to try and get tickets but the price was still around £100 with every man and his dog looking. I thought it about time to try some other methods of getting into the ground and found the student entrance where they were letting in students for free with their ID cards. What...a European ground holding only 15,000, a Prince's sports toy and bloody students get in for free!

Unfortunately, my French was nowhere near good enough to convince the bouncer that I was actually French but on a year out in England which was why I had an English NUS card! I was told in no uncertain terms to leave! I then tried to get in on the back of a party of schoolkids by pretending to be a teacher, and did my best to look official and shepherd the kids in, but this was foiled as well. Just as I was despairing, I saw some bloke with a crowd of people around him, and got a ticket off him for £40, which was not too bad. I thought I might was well try my luck and get in the United end anyway but as it turned out I needn't have even bothered getting a ticket.

As seems to be the norm with United away in Europe, the security just couldn't handle the occasion, and the area outside the United section was chaos. Crushes were developing the tiny entrance protected by flimsy barricades and surprisingly few old bill, and in the end everyone, ticket or not, was carried through into the ground in waves. So much for the promise that the game would be treated as a warm up for the World Cup and those without tickets would NOT get in! Once inside it was obvious that just about everyone had got in one way or another as Reds were represented in all parts of the ground.

Here we meet up with Barney who had spent some of the day in the infamous casino - after not getting in to the main suit & tie area reserved for those with incomes similar to Martin Edwards, he had settled for the downstairs area (which of course he fitted into perfectly as this area often played host to drunken students!). The Eric Cantona number luck at roulette that had served him so well in Amsterdam airport on the way to Turin was once again in residence as number seven came up to net a hundred odd quid. Having completed his jig of delight and stopped punching the air victoriously he realised his faux pas as those around him were casually winning and losing sums of up to £20,000 in one go and not batting an eyelid!

The game itself was poor, but it was what could be called a 'professional' performance, and was played in the most tremendous atmosphere for a long time. The Calypso got a mighty airing, and there was a deafening Forever And Ever from ALL parts of the ground - amazing stuff that made the hairs on the back of your neck stand up. Faz, a top lad and star throughout the whole trip, had even managed to get himself right next to the ITV commentary box, and could be heard back at home singing songs all the way through the second half! It was a shame that the game couldn't match the atmosphere.

The 0-0 result was satisfactory, but there were many who felt that not getting the away goal might be costly (and how right they were to be). These were the days when going for the 0-0 draw seemed the best route to qualify. After being caught slacking early on in the home leg again this policy - at long last - was replaced by the away style of play that Utd knew best - attack. At the time though we were not too displeased with the result and after being kept in for 30 minutes at the end (to protect us from the baying mob of millionaires outside presumably) we headed back to Nice in search of a drink.

A short train journey later and the jam-packed train pulled in to Nice where everyone proceeded to pour off

the train and over the tracks, thousands repeatedly chanting 'UNITED' - a memorable sight of the massive travelling support in action - nobody else does it like the Red Army and in moments like these you just can't help but be proud of being a part of it all. First stop is an excellent Cuban bar serving some of the nicest tasting alcohol ever known, and before long there are several familiar faces around joining in the session. And what a session it turns out to be - we leave the Cuban bar and after a fruitless search for another bar we stumble across a small karaoke bar still going strong. Bar prices are outrageous (£4.50 for a small bottle of beer!) but it's the only place serving and it's full of Reds having a great crack (including the two lads that helped me jib into Arsenal away that year - much appreciated, you know who you are!).

It's baffling to see the barman running out to a supermarket round the corner buying more and more crates of beer (presumably buying each crate for what we pay for one bottle) but that doesn't stop us from drinking it and a memorable evening is had. We are treated to some dreadful singing, bizarre dancing and general drunken Euro Away behaviour as the night goes on till 7am! Along the way three well known United boys get up and serenade us with Like A Virgin, Anglo-French relations are furthered in various dark corners of the bar, and any non Red singers (singing a selection of banal French numbers) are shouted down with United songs! Mental.

The walk back to the hotel brings strange looks from French businessmen making their way to work as we greet them with chorus after chorus of Eric songs. The hotel is finally reached where breakfast is in full swing - a couple of ham and cheese rolls, a small reservoir of orange juice and its up to the room to throw my stuff back into my bag and board the coach! It is around this stage I slump into an alcohol induced coma and sleep virtually the whole way back to Calais where I wake up in a pool of sweat courtesy of a broken down air-conditioning unit and the unusually hot weather outside. By now I am feeling about as ill as it is possible to feel without actually throwing up, and I positively pine for my own bed and 12 hours sleep. This utopia is finally reached midway through Friday morning, and ends yet another superb Euro Away.

Alas 1998 was not to be our year and the lack of away goals was to cost us dearly as we exited the competition on the away goal rule, gutted again that a home second leg win wasn't to arrive as many expected. Next year was to show that the away leg second was better for Utd. Monaco hurt, and being beaten by a team who were rated eighth best raised serious questions about our European stature. But injuries to crucial players, fatigue and playing a crucial tie during a bad run - and bad luck - all played their part, but it was the end of the dream for another year where we had once again been shown lacking in the latter stages of the competition. We consoled ourselves with the thought that we'd be stronger for the experience next year, and might finally be in a position to take that extra step. But the team (squad) that night showed that additions, whatever people said, were needed for us to succeed. Who was to know that the mammoth buys of Jaap and Dwight were to be the final pieces of a long played out jigsaw puzzle.

And so to 1999, and what a year it was to be! With the League and Cup double already secured, it was off to the

Nou Camp for the European Cup Final. I hazily recalled an especially drunken night out before the final League game of the season where Nigel the Ginger Prince informed everyone of the simple equation - 3 games, 3 wins, 3 trophies. Two down and one to go - game on!

The events of the final in Barcelona have been chronicled in more detail elsewhere in the book, but on a personal note I will never forget some of the goings on that evening. The four of us that were stood together on the bottom tier had virtually resigned ourselves to defeat as we glanced up at the clock showing 45 minutes gone. Then all of a sudden there was total and utter bedlam - that first goal sparked celebrations the like of which I very much doubt will be seen ever again. It was utter chaos as those all around us went mad, running, jumping, hugging, punching the air with delight. The second goal was one of the most surreal moments I have ever known - from being down and out we were the Champions of Europe. The sheer emotion of the moment was almost too much to take as what we had all hoped for and dreamed about had suddenly, dramatically and gloriously come true. All around me people held each other, tears flowing down their faces as the realisation of what had just happened dawned upon them. It was a feeling that I had never known before and doubt I will ever experience again, but one that I will never, ever forget. These truly are unforgettable times.

For me winning the European Cup has always been THE dream - I have been lucky enough to have been born into an era where bar the abominable sides of the late 80's, the club have been unfeasibly successful. The majority of my match-going life, the 1990's, has seen us collect a haul of trophies that would have been unthinkable for those brought up on 70's and 80's United. I have also been lucky enough to have emulated both my parents, both of whom were at the original final at Wembley in 1968. Some people may ask where we go from here but there will always be something special about watching United, no matter what. Its not simply a case of going to watch a game of football, its much, much more than that. A flag that I first spotted in Porto (and was glad to see again in the Nou Camp) sums it up perfectly - quoting from the Stone Roses classic:

One Love, Don't Need Another Love, MUFC.

HARRY LINFORD

I would like to take this opportunity of paying tribute to a great friend, Harry Linford, who sadly passed away in Spain shortly after the European Cup Final. Aged 42 he has left behind his lovely wife Diane and two young ladies in Natalie and Carmel.

Reds knew him as Harry The Hat as he was never without a baseball hat on at football. He sat half-way up behind the goal slightly to the right in K-Stand. He was a real character who will be sadly missed by so many. It will be strange not picking Harry up for every home game. A man who would quite literally do anything for his mates. Harry was from Preston, worked in Manchester and had followed the Reds since the early Seventies. He, like all of us, was thrilled with the Treble and I will treasure the two moments when we cried tears of happiness together in Rotterdam and Barcelona. Rest in peace mate.

Martin Day

THE RED BUS
FROM POLISH LADIES OF THE NIGHT TO SPANISH RENT BOYS
Martin Day

Martin, 37, is six foot one with the slim frame of a 19 stone weakling. Eyes green, inside leg 31 inches, large belly and no dick. He is married to a gorgeous lady with a son of eight called Liam. As Martin says: "A boy who is everything a father could wish for". He lives in a semi that needs a bit of DIY but where does a football fan find the time to decorate and all that crap. Add to that, that most of his spare time is taken up by his role of Secretary of one of United's many Supporters' Clubs. When the season ends for most Reds, he has membership forms, newsletters, reports, etc, etc, etc. United takes up most of his life and what a wonderful bloody life it is - all that silverware with trips to Tokyo, Rio and numerous European countries to look forward to (Book 3 maybe?). Martin says - 'enjoy the book and tell your mates to buy one as well! Thanks to all the reprobates who contributed to this masterpiece. Oh, and this book will self destruct when Liverpool next win the league!'.

"Stop the bloody car, she's gorgeous". "It's a bloke!"

Our European adventure started way back in August 1998. I had booked twelve of us onto a flight from Heathrow to Berlin for £70 return. Lodz was our destination but as everyone knows - it's very close to Berlin. Well, that's what some bright pillock said. Us Northern folk travelled down to Watford on an evening train where Ricky meets us at the station and takes us to his local for a couple of Shandies before bed. We were up at 4.30am to get to Heathrow for the 7am flight and all passed without incident as we hire two eight seaters in Berlin as the numbers have swelled to fifteen with the inclusion of Hugh the Busker and two lads from Chesterfield. Hugh was to become an ever present on our travels, always with his large Weston Super Mare flag under one arm and his guitar under the other. That was and has been his baggage all season, no sign of any toiletries or clean knickers. He is one of those very rare - in fact almost extinct - United fans who does not partake in the wicked brew. More of Hugh later.

We arrived at the Berlin hotel early Tuesday afternoon and we all followed that famous Red drinker Barney knowing our first Euro beer was close by. Well bollocks to that. Mr Barney has a weird fascination for Berlin history and wanted to see the sights. Asking a German the direction to Hitler's bunker had the result of our little army splitting up until later that night. So me and the Kent lot went off to find a few steins. One of our group well known for using tissues in his room did not venture out when he found his favourite ever TV channel called Fucky Fucky. Tosser!

We all meet up in the hotel bar where that famous drinker Barney is consuming milk and as the evening gets later we had to wait on the arrival of Steve the Greek who was travelling by train from Athens to meet us for a night out. A bit similar I suppose to getting the train from Eccles into Manchester for a night out. The journey took Greeko two days and after he finally arrived it was into town for a few Becks and the customary Irish gaff for a warm pint of the black stuff. As most people who know us will be aware we always seem to find the red light district and Berlin was to be no exception. Now if any member of our party partook in the oldest business I am not allowed to divulge. All I will say is 'you dirty bastard, she was gorgeous'. Please let it be noted however that Barney did have a beer before bedtime.

Wednesday morning saw us all on the road by 9am making the three hour journey to Lodz. As Berlin was on the border with Poland we did find it strange that it took us three hours to reach the Polish border. And the roads in Poland are what can only be described as the worst ever. As we started to travel through this country we discovered that there was something that could catch on in England. Where we have flower sellers on our main roads the country of Polska has prostitutes. This was in fact to become a problem for me at the wheel of the car as all of a sudden my passengers were in no rush to reach Lodz. In fact if I went faster than 6 miles an hour I was severely reprimanded. Of course none of the gentlemen wanted to spend the three Zlotties - well, not until the return journey.

We eventually made Lodz at about 3pm and quickly met up with other Reds who had travelled by an aircraft (strange). The local brew was by now flowing in a brilliant bar and it was a merry bunch who made their way to the stadium. Arriving we now had an hour to spare before kick-off and time to get the beer in so I order 20 bottles of beer from a street booth. Well, sorry lads, how was I to know it was non-alcoholic.

After receiving abuse we walked straight into football violence. We could not believe Reds were fighting. In fact it turned out to be a mob of Legia Warsaw fans attacking Lodz - strange. Anyway, the match was crap, United's support about 400 and we were on our way to Barcelona in May.

The journey home saw one of the party enjoy a picnic in the woods with a Polish girl - the only Red I know who resides in Merseyside! On reaching the airport we found the lads in the other car have been done for speeding and had their car broken into in Lodz. All good fun. The trip cost us £119 each.

John and I do the Red Bus where for the last few seasons we take coaches to Euro aways. This season would see us run at least one coach to all the matches. Brief highlights below, culminating in the Final.

Munich. And the bloody beer festival. The biggest problem organising the trip was the accommodation as Munich apparently gets rather busy during the Oktoberfest. We ended up staying in four different hotels, one of which turned out to be a youth hostel where you had to be in bed by 10pm. Sorry, you whippersnappers. We made the Bar of 111 Beers our home for the next couple of days where the majority of us stayed together including a certain Sale gentleman who had travelled with us at the very last minute telling his wife that he was working in Blackpool for the week. This chap chatted up a Fraulein in the bar and we would see Helga again this season in Barcelona. Love moves in mysterious ways. On matchday it was off to the beer festival. If you haven't been - go, it is brilliant. Good beer, food, singing, all nationalities, more beer and more beer. Bloody brilliant.

The match is well documented. Two people I know however - one of each persuasion I should point out -

were rather enjoying each other's bodies in the United end. When United went 2-1 up early in the second half to celebrate the goal, the song went, 'put your hand up if you had a blow job', if you get my drift. Teddy had a good match and we should have won bar the last minute. It was back to the 111 Bar and I think we got through 27 of them on the Tuesday so a few more to sample.

Brondby. Most people had opted out of travelling on the Red Bus for this trip, so 25 of us set off for a perverts paradise trip. Tuesday lunchtime we reached our first overnight stay - the wonderful city of Hamburg. We headed to that main road and myself, Jon, Brian and Martin had no option but to get pissed. We were joined later by Russell and the Fleetwood lads. As the night drew in we were somewhat merry and in the two visits to Hamburg I still have seen nothing but that main wide street. We eventually met up with the other members of the coach and a great night was had by all, even though some gentleman kept disappearing into the big house next door, called Enfuck Ladies. Never did find out what was in there.

One of the lads from Huddersfield got lost and ended up in a bar where a man was very friendly to him. A bar just full of men in fact. Oblivious, the lad invited him back to his hotel room when the stranger said he had missed his lift home. The lad is just a little gullible. Anyway, lucky for the lad, his room-mate scared the German off.

Wednesday we reach wonderful Copenhagen at about 2pm. It was pissing down so we decided to all meet in an English pub in the main square. When we arrived beer was about £6. Bollocks to that and into a little Danish bar near the station where the beer was about a quid. Getting into the stadium was a novelty - no police anywhere and stewards who were just bewildered by it all. A great result meant drink was needed so it was into the stadium pub under the Main Stand. A tremendous drink was had by the 50 or so Reds until there was a problem between a blonde girl, a Red, her Liverpool supporting boyfriend and an ashtray. Back into town drinking in various bars which included a nightclub where the lads all thought they were John Travolta...not.

Thursday came and now the 24 - we had lost one in Copenhagen - landed in destination number.3, wonderful Amsterdam, a city I have only visited 23 times and quite frankly can't see what people get excited about. After checking in guess where we ended up? More bleeding naked women, drink and funny cakes. Needless to say everyone was skint by 6am. This had been one hell of a week, the only question was would we be fit for the next trip.

Barcelona here we come for our first trip there this season. A full coach and mini-bus had made the trip and a hotel (if I can call it that) just off La Ramblas. The Tuesday is a bit of a blur, photographs that I have seen since would suggest that I had been drinking. All I can do is move onto Wednesday where my drink intake was water, all day. A day where I was as rough as a bear's botty. Me and Jimmy did the old tourist bit until about 5pm when we went to meet Ankle Biter and the Worm in the Barca Ultra Boys Bar. A good couple of hours spent with a few Barca fans who pay £100 for their season tickets. That includes all Cup games. A fantastic match followed resulting in me having a few drinks into the early hours of the morning.

Now if you went on all three trips in the group stages with the Red Bus it would have cost you £400.

The Quarter Final match in the San Siro against some goofy looking Brazilian and his team of Ginola-esk cheats. Anyway, we stuffed 'em. Once again the Bus was full with an over-full mini-bus as well,, the hotel by Central station where the evening got underway with a Yorkshire lass who was not shy in showing her large bosoms (strange). The stadium was great when all lit up together with the 10,000+ Reds and the result was fantastic.

Turin was next and I for once was convinced that it was the end of the road. We were playing possibly the best side in the world over the past five years. Well, what I will say is that this match will go down in folk lore. 2-0 down and we were in for a hiding. The next hour of football was quite simply bloody wonderful. When the final whistle went, whilst all around Reds danced and jigged, sang and shouted, I was there, crying inconsolably. All my life I have followed United, home and away, abroad and my dreams of seeing my love in THE FINAL. Just a dream, one of those fairy tale dreams that never come true. But it bloody well had. Manchester United Football Club had made it into the European Cup Final.

I was still sobbing. Being comforted by friends, true, true friends, people that I have travelled thousands of miles with. You know who you are and I thank you all. Barcelona here we come.

Sorry to have got a little sentimental. The day after the semi I did not return home with the Red Bus. I got the overnight train to Barcelona. Hotel beds were needed. Two days I walked the streets of Barca and Stiges and returned home with enough beds for the Red invasion.

Of course the events in Barcelona are well chronicled later on in these pages. Needless to say plenty of tears flowed again. It had been a marvellous season. The Red Bus went to all of the games for under a £1,000 per head. I had met plenty of new friends along the way as well. Hugh the Busker - still to hear him sing, the Fleetwood lads, all the Kent kunts and many, many more to mention. There is nothing quite like following your team abroad. Thank you Manchester United.

EAT F**K ALL, SLEEP F**K ALL, DRINK

JP

LKS Lodz 0 - Manchester United 0
European Cup Champions League, 2nd Qualifying Round, 2nd leg
August 26th 1998, Stadion LKS
Schmeichel, Neville P, Irwin, Stam, Johnsen, Keane, Beckham, Butt, Scholes, Sheringham, Giggs.
Subs used: Solskjaer.
Attendance: 8,000

JP - young, gifted and red - is a contributor to Red Issue, regularly writing his Euro away travel reports. Mark our words - this lad's destined for great things at Old Trafford!

3am Sunday morning, Ostend train station. Another season of mad European adventures was upon us, and as ever, we were fucked. The day before at West Ham had seen one of THE classic away days, obviously nothing to do with the 0-0 result, as the Red Army 'visited' the Boleyn Ground for the first time since (but this time without) the infamous balaclavas. The twenty or so United who were spread about the last train out of London ensured the hector had his work cut out and once in Dover all eventually boarded a ferry to Calais after the Ostend one had apparently succumbed to a fire. The ferry company laid on a coach to transport us to Belgium which, when it eventually turned up, presented a chance to get a bit of kip. For the most part the chance was passed up and it was a weary band which bailed off in Ostend.

It had been a long day and the "late-night attractions" were as unwelcoming as they come, but one lad still felt obliged to indulge for a mere £50. Meanwhile the rest of us tried to keep warm before the first train which was a good two hours off, whilst a few amused themselves with "spot the Belgium nonce" which led to much abuse of any dodgy-looking local. It's at times like these that you resolve to fork out in future for the luxury of a direct flight rather than poncing about with late-night ferries and early-morning trains, a resolution that lasts until the time comes to book the next trip.

As ever it was first stop Amsterdam. A few of our group with less spare time but more spare cash travelled "par avion" and arrived at various times during the following 24 hours, bumping into us almost on arrival as we patrolled the seedier reaches of the city. The usual suspects indulged in the usual activities throughout Sunday and Monday, before the night train to Berlin which, with connections, would enable us to get to Warsaw for Tuesday afternoon. As we assembled on the platform after 36 hours in the Dam we were a pretty sorry sight, with everyone well caned - one way or another. At the border stop Customs didn't appear particularly arsed that not all of Amsterdam had been left in Amsterdam, content with a straight answer to their questions despite the obvious "foreign" aromas. After negligible amounts of sleep on the overnight train, we were in an even worse state on arrival in the construction site that is Berlin. With only about twenty minutes to wait it wasn't long before we were enjoying quality meals on the train to Warsaw, which were being served up for all of £3, putting Virgin West Coast's dodgy sandwiches to shame.

Eventually arriving in a very grey, damp Warsaw there was the mandatory 10km-trek-with-large-bag to negotiate before a vacant hotel room could be found and we could see the sights. Once everyone was sorted we descended on "Champions", a bar across from the station which evidently set out to attract a high class clientele, with beers at £2 a throw, but instead had to make do with us after being made base-camp by the early arrivals in Poland. Despite Warsaw being heralded as a rapidly improving city as a result of the Western influence, the old regime was still very much in evidence and finding a decent bar wasn't exactly easy. It didn't help that none of us had picked up a map to find our way around so the only thing to do was to jump in a taxi and say "Irish Bar" (apparently located in the Old Town) but the obvious language barrier proved to be just that. We were dropped off at some shady looking place full of locals "enjoying" what was supposed to be a Rolling Stones tribute band, singing in Polish. The length of time it took to get served ensured that we were soon on our way, looking for another bar and thus setting the pattern for the night.

It turned out that as we were meandering aimlessly along, elsewhere in the city one group of Reds ran into a bit of trouble with some locals which was quickly sorted out with the assistance of some older hands. The Old Bill were quickly on the scene and the group of Reds were all nicked, many of whom were completely innocent, whilst the older, wiser Reds had spotted the danger and rapidly departed to continue their marathon session. The Reds who got nicked were treated to two nights in a Polish nick before being hauled up in front of a judge and ordered to pay £180 each, before inviting them to return to Poland anytime, once payment was settled.

Our night hadn't been much better. As it dragged on everyone went their separate ways and a few of us stumbled upon Arena, which was a "dancing" club with services rendered for roughly a tenner. Not that by 3:00am any of us were in any state to take advantage of this and the last half hour before closing was spent singing "We'll Never Die" into a pint pot. We retreated to the Marriot Hotel where some Reds were staying, for yet more refreshments only for the bar to be closed. It was clearly time to call it a night as the conversation turned towards going to Lodz in hired limos and I wandered off just as the sun was rising over Warsaw.

Wednesday morning. A sense of deja-vu in being woken up on a cold floor in someone else's hotel room in a far-off land. So much for the limo as there was a coach leaving from the hotel to Lodz in ten minutes time. "It should take about two hours" was what the tour operator had told the Reds whose coach it was. The previous season a two hour coach trip from Budapest to Kosice had meant five but here the roads were marginally better than the Slovakian one lane dirt tracks and we arrived in Lodz under police escort(?!!?) at about 2:30pm. This would have been too late to play in the return leg of a match with some Lodz fans that had somehow been arranged. A coach-load of Poles had turned up in Miles Platting at seven in the morning before the O.T. leg and went on the piss before losing the afternoon match 8-0. Despite the Poles' careful preparation, the return never actually took place as those who had arrived in Lodz in good time, and had been pencilled in to play, were too busy downing the complimentary loopy juice laid on by their hospitable opponents. Those of us who had to pay for our beers couldn't exactly complain at 60p each.

With kick-off approaching we reluctantly had our first food of the day in MaccyD's before setting off for the ground. Being unable to locate the United section we walked straight into their main stand, ignoring the protestations of a steward. We soon discovered what his problem had been (apart from our lack of tickets) as we found ourselves in the UEFA "executive" section, which was actually an old gym with a few tables laid out for a half-time buffet. We were surprised to see the teams go past on their way to the pitch and promptly followed them down the tunnel before locating spare seats next to a Polish journalist who had no reason to suspect that we weren't the English scouts we purported to be.

The game went by with no action of any note except the feast we helped ourselves to at half-time. Needless to say there were quite a few other United lads onto the same scam. The second half began with a downpour and it was heartening that our executive seats were in the only covered section of the ground, despite the leaks in the roof. The Lodz fans created a good atmosphere with Beckham being singled out for abuse and we were glad that safety restrictions had limited the crowd to half its normal capacity or it could well have been quite intimidating for the Shirts. The 400 or so United fans had their numbers increased by a load of Legia Warsaw barmies who had taken a liking to United back in '91, although from our privileged position we didn't hear them all game. The second half was even worse than the first and we were soon back under the stand stuffing ourselves but this time there was free booze as well. A couple of bottles of vodka were swiped for later on and we proceeded to munch our way through Fergie's press conference, doing our best to disrupt it while the players were being mobbed as they tried to get some scram from what was left of the buffet.

Once back in the centre there wasn't much open so we retreated to the hotel bar and drank UEFA's vodka till 5:00am ignoring the soap opera being played out by a couple of police, the barman and a few other Reds, over who was to pay the bill. The coach back to Warsaw left three hours later and although we were definitely on it, the state we were in meant it is impossible to say how. The coach dropped off at Warsaw airport which was alright for those with flights straight home but wasn't much good for us, so two of us tried to jib a flight rather than face the 20 hour train journey ahead. We gave up at passport control after several thwarted attempts to get through without a boarding card. Instead we ended up jibbing a bus back into Warsaw, which obviously wasn't intentional, but we just didn't know where to get a ticket from. Or so the inspectors were told as they demanded £20 each off us, but we had learnt our lesson well in Nice the previous year and weren't going to get stung again - the inspectors gave up just as we were going back to sleep.

There was a train back to Cologne that night so the rest of the day was spent back in Champions Bar recovering from the previous night. Some of the lads who had been nicked on the Tuesday were in there enjoying their first meal and beers since being released whilst we all waited in anticipation for the draw which was live on Eurosport. It turned out as good as we could have hoped for, what with the way the teams were pooled, with a nice mix of destinations of Copenhagen, Munich and Barcelona. It was even suggested that it was better to have finished runners-up last season just to have our draw (rather than Arsenal's) this year. As the afternoon wore on someone mentioned that the adjoining Marriott hotel had a swimming pool so a couple of us took advantage of its facilities for a much needed sauna, swim and shower before the week caught up with us on the 14 hour overnight journey. The next morning in Cologne two of us decided that we'd had enough so we headed off home whilst the rest returned to the Dam. There was a chance that we would make it back that night but only if we caught all the connections. However as we had a bit of spare time in Brussels, we made up for our failure to jib a flight in Warsaw airport by jibbing the Eurostar to Waterloo, getting back to Manchester just less than a week after setting off.

June 1999...

The contrast between, LKS Lodz 0-0 United, and the finale to the season in Camp Nou could hardly be more striking. Those who started their 98/99 European travels in Poland will certainly have appreciated the colour and splendour of Barcelona. Few, if any, actually expected Lodz to be the first step on the way to winning the European Cup, despite many commenting on the probability that we would win it this year, simply because we'd qualified as runners-up. From the drabness of Poland to the Oktoberfest and the poignancy of Munich onto the rain and goals in Copenhagen and the unbelievable game against Barcelona. The thousands living it up in Milan and then the mass pessimism before the game in Turin. Some of us had been telling everyone that we'd go through but few others believed it. For some reason the confidence was still in evidence even at 2-0 down but it was well founded and we were going back to Barcelona, the culmination of everyone's dreams.

As for the final itself, everyone's got their own memories and their own stories but after the intensity of the actual victory, the rest of the night, the rest of the week, was just very, very strange in a way that's hard to describe. It probably just didn't sink in, especially still being in Spain for the homecoming and with no football after the final for two months. Now, a number of weeks later, I'm starting to get my head round it. Apparently, it can't get any better than Barcelona in May. Whether it can or it can't isn't really important. For now, if you prefer "European Champions" or "Champions of Europe" doesn't matter. Just put "Manchester United" before it and appreciate what that means.

GETTING OUR OWN BACK
Rob Pattinson
Bayern Munich 2 - Manchester United 2
European Cup Champions League, 2nd group match
September 30th 1998, Olympiastadion
Schmeichel, Neville G, Irwin, Stam, Neville P, Keane, Beckham, Scholes, Yorke, Sheringham, Blomqvist.
Subs used: Cruyff.
Scorers: Scholes and Yorke
Attendance: 55,000

Rob, 26 years old, fat bastard, IT Manager, and United We Stand stalwart, has just moved back to Manchester after living it up down 'saath' for a year. Thought last season was the best ever, not just because of what happened on the pitch but also the craic we had off it. The number of lads going to each match just seemed more and more, and providing you steered clear of Old Trafford on a match day until 3pm the prick count at matches didn't seem half as bad as other seasons. He spent the summer in rehab after the goings on during the season (however we just think he's being his usual drinking lightweight self), and also recuperating some cash from the most expensive season ever.

"Ted's Got Life, Na-na-na-na-na", Ted's got life...We laughed and sung this song, but really it was no laughing matter, Ted was "doing bird" for doing nothing!

Bayern Munich away last season, was, for me one of the best European away trips. Even though the match was pretty shit and the result disappointing, something about the Wednesday night after the match made it one of the best nights ever...

The trip started for me in North London. I drove to Gatwick to catch the flight with Benno to Munich, where we were meeting the lads from Manchester as their flight arrived about 20 minutes after ours. Lears, managed to get himself on our flight at the airport so the three of us plotted up in the bar to start getting in the spirit of the first Champions League away game of the season. Everyone was on this trip, most hadn't bothered with the trip to Lodz, so everyone had a bit of cash saved up after the summer, and a trip to Munich during the Oktoberfest couldn't be turned down.

After a few beers at the airport, we chipped in for a load of duty free cans of Heineken and boarded the plane excited about another Euro season which really started with this match. Much of the talk revolved around United's chances in Europe this season. To be perfectly honest we all thought we had a good chance, however, I was a bit reserved and thought Arsenal had a better chance after some of the displays that they had put in at the time - how wrong I was!

When we arrived at Munich airport we were fairly charged up and looking forward to a good night out on the town. A load of us had been to Munich on the way to Vienna in 1996, so we knew about a bar which we called "The Boxing Bar" near the main station. We had a cracking all-dayer in there in '96 and one of the lads, Knighty actually fell in love with the place.

The Manchester crowd, Mitch, Jepo and Smithy stumbled off the plane and met up with us and we all caught the rattler into Munich. Again the chat was about the first real Euro of the season and how good it was going to be.

At the station we argued about which way the Boxing Bar was, and then eventually found it and ordered drinks. The bar was packed and people were spilling out onto the streets. Grant, Franny and Rob told us how it had just "gone off" in the Beer Festival and how Kilburn, Shed, Damien, Ted, Gary and Steve had been nicked after a fracas with the security in one of the beer halls. We didn't think much of it at the time, "Oh they'll be out by the match", "Nothing really happened anyway", "The Police are just overreacting", it's nothing new really for lads to get nicked on European trips, especially when it's Ted!

In the past 5 seasons, Ted had Tonsillitis in Barcelona in '94, he nearly died in Dortmund with Glandular fever, missed his flight home in Milan this year, and got nicked in Munich, which nearly lost him his job and also stopped him from travelling to Barcelona or Brondby!

The night drew in, the bar was full on United and crap rumours were being bandied about as per usual when anything happens to do with trouble. "The police were out of order, we weren't doin' nuthin", "It was mental, there were 200 of them!!". On this occasion however it seemed that the police had overreacted and the lads hadn't really done anything at all. At the time it didn't seem too bad and we just got on with the night ahead.

I left our lads to go on a session at a hotel just out of the centre of Munich, which after a good few hours, Fass, Benno and myself returned to the centre feeling a bit worse for wear. I couldn't see my watch, but found out it was 4:15 so decided to go up to Benno's hotel room to spy on the bird he had seen undressing earlier in the opposite apartment.

The day of the game started badly. We were sat outside the Boxing Bar again when it was confirmed that the lads had definitely been nicked and no one knew when they would be released. To make matters worse, as we sat there Steve was arrested by the German old bill and whisked away with about 35 riot police surrounding him like he was a fucking terrorist - tossers! All this had put a bit of a dampener on the day, but we decided that having had our fill of the Boxing Bar, we would make our way up to the Bierfest to see what was going on up there.

About 25 of us sat round a massive table and got involved with a massive "stein" of beer each, which:-

1. Was too fucking heavy to lift.

2. Tasted like shit.

3. Was warm and flat by the time you got to the bottom, and

4. Blocked your view of the person sat opposite you!

On top of this there was that shite "OomPah" crap playing in the background whilst loads of Europe's worst dressed nation slapped their lederhosen and spilt beer down their leather vests!

We soon got bored of it in there and went outside. However, as we stood on the balcony, the old bill came up and nicked another couple of lads near to us. I don't think they were particularly fussy who they arrested, so I kept my head right down as I didn't want to join the rest of the lads in the nick. I later found out they arrested a lad from Urmston who was making his debut at a match, is not even into football violence, has never even been seen with the 'firm' before, and is usually so stoned on weed to even speak to people let alone fight. On top of this - like a few of the others nicked - he wasn't even in the country at the time of the event the previous night!

After a few more beers, we decided to make our way up to the ground. We bumped into Smithy and Jepo, who, after having food poisoning all day from a couple of snide Bockwursts, had realised that Smithy (Britain's worst organised man) had lost the match tickets, the plane tickets and his brain!

We then proceeded to hammer them for being soft, disorganised fuckers, then they explained how it was their worst ever Euro away, so we went easy on them!

I managed to get another ticket although I didn't really need one as the gates were wide open. The match was OK, we went fucking mental when Yorke equalised on 29 minutes, then even more so when Scholesey ran through and scored on 49 minutes - then dismayed at the end when Schmeichel made a rare error and dropped us a couple of points. I seem to remember it was pissing it down as we came out of the impressive stadium, however I can't really remember as I was pissed! My comments were "Fucking Schmeichel", "useless Danish twat, past his best, get rid of him" and "we'll never win that European Cup when we can't get a good result on European soil" - humble pie for me at the end of the season, what a tosser!

I had heard Spandau Ballets "True" on the radio on the way to the airport and couldn't get it out of my head. Next minute we were sat on a U-Bahn back to the traditional Boxing Bar, with all 10 of us singing "Ba-ba-ba baaaaahaaa, I know this, much is true", classic. Then came the ballads of me and Benno, reeling them off - Dr Hook, Leo Sayer, Eric Clapton, Rod Stewart. We were all absolutely shattered, Benno and I hadn't slept for a couple of nights, everyone else was hungover and even a bit subdued. Most of us (apart from alcoholic Grant) decided

that we would have a few drinks then probably get our heads down and make the most of Thursday, only it didn't quite happen like that.

See, you know when you have a spontaneous piss-up it usually ends up being the best night out you've had in ages? That is exactly what happened on this night in Munich, it actually turned into one of the best nights ever! We plotted up, about 10 of us around a table and started ordering the beer. The songs started again, first of all a few love ballads sparked by Benno and me, then at Teds' misfortune "Ted's got life", then a few rock classics by Rob.S and Franny, then TV classics (Franny and Rob are telly addicts), then a full rendition of Stone Roses, Hotel California, and topping it all with the full version of American Pie - the whole fucking bar was joining in, Germans and all "vy vy Miz Americaan Pie", absolutely brilliant. This went on for a good couple of hours, the songs got more abstract, louder and the laughter increased! Eventually as pissed up singing normally does, we reverted back to the good old United songs, the full versions of Willie Morgan were sung, The Flowers Of Manchester, any old, long United song was better than the last.

People were coming past the bar and stopping outside, Bayern fans clapping along, Benno stood up on tables as we all sang "Beano's fucking magic", and "Na na na naaaaaaa Beeeeaaaannnnoooo", (he's 39 going on 9!!).

Some German geezer came over and said the barman would like us to leave but he was too scared of us. I don't know why, we were in such good spirits that we didn't have a malicious bone in our bodies at the time. Classic! Eventually it all calmed down and we went to crash out. I got my head down in the absent Ted's bed and slept, and I mean slept!

Most of the lads had gone early the next day back to Manchester, but the rest of us, just relaxed and had a few beers with the money we had left before returning home, still with no sign of Ted.

When I got back to the airport I proceeded to drive up to Manchester, I rang every single person around the table that night and everyone agreed it had been one of their best ever nights, I suppose you just had to be there really, we still look back on it now, it's what European travel is all about.

As for the more unfortunate lads on the trip, Smithy and Jepo decided to go back to the hotel after the match and described it as their worst Euro' ever! Not as bad as for Ted and the rest of the crowd though. Ted was in a German prison for ten days with shite German food, cost him a fortune in solicitors fees and nearly his job. Ted, however was one of the more fortunate ones - Steve, Steve and Gary were locked up for months, and what for? The treatment they got for something so minor was a fucking disgrace.

Aah well, look on the bright side, at least we got our own back on the bastards in the final, altogether now "Who put the ball in the Germans net...!"

WONDERFUL, WONDERFUL COPENHAGEN
Nigel Appleton

Brondby I.F. 2 - Manchester United 6
European Cup Champions League, 3rd group match
October 21st 1998, Parken Stadium
Schmeichel, Neville G, Neville P, Brown, Stam, Giggs,
Keane, Scholes, Blomqvist, Cole, Yorke.
Subs used: Cruyff, Solskjaer and Wilson.
Scorers: Giggs (2), Cole, Keane, Yorke and Solskjaer
Attendance: 40,315

Nigel, 41, now works as an Independent Financial Advisor from his home in Chester, moving from his previous employer last summer, a move not totally unrelated to the fact that the number of days off required per year to watch United were starting to exceed the "official" holiday entitlement. He has a love and commitment to United matched by very few and to say his life is ruled by his "obsession" is quite possibly one of the all time understatements.

When one reflects on those glorious eleven days at the end of the season, during which we completed our third double in the last six seasons and then eclipsed even that with possibly the greatest comeback in the history of football, it is easy to understand why Manchester United means so much to so many. However, it wasn't always like this, as anybody who has watched us for more than a few years will testify, and no doubt at some time in the future we will again experience depressing and barren times. But, enough of this philosophising. Hopefully, the following recollections of my trip to Copenhagen will give a fair reflection of what a typical trip watching United in Europe is like for me, and many others, and long may they continue!

When one looks back at the Euro away draws enjoyed this season - Munich, Milan, Turin, Barca (twice), it becomes easy to see why perhaps this fixture was viewed by many with the least anticipation, with the exception of Lodz in the preliminary round (great trip!). As the game was also sandwiched between visits to Munich (during the beer festival) and Barcelona (the very mention of which has always got the pulse racing) it became appar-

ent that this would represent the smallest Euro away following of the season, again with the exception of the visit to Poland.

I, however, looked upon the draw with a certain degree of deja-vu, as having never been to Copenhagen - or even Denmark for that matter - before in my life, this was to be my second visit within three months. Remembering the great time the city afforded us on the pre-season visit there I was certain that another memorable trip was in the offing, and so it proved.

With the downward trend in air fares over the last few years and the increasing popularity of United games in Europe a good deal of advance planning is now required in order to obtain the most cost effective way of travel and so it was that I had the pleasure (again!) of driving a car load to Stanstead for an 8am flight with those nice, cheap and cheerful people at Go! "Long may the discount airlines prosper!" I say. It's just a bloody shame that the landing fees are so expensive at Manchester to save me the bloody drive.

With the advent of the expanded Champions (!!!) League I seem to spend so many hours airborne these days that flights tend to pass with numbing monotony and fortunately, as this is not a long journey, before I become totally comatose we are checking in at our hotel in central Copenhagen.

Locals wear Utd. colours at Brondby

Now this was the sister hotel of that stayed in during the pre-season visit and was definitely the ugly one of the two, though it did carry a 3-star rating. It was only later that I discovered star ratings in Denmark are not awarded by an independent agency - as in England - but by the hotels themselves - makes you wonder why they're not all five stars really!

A bar (surprisingly...) called Rosie McGees was to be the early evening rendezvous, and for the benefit of those who have not been to Copenhagen this place serves up the largest rack of ribs ever seen (even Phil who has the biggest appetite in the world struggled to finish the beast off!). Just a pity the beer kicked in at about £3.50 for a pint.

After the pre-season game all the United players had a beer, or two, or...in here, and I remember at the time meeting Peter Schmeichel as he left the gents. I hadn't realised until then how big he was as he literally filled the door frame. Upon returning to the bar he offered to buy all the Reds a beer, which we politely declined but nevertheless...a top man! You will be missed Peter.

However a different sight met me this time - the legendary Drunken Dave, complete with multi-coloured Afro wig and toy mobile phone! Not a pretty sight I can tell you. By this time early evening had arrived and some time travel seemed appropriate - to the uninitiated this meant a trip to Christiana Park - but with the assistance of a taxi and not a phone box!

Christiana Park started as a hippy commune in the 1970s and declare itself an independent state, together with government approval and it self-policed with rules such as 'no theft, no violence and no hard drugs'. However, softer "recreational" drugs are available in abundance and represent one of the few sources of income the commune dwellers have.

It is easy to imagine walking into the appropriately named Woodstock Bar (which is reminiscent from the outside of the worker's hut in the TV series 'Auf Wiedersehn Pet'!), that you have been transported back into the 70s - as a sea of dope smoking, beer drinking, bearded hippies meet your gaze. Add this to the not unpleasant fog like atmosphere and it takes a few moments to remember that you are actually only a mile or so away from the centre of a European capital city.

Whilst we indulged ourselves with the cheaper beer and enjoyed the general bonhomie, a local female, who resembled a cross between a hippy and an eskimo approached us with what appeared to be the Olympic Torch, but which she explained was in fact a peace pipe. Upon smoking this object one of the lads almost burnt down the entire hut and its inhabitants such was its ferocity. Anyhow, the peace bit seemed to do the trick, as within a very short period of time another of our party - who shall remain nameless to protect the innocents at home - had disappeared with said female for some free instruction in hippy carnal practices!

By this time we were all feeling pretty, er, chilled out and it seemed the appropriate time to return to the real world, but not before we stumbled upon the biggest band (probably) of 1998, the Manic Street Preachers, performing an impromptu gig in what can only be described as an oversized barn, full of spaced out Danes. Security at the barn doors was fairly thin on the ground and we managed to jib our way into the gig to catch the final three tracks and the band taking the piss out of the Danes about Wales defeating them the previous week (Welsh Phil loved that I can tell you!). The night was getting stranger by the minute and it wasn't even the witching hour yet,

A tardis - sorry taxi - was finally found to return us to the centre of Copenhagen and some form of 1990s normality and the evening continued in a now familiar sort of way - drinking in those student bar and late night disco type haunts that seem to attract themselves to me whenever I'm in Europe, and bed was eventually reached, in time honoured fashion, as breakfast was being served.

We discovered during the pre-season trip that as Scandanavians are absolutely mad about everything connected with English football, and United in particular, they will always arrange an afternoon pre-game function in a local disco, which seems to entail hundreds of replica

shirt wearing locals going absolutely ballistic whilst watching United videos and listening to all those dreadful records that our club has produced over the years. But the upshot of this is that they are desperate to get rid of their money in exchange for anything connected with United (scarves, badges, etc) and so it was that a well known fanzine editor loaded up with more out-of-date fanzines than was humanly possible to carry, descended upon the throng to dispose of his unwanted luggage. I watched on with amazement at the copies he and a few helpers got rid of - it was absolutely ridiculous.

Another thing with these do's is that it attracts all sorts of local media types from TV, radio and newspapers, and as I was propping up the bar (no selling for me) I was approached by a guy from the press, who was dressed in the worst Union Jack shirt I have ever seen. I don't recall too much of what was said but I do recall him asking: "Why is it that most fans from England do not wear the team's dresses?". I was by now becoming a little wary about this man's intentions until his colleague explained that by "dress", he actually meant "kit". That was a relief! Imagine my surprise the following day to find my mugshot, together with said interviewer, on the back page of the main daily paper!

The weather outside was typically English (pissing down!) and so we did not venture too far before heading off for the game, for which we had acquired, through a friend in England with a Danish contact, half a dozen seats for the Main Stand.

Unfortunately, due to having our own United end tickets spare, which we couldn't give away, we missed the opening five minutes of the match and were ecstatic when Ryan Giggs scored the opening goal after some 20 minutes. It was only after we had settled back into our seats that we were informed by the Danes behind us that this was in fact United's second goal, as Giggs himself had opened the account in the second minute, whilst we were still outside attempting to shift the aforementioned spares.

All credit to the Danish fans, as they showed to the full their knowledge and appreciation of the English game, despite having to put up with our inane ramblings throughout the proceedings, and the thought that they may be bitter in defeat never even came into the equation.

The game itself was a fairly routine affair with additional goals from Cole, Keano, Dwight and Ole resulting in our highest European away score since we beat Borussia Dortmund (remember them!) 6-1 in 1964. I bet there weren't many in Copenhagen who had seen that match live. The only downside to the result was the indifferent performance of our own Great Dane, who was going through probably his most inconsistent spell since arriving at Old Trafford, and who was at fault with both Brondby goals. I think we can forgive the great man one poor spell after what he has achieved during his time with us, and not least of all with some of his performances in the latter stages of this season (eat your heart out Dennis Bergkamp).

We had, on our previous visit, found a bar by the ground - in fact attached to it - and this was our rendezvous afterwards. A few beers to allow the traffic to clear is always a good move in my eyes and the only potential aggravation in this bar came from an Everton fan from Doncaster (postcode L something...I don't think) who was winding my mate Alan up, bad style. Now, Alan, to the uninitiated, does not have the longest fuse in the world but his parting shot of: "This conversation is now over - F**k Off!", before calmly walking away, has to be a classic at any time, and we duly departed for the nearest taxi. Alan, having left the bar with a bottle of beer in one hand and a tuna bap in the other, then proceeded to produce another classic act. Getting into the taxi, the driver told him he couldn't drink in the vehicle so promptly drank up, only the be told then that he couldn't eat either, which led within seconds to the driver receiving the said bap between the eyes!

The rest of the night's activities followed that all too familiar role of beer, more beer, another bar, more beer, another club, etc, until I vaguely recall we found the Absalon Disco (top club) which was packed with Reds and a fair number of attractive locals! What was left of the night then seemed to disappear into a drunken haze, but I am told that a top night was enjoyed by all present, and another breakfast time return to bed followed. Fortunately the flight home was not until late afternoon, which at least afforded us a few much needed hours of shut-eye.

To briefly summarise the trip: loads of beer, a brilliant laugh with the regular travellers, very little sleep and an empty wallet - the usual ingredients of a Euro away. Add to that a bagful of goals and we've had an excellent three days in a great city for United's first ever competitive fixture in Denmark. Despite promising myself after not seeing her in the summer, I've still not managed to see that bloody mermaid though! - ah well, maybe next time.

And all that remained was a short flight back to Blighty and that bloody drive home from Stansted - pass the matchsticks for the driver please! The sobering thought on the way home, bearing in mind how quickly these games come around nowadays, was that it was only five weeks to Barcelona, and guess where we were flying from!

BARCELONA!
Phil Holt
Barcelona 3 - Manchester United 3
European Cup Champions League, 5th group match
November 25th 1998, Nou Camp Stadium
Schmeichel, Neville G, Irwin, Brown, Stam, Keane,
Beckham, Scholes, Blomqvist, Cole, Yorke.
Subs used: Butt.
Scorers: Cole and Yorke (2).
Attendance: 67,650

"He loves the life and lives the life".

Barcelona by Freddie Mercury...a song title I was to hear many times during this long and wonderful season.

My goal has always been to see us win the European Cup but to achieve it in the manner which we did has exceeded all my expectations. Not only the final, but the whole tournament was a classic one from start to finish.

Each game was memorable in its own right yet Barcelona stands out as the place where we visited twice - once in the league stages where we were full of hope and confidence, mixed with nervous trepidation, and once for the final, the biggest and best event ever. The first

game in the Nou Camp, played out in a bizarre half-full stadium as their fans had given their chances - slim - the ghost, saw one of the greatest attacking matches ever seen in Europe. United showed that the bagfuls in Brondby were not a fluke - we now had an attack that the rest of Europe feared. It was a great match and enabled us to know exactly what we now needed for us to qualify in the last group match.

It has meant so much to reach this stage that I never felt we would lose, but what an adventure we all had on the way. Here are some of my recollections of this wonderful city and our two visits:-

MOST GENEROUS AWARD
The barman who gave me and Andy a bar tab at 9am when we had run out of pesetas after drinking all night. We promised to come back and pay him but he let us get so pissed we never found the bar again - sorry senor.

BEST NIGHTCLUB AWARD
The Velvet wins hands down yet again as a willing receptive for our post match celebrations. We have been frequenting this club for years now and still aren't bored with the David Lynch inspired toilets.

BEST SHIRTS OFF DANCING AWARD
'Sit Down' celebrations from James nearly shaded this one for the Velvet Club again but the little bar on La Ramblas takes it as I simply can't remember the fact that I, along with several of my equally stupid chums, were dancing topless with a gypsy match-stick seller, oblivious to the police trying to hit us with their batons!

WORST MEMORY AWARD
To me for forgetting the above and having a £100 bet with Eddie that it never took place and being proved wrong by too many neutral witnesses.

BEST CENTRE FORWARD COMBINATION
Cole and Yorke for their brilliant contribution to that thrilling 3-3 draw in the group stages - or was it Ole and Teddy for their never to be forgotten Munich destruction? Pure magic.

BEST CHAMPAGNE AWARD
To the German who, totally uninvited, sat down in a grimy pavement bar with us after the final and purchased three bottles of champagne for 17 of us. Gracious in defeat and heading towards forgiveness. Vielen Danken.

BEST POOL AWARD
The Stiges Maritime on match day. Sat around the pool all day with none of the usual hassle. Well chilled and the best build up to the best match.

WELL PAST SELL BY DATE
To the dodgy old tart who ushered us into a bar and walked us to a table in total darkness followed by trying to get us interested in a bit of nether region action. Non gracias senorita.

SEX ON THE BEACH AWARD
To several gay f***ers, regularly seen shagging on the beach in Stiges at 4am, more than one of them feeling the worse for wear after meeting some of our Cockney chums on the way home from their regular karaoke session!

MISSING LATE GOALS AWARD
Mr.Taylor leaving in order to remonstrate with our German friends at the other end. Surely he never made it back in for the goals?

MISSING LATE DRINKS AWARD
To El Molino in Sitges - open 24 hours and found easily when passing in a taxi but desperately well hidden

when I've got a bet that it's "just around the corner" and that "we'll be in there with a drink by 5.30am". Many thanks to the local who picked me up as I ran into the road and drove three of us to the bar for 5.29am!

BEST CROWD CONTROL

To David May for his superb marshalling of the post-match celebrations. Even if he's not good enough to get in the team can we not get him to replace Keith f***ing Fane and that infernal Barcelona song!

ULTIMATE RESPECT AWARD

To Sir Alex Ferguson for being himself.

RIP AWARD

To Harry Linford, died in Spain a few short days after the Final - much loved, much missed.

CONCLUSION AWARD

To me for managing to complete this with a very short deadline whilst enjoying the pre-season tour of Australia, hence the briefness. It really was a magic season which will never be forgotten by anyone involved. I went to every game along the way and loved every minute of it. I travelled far and wide with some of the finest people I shall ever meet and would like to thank every single one of them for the memories.

LIFE IS BEAUTIFUL
Teresa McDonald
Inter Milan 1 - Manchester United 1
European Cup Quarter-Final, 2nd leg
March 17th 1999, San Siro
Schmeichel, Neville G, Irwin, Keane, Johnsen, Stam, Beckham, Berg, Cole, Yorke, Giggs.
Subs used: Neville P and Scholes.
Scorers: Scholes.
Attendance: 79,528

Teresa, a mother of three and a grandmother of three is 63 years of age and if she hadn't fallen for Manchester United in such a big way, might now be living the life of riley in the sun. As it is she now collects her pension (to pay for the next trip), swims daily, listens to jazz, watches the movies, has an embarrassing shrine to her God - Eric Cantona - in her bedroom and is probably (is) the biggest football bore the world has ever seen. Any intellectuals out there might encounter her at her other role play - offloading old books at antiquarian book fairs. Beware the soft sell, it all goes to fund her United habit.

Italian film director Roberto Begnini's 'Life is Beautiful' swept the boards at the 1999 Oscar ceremony. Set in fascist Italy during the Second World War, this controversial movie takes great delight in sending up the Mussolini regime. Begnini himself in the film sets the stage when he is applying for a job as an upholsterer and delicately wants to discover where the proprietor's politics lie. The man's two children are fighting each other and the owner yells at them "Benito, Adolfino...stop fighting". Begnini awards himself a small chuckle. Two weeks after seeing this great movie I turned up in Milan for our European Champions League tie against Inter Milan.

Several decades on from the film setting, there is always an underlying menace simmering under the surface at Italian football stadia, and for me the image of Mussolini's black shirted thugs presents itself in the form

of the uncompromising and uncommunicative riot police who await (mob handed) for the football supporters travelling from England. I realise that they may think they have an axe to grind - Heysel (but we're not Scousers) will never be eradicated from their, or our, memories. But you always arrive in Italy with a gut feeling that in such fine surroundings, fair play and justice will not be on the agenda at the ground.

In addition, the moral panics and media hype from certain sections of the British press add to any build up of pre-match tensions. We hardened veterans of the European 'Reds on Tour' brigade can safely predict the media reaction to visits from Manchester United supporters at the bigger stadiums and matches. In the weeks leading up to the match the tabloids will be awash with scare stories about the lack of safety for the fans because of the availability of wide-spread black market tickets and the problems of segregation between rival supporters, quoting a club spokesmen appealing for United fans not to travel. The tabloids conveniently overlook the fact that their own papers have been carrying adverts from independent tour operators offering package deals and match tickets along with hospitality packages. Ask yourself, if you couldn't get a match ticket from United and you could afford to pay over the odds for a package deal, what would you do? It is also by the by that there seems to be a total lack of regard for security pre-planning at the grounds to sort out proper safety control measures in advance and that it is sometimes alleged that the club actually turns down an extra allocation of tickets, as was rumoured about the Milan fixture!

The press will then say after the event that nobody realised that there would be as many Reds travelling as they did, even though every clued up Red could give a fair approximation of the real number beforehand and then there will be a jibe over how they'd wished we hadn't travelled unofficially as if the ensuing chaos and incompetence at the ground is somehow our fault.

The enduring hypocrisy of the British press never ceases to amaze. As I write this piece we have won the unique treble, yet the constant sniping and undermining of Alex Ferguson and his team throughout this season, starting with the vilification of David Beckham and then to be later accompanied by a Uriah Heep sycophancy was flesh crawling. The over-the-top fawning at our achievements after so much stick and bile words leaves a bitter taste in the mouth.

The background to our match in Milan had the usual painting of a scenario of warring, ticketless fans marauding their way across Europe although we will take thousands to the match, the vast majority will behave impeccably yet somehow the local press will pick on some 'un hooligans el Manchester' story whilst back home the tabloids print a story of 'trouble the night before the game'. I'd like to know what it would be like if 8,000 tabloid journalists went to a foreign city for a few days and then see the headlines...

The next prophecy that we can expect on certain big European trips is that - and we can set our watches to this - we will arrive at the ground and find unbelievable chaos as those working at the ground will seem to have no idea what their stadium is actually there for (getting people in safely), with ensuing crushes, safety hazards and potential disasters that English grounds simply would not get away with.

UEFA will either deny the crushing, etc, or say they knew nothing about it, the police will either be non-existent or ridiculously violent, the gates will either be one inch wide or closed, English speaking people and United officials will also be non-existent and the club security firm (the dreaded suits) who are all on our freebies and at least should be seen to be doing something will - in 100 cases out of 100 - probably laugh at the Utd fans asking for their help to sort the mess out or walk away. Oh, and as a token gesture United will be fined because - at the end of all this - we let off a few flares inside the ground. The crumbling, dilapidated stadium will, of course, get off scot free.

The match ticket (every Euro away bar the last two) won't be checked and the home end is easier to get into than the away section. It's lucky we're so well behaved - imagine Leeds fans - but the terrifying thought remains that at one of these fixtures there is a tragedy waiting to happen. Those of us who have seen first hand the crushes and incompetence realise how Hillsborough happened and subsequently covered up. Because we've seen it so often - Galatasaray, locked gates and baton charging. Porto - the same. Feyenoord - locked gates for 45 minutes because the police lost control. Turin - baton charges. Munich - a lack of segregation that was comical to the extreme. Fenerbahce - a nightmare stadium.

So as I made my way to Milan - with stories at least a month before saying that the home fans had begun using all sorts of missiles on the away fans to vent their anger at their team with little done by the authorities - it is safe to say that I had a very prophetic and sad vision of what to expect come matchday.

But once again take away the baton and the local population was friendly and welcoming. Milan itself has slightly more to offer the visitor than Turin. No wonder they call it the Turin Shroud - the whole bloody place is under a shroud. Yet the tabloid story - along with Fergie saying that: "I am not convinced Ronaldo is not going to play. When the Italians tell you it's pasta I even check under the sauce to make sure it really is" - was of 'Soccer thugs in Milan riot', when the only riot we saw was the crush to be served in bars that stayed open late.

On the match day a few of us took in what seemed to be the only sight worth seeing - the large cathedral - although in fact it was the arcades with Prada and Versace window displays that took our attention over a cathedral packed with Japanese tourists and pigeons, rather like Trafalgar Square.

We'd intended meeting everyone at the Red Indian Bar for the usual pre-match session and sing-song. But it was closed - so a small cafeteria nearby was chosen, serving sublime red wine and snacks for an elongated thrash as we read of Fergie's pre-match psychological ploy - which worked an absolute treat and perhaps was a key-factor later that night: "There will be a lot of scheming, diving and referee baiting. I think the Italians will go through their whole repertoire. I hope the referee is strong". The Italians had fallen for it hook, line and sinker - Gianluca Palliuca: "Manchester United are scared and have to resort to this sort of attack", and especially Milan coach Mircea Lucescu fell into the trap. Lucescu said: "The messages coming from Alex Ferguson might incite crowd trouble and will certainly make for a bad atmosphere. I have

always believed in the English sense of fair play, but Ferguson is from Scotland where they don't have fair play apparently...maybe he is afraid".

The session took hold however and I seem to recall finding the Red Indian open and even more hazily attempting a conversation with United folk hero Pete Boyle. Although I know now never to repeat drinking with Kevin as his wine buying prowess was similar to a billionaire in Harrods. We boarded a bus to the stadium with every intention of gaining access at a reasonable time before kick-off. One of our party couldn't handle the Kevin approach to pre-match time passing (drink until you drop) and feeling like he needed to be sick and/or go to the toilet he departed down a side-street. We didn't see him again that day, apparently he'd found a small hotel nearby and headed to the toilet for a pee, then spotted an open bedroom door and before he knew what was next he was being woken up be a phone ringing in a hotel room he didn't belong in! He'd fallen asleep until nearly half-time and all he can remember about this stepping stone to European Glory was seeing Ronaldo's bald head on the pitch and that's it!

This left me and Kevin the task of hailing a taxi before the game - for once a success. My immediate reaction to arrival at the ground was 'at last an Inter fan' as until then we hadn't spotted one fan around town. To our alcohol induced credit, we'd arrived at the stadium at least an hour before kick-off. As is always the way those who arrived after kick-off or jibbed in the open gates didn't know what was to happen next and the trouble there had been.

As we arrived at the United section we were amazed to discover that there were only two gates for the United contingent, this after a decision had apparently been made to put the unofficial and official United support in together - an estimated 7-8,000. At this time there were only a few dozen milling around and all seemed quiet on the Western front but knowing what we know, things did not look good. I should have remembered Begnini's film - never underestimate the nature of the beast which can beat in the Italian heart. I noticed that the police were only allowing one or two people in at a time and then, most bizarre and ridiculous of all, they would close the gates for a time. This opening and closing ritual led to a growing crowd to be kept waiting for no reason whatsoever and as more people arrived a crush developed. In these situations we expect little and get nothing - no English speakers, no bi-club stewards to communicate with - 'no nothing'.

The congestion led to severe crushing and then - unbelievably - police baton charges. Two large main gates were permanently closed (where we could have all got through under 'normal circumstances' and with the small turnstiles being opened and closed randomly it soon became apparent that chaos was just around the corner. More people were arriving and I crept under a protective metal barrier before the turnstile to gain some protection in the crush and panic. The police were now allowing - baton charges apart - people in on an ad-hoc basis. Presumably if they liked your face. This was so slow it was never going to cope as time and more people progressed.

I have developed a mind-boggling technique in these all too frequent situations - scream like a banshee - and it usually works and which managed to get me through the turnstile. But what about those to come? My ticket unchecked I got in with bottles of wine and water and the only difference from the usual chaos was that we didn't have our coins confiscated which are then presumably handed to the home fans to throw at all of us.

'Safely' inside the perimeter fencing I concentrated on obtaining as many photographs as I could of the inadequate policing and police brutality as the appalling scenario built-up. An OAP dodging baton wielding riot police was proving quite a task but we cannot let other Reds down when this occurs. Despite warnings I took photos of Reds staggering through the small turnstile after being hit. Outside there were United fans being crushed against the wire mesh and gate 14 which could have solved all the problems remained firmly closed. People were yelling for help - people losing their footing - and once again a 'suit' laughed at me as I pleaded for assistance. The request for someone in charge or someone who spoke English resulted in a baton to those outside and one Red was battered, got in the ground and promptly collapsed in a heap. Where as in Turin for the next round there were a number of medical helpers to cope with the large number of Reds cut to hell after the 3rd went in and the Juve fans rained missiles down - here you wouldn't have found Doctor Who let alone anyone else.

Finally Gate 14 was opened and a melee of people fell or walked through. Whether it was pure luck or panic which caused them to finally open the gate I've no doubt it saved lives and this is not an exaggeration. Those with or without tickets began scrambling in - the look on Euro away virgins one of shock and those veterans of 'not again'.

It wasn't really much better once in, as there was simply not enough space where everyone was heading to cope with the large surge in numbers. One well known Utd official was seen to walk away from the ground in disgust at what he'd witnessed. Yet again UEFA, Inter officials, United suits and the various boards and committees just shake their heads and blame 'el hooligans'. Not true matey.

By now desperate to use a toilet I discovered the inevitable - no female loos. Myself and a couple of women had to navigate the urine soaked floor of the men's toilets. One guy stood guard as we used the only cubicles they had.

My usual gripe is about the poor standards of European grounds. Supposed top notch ground - such as the San Siro - are now either decaying, out of date or have a sub-standard infra-structure. It isn't a plainly stupid question to ask why it had been arranged to put so many United fans together without either working out that there weren't enough gates or that they wouldn't cope.

Due to my David Bailey exertions I had been overtaken by the odd thousand or two and as I endeavoured to reach my seat (alright, any seat) I encountered a solid phalanx of United fans blocking all the stairways, themselves trying to get in. Yet again a potentially dangerous situation was developing and I went back down to try and gain access at ground level. I did but it was impossible to see more than 30% of the pitch. Great. The game was well under way so I noticed a door open onto a rather plush lounge and thought 'go for it'. They guy at the door didn't see me slip past him. From the window you could see the whole pitch. As I got my bearings (these things have a

habit of completely sobering you up) I noticed a room full of mafia type suits - only Al Pacino was missing to set the scene. Too late - "out, out you get". I'm not having this I said to myself after what I'd just witnessed. "Where is someone in charge?", I heard myself foolishly yell, but it was too late and anger grew as I let rip at all and sundry. They couldn't organise a piss up in a brewery - even leaving a 'complimentary' programme on the seat for each place which were grabbed by the first people in the ground - cue thousands of programmes in the possession of just a few people! Life was not so beautiful all of a sudden. If leaving with dignity after being pushed out is the correct description, that is what I did. I did shout a parting gesture that they should see Begnini's movie.

I tried to climb the staircase again but I was met with a solid body. Our biggest game and I was missing the drama unfold - and the truly great result it turned out to be. Eventually I met up with a couple I had met in Porto who had had enough of this farce and we decided to give up the ghost and attempt to see it at a hotel nearby. This we did - in a bar full of United fans with similar tales of woe (count yourself lucky if you weren't caught up in it all) but all able to share - in a surreal location - the wonder and joyous behaviour when Scholes scored, meaning we were through after the worst tension - as Inter piled pressure - that I can remember...at the time. This saw the Inter fans leave en masse - not before they threw everything bar the kitchen sink at the celebrating mass of United fans.

Nights like these are truly great - even if the trip for many hard-core Reds wasn't on a par with any of its predecessors - but should you pay out a small fortune on the trip to be denied the right to see a game of football?

Bear in mind we'd got to the stadium an hour before kick-off - virtually unheard of at Old Trafford these days. There you can stroll (even if you were a continental away fan) into your actual allocated seat fifteen minutes before kick off. You can expect a civilised standard of behaviour from the police and stewards and not be intimidated nor ripped off by exorbitant ticket prices (£56 in Turin) - paying £20 at United. United have wonderful facilities yet a stadium praised like the San Siro - called one of the finest - was nothing short of a cesspit. Mutton dressed as lamb as my Mum would say. And don't even ask about all that media hype about the massive security operation checking for tickets a distance away from the ground, before we got to our turnstiles. Utter rubbish again. It is madness to think as the Millennium approaches that we have feelings of fear and dismay whenever we get an Italian side - a Euro away where the police are empowered to do what they may and will as we go to games in the lap of the Gods. They can beat us, stop us seeing a game but nobody cares or really listens. And you know what, it will happen again.

It was after a defeat against Parma where the police knew that all sorts of missiles were now being thrown at away fans but no checks were made for such a volatile game with their season all but over if defeat occurred. So on returning home the following day I eagerly scanned the papers for reports of the mayhem. Not a word.

I began to imagine that I had dreamt it until I got back my camera film and David Mellor took up the cudgels on his radio show. It says a lot when Mellor is your only friend. He has a vested interest after his son was treated badly in that Rome madness at the England game but, give him his due, he gave air time to callers so that they could all recount individual and different tales of terror. It's all about being in the wrong place at the wrong time. When will something be done - and that pointing of the finger includes United (we could give you some suggestions) as well as UEFA - or will it take something worse to occur? Yet you get to my age and nothing surprises you anymore. So it was that in Milan I was told by a Red that he had allegedly met a UEFA delegate and he had seemingly told him that the draw had already been made (two days before the real one) and it was Juve home, first leg. Surely not!. Come in UEFA, your time is up.

For the European Cup Final I had the right timing and the right place. I walked straight into the ground, found my exact seat (a first) and watched the entire game in a ground that is showing decline but can handle it. I love my European nights. When you've been once you either can't get enough or it is your first and last. I've been addicted for years - but I'm not addicted to the constant threat of intemperate, violent police behaviour I've encountered at too many Euro aways to keep count.

The bodies in charge need to get their act together, proper liaison between the clubs, fans, police, more United stewards - not suits - and English speaking assistants. It needs to move into the 21st Century and work out that people paying a fortune for these trips need to be treated with the respect that we'd get if we'd travelled that far for the opera or the like.

I'm not going to let my memories of Milan be destroyed by the actions of the incompetent - there was so much talk of destiny after the culmination of our season in the 90th minute in the Nou Camp yet Henning Berg's dramatic clearance in both ties against Inter are as fate-filled as they come. They did as much as anything to get us to those dying stages in the Camp Nou. As Fergie said: "Milan was a massive step forward for the club...you have got to advance beyond the Italian sides...it was something that has eluded us before...it's a European coming of age...I think we are entitled to feel that with Inter out of the way we can go all the way". He knew the significance of the result and opposition.

Yet my own guess is that after Barca, many more United fans present will want to travel with United and soak (sic) up the atmosphere in different settings. A Euro away for them should not be how it has been for so many others - treated like vermin by local blackshirts and generally disempowered. We're not all angels but as 60,000 showed in Barca, United fans know how to behave. How to enjoy. How to support.

And onto Barca. Those privileged (which is what we were) to be there on Sir Matt's birthday will carry the memory until they die. I cannot categorically claim that I won the Cup - that's Ole's right - but collectively my own endeavour went a long way to securing victory. Ask Kev and Tony. They witnessed my last desperate act. As the board showed 3 minutes to go, tears welled up that I may not see this again. Then I yelled 'fuck it'. I had been wearing my special 'Happy Birthday Sir Matt' shirt but I hurriedly put on my United Champions League shirt which I'd never seen us lose in. Sheringham scored as I pulled it around my ample gut. Tony and Kev just looked at me and said: "F**king hell". Then Ole scored and for 90 seconds I just knew that the spirit lives on. Sir Matt, 60,000, me,

myself, I, all of us won it that night with a little help from the team, of course!

Right now, you're right Roberto, life is truly beautiful...

TRIPPING IN TURIN
Andy Mitten
Juventus 2 - Manchester United 3
European Cup Semi-Final, 2nd leg
April 21st 1999, Stadio Delle Alpi
Schmeichel, Neville G, Irwin, Keane, Johnsen, Stam, Beckham, Butt, Cole, Yorke, Blomqvist.
Sub used: Scholes.
Scorers: Keane, Yorke and Cole.
Attendance: 64,500

Andy Mitten, 25, has edited the fanzine 'United We Stand' for the last ten years. He is also a contributing editor on the Manchester United magazine and freelances for a number of publications from WSG, Japan's best-selling football magazine, to the British Tourism Authority's Rough Guide to the U.K. His ambition was to see Manchester United lift the European Cup. Now, it's to see The Smiths reform.

Deep down, even the most optimistic United fan knew it would be a tall order to beat Juventus in Turin. Juve's performance at Old Trafford had left us in no doubt as to their capabilities and given that United had never won on Italian soil - and lost our three previous games against Juve there, the omens on us reaching the final weren't good.

Of course the British press talked up our chances, peppering copy with Fergie's 'of course we can win' type quotes but I, for one, thought our European aspirations were about to close for another season.

Plenty of United fans thought we were in with a fighting chance - over 5,500 booked onto trips to the northern Italy's fourth biggest city, most arriving anywhere but the industrial landscape of Turin. Stories in the Manchester, 'We'll ask you for a 500 word article and then cut it to 200, patronise you by taking out any decent words and add a cheesy headline' Evening News saying that United needed 15,000 tickets were out of touch, the 6,000 ticket allocation was more than adequate, given that the trip to Milan had been just five weeks previous. Adequate for United, but not, it seemed for Juventus.

A week before the game came one of the most ludicrous stories of the year. Juventus fans were outraged at the allocation of tickets leading the the stadium manager at the Delle Alpi to say: 'We could sell 200,000 tickets for this game. Of course everybody wants to see it but it's the fans who don't normally come to games.' The hypocritical twist in this story is that Juventus are moving to a new smaller 40,000 stadium because the Delle Alpi is 'too big'. The stadium has sold out on just three occasions since it opened in 1990. Part-time supporters on a grand scale. Then again, charging £56 a ticket, the price they charged United fans, will hardly encourage the working classes of Torino out of their flats and into the stadium.

Thirteen of us flew into Pisa on Tuesday morning, splitting into two groups on arrival. One, a group of anoraks who wanted to see a bit of Italy and therefore

site end of the ground, the 2,000 travelling Marseille fans looked equally impressive.

Bologna took an early lead and could have sealed the game on many occasions but with two minutes to play Marseille were awarded a penalty. The penalty was converted but ordered to be retaken. When it went in the Marseille fans went mad, throwing flares into the neighbouring Bologna fans. The Bologna players were as devastated as their fans and resorted to kicking their opponents until the final whistle. At that point the Marseille players snapped and there was a huge brawl by the tunnel as the players left the field. We let them sling it out, our time was to be better spent in an Irish pub full of Bolognese students.

hired a car and headed up through Tuscany to Bologna. The other group, for whom adjectives like 'shit' 'boring' and 'gay' would be used to describe the Pyramids, the Empire State Building and Mount Everest, jumped on a train north to Genoa to indulge and gratify themselves in a variety of ways.

The reason we chose Bologna was because the local side, the originally titled 'FC Bologna' were playing Marseille in the UEFA Cup semi-final second leg. The first leg had been goalless so the tie was perfectly poised for Bologna to qualify for their first ever European final, a feat made all the more remarkable by the fact that they had reached the semi having trawled through the various rounds of the Inter Toto cup last summer. Marseille, on the other hand, were trying to re-establish themselves on the European stage, six years after their European Cup win which was followed by the bribes scandal that rocked French football and saw the club demoted.

After a four hour drive through the Manc-esque rain we arrived at the Stadio Communale and went in search of tickets. Touts were aplenty, asking £33 for tickets behind the goals. We paid £17 off the tout who had sorted us out in Rome a month earlier and went into the centre to find some accommodation. The 'four star' hotel by the station may have been four star by a Burnley's hotel standards but it made the Greatstone look like the Dorchester. Sagging single beds, early 70s decor and the clinical smell of a hospital ward. It was the only hotel with vacancies though so we booked a double and got four in.

It was the biggest game in Bologna's history and their ultra's had done their preparation with the usual impressive display of flags, banners, drums and flares. At the oppo-

It was raining again on Wednesday morning and the mood in the anorak party was different. Conversation in the car to Genoa centred on how desperately we wanted to win the European Cup. The consensus that we'd settle for European Cup and no other trophy this season was not unusual although the suggestion that we'd be happy to see United relegated to the Conference just to win the European Cup was taking things too far. After meeting up with the 'ten men' in Genoa we began the drive back through the mountains to Turin. Juventus attract support from all over Italy and all roads were full coaches of Juve fans. Despite efforts to get to the ground early, road works meant that we didn't arrive until half an hour before kick-off. The others made their way around to the United end whilst I went to pick my ticket up on the other side of the ground. It wasn't there.

There was only ten minutes to kick-off and I was ticketless and desperate but touts were everywhere with bun-

dles of gear and the price of tickets was on the floor. It was a buyer's market and I picked up a 110,000 ticket for 50,000 lira (£17), albeit in the home end. So much for all those millions of Juve fans wanting tickets.

The seat was directly opposite the 5,500 travelling United fans who had been allocated prime seats by the pitch and I had barely sat down when Inzaghi put Juve a goal up. I wasn't too concerned. United had to score in Turin and that was still the case. When the same man put Juve two up after just eleven minutes, my world caved in. As the Italians celebrated wildly around, I just put my head in my hands and started to ask a million question, questions which had no immediate answers like: 'Will we ever learn in Europe?'

The Italians soon realised that I was a United fan but far from being aggressive, they shot me sympathetic looks and shrugged their shoulders as if to say: 'there's always next year.' I was sick of that sentiment as I sat there wondering if fate would never see us reach another European Cup Final. That god had taken from United at Munich but given with the win in '68 and that was our lot. That he had given us Ralph Milne and it high time that he repaid that debt with a big fat European Cup.

Then Roy Keane scored - a perfectly placed header. Then Dwight Yorke scored with an even better header. Get in there. The United fans were going mad opposite. The Juve fans on the curva nord were throwing flares into them but they were being returned just as quickly. Conscious that a celebration could get me a kicking, I remained seated and looked like I'd just turned schizoid. This was magnificent.

At half-time I tried to get into the United end but the police were having none of it and I had to settle for an espresso knocked straight back. The second half remains a blur. It was tempting fate I know, but all I could think of was how we would all get to Barcelona. Would we fly, drive or go by train. Who would be coming. Who wouldn't? Incidents just passed by as clock watching became an addiction. When Cole scored the third it signalled immense relief. The Italians began to leave but not before shaking my hands and wishing United well in the final.

'Stam, Cole, the best in Europe,' said the bloke next to me. As the final whistle signalled celebrations from the United camp and fans, the home fans sportingly applauded the reds off the pitch. They appreciate quality when they see it.

Adrenalin was pumping through my veins. I wanted to celebrate but I couldn't. I decided to run down to the emptying curva nord terrace by the United fans and get through the Police lines to meet up with my mates. I ran down the steps from the third tier onto the concourse that circles the whole stadium, and began to make my way round to where the United fans were. Passing a souvenir stall, I saw a United scarf. I wanted one. I've not worn a scarf to a match for ten years but I wanted a United scarf.

'Costa?' I asked the assistant.

'25,000' he replied in English.

He was beginning to pack the swag away and there was no way that United scarves would be sold to Juve fans in the future so I tried to haggle.

'I give you ten,' I replied in a phony accent.

'No, it is not possible.'

'Please?'

'No, I'm am sorry.'

I had 25,000 in my pocket - I had 50,000 lira, but I didn't buy the scarf. I don't know why, I just didn't buy it. Instead I began to jog further around the concourse towards the United fans. A second later I was lying sprawled on the ground. My first reaction was that I'd ran into a concrete bollard, but as I pulled myself up I realised that even that was wishful thinking.

'Fucking Inglisi,' shouted the Italian above me. 'Fucking Inglisi.' He'd spotted me trying to buy the scarf and he wasn't impressed. He chased after me and booted me in my leg. I'd gone down. There was a commotion. The mood changed instantly and the roar, that roar you only hear when it's kicking-of, went up. Petrified, I ran towards to stewards wearing flourescent bibs, chased by what was now a baying mob. I tried to reason.

'I'm Torino,' I remonstrated.

I couldn't have said anything worse, but I didn't have time to think.

They hate Torino.

'I'm Juve, I'm Juve. I support Juve.'

It wasn't working. A punch landed on the back of my head knocking me to the ground but I got up straight away. Surrounded by around a dozen stewards, I continued, 'I'm Juve, I'm Juve.'

It all happened in a split second, but what the stewards did probably saved me from the biggest kicking of my life. They managed to stem the mob back and told me in no uncertain terms to get the fuck away. Quick. I started running down the slope out of the ground and after a while I looked back. Three or four of them were giving chase but they were a hundred metres away and I could get lost in the crowds still spilling out of the stadium.

My elation had turned to intense fear and paranoia. In a bid to remain incognito I took

Reds from here, Reds from there...

Celebrating in the usual restrained and dignified fashion !

my jumper off and tied it around my waist and began to follow a large group of middle aged and middle class looking Italians away from the ground. Adrenalin was overriding every other emotion in my body and I didn't even notice the pain in my left leg that was to disable me for the next five days. I walked, I just wanted to get away from the ground, but after a while I realised that I was heading the wrong way back to the car. I turned around but the paranoia was killing me. I felt that everyone knew I was English so stopped at a stall to buy a Juve scarf. It cost me 20,000 lira (£6) and I began to tie it around my neck. I felt better and started to jog back to the ground. The first group of fans I jogged past realised that I wasn't Italian because they walked into my path and one said, 'Inglisi, we kill you.'

I ran back to the exit where I expected to see United fans but they were still in the ground. Gaining a modicum of composure, I worked out where I thought the car was and five minutes later, arrived. It was then that I noticed that my leg was writhing in pain. It seemed like an eternity for the others to get back but when they did, they were as high as a kite on United's performance. We started back on the drive back to Genova and the roads were full of Juve fans returning south. We couldn't help but rub the result in and they didn't like it one bit, threatening to slit our throats from the safety of a coach and acting like the cowardly Italians that had jumped me outside the ground.

The result didn't immediately sink in. A copy of Gazzetta Dello Sport was purchased the next day and, although my Italian is as good as my Arabic, it was possible to decipher what they were saying and in contrast to the comments after our game in Milan, the observations were highly favourable. It made my so proud that a football team from my home town, a much maligned industrial city in the north of a small island of a small continent, was being heralded by usually critical the Italian press as the best in the world. The best football team in the world! Manchester United!

Any Italians we met were equally as gushing in praise, Juve fans or not, and whilst United have not yet been crowned the champions of Europe, we almost felt it just

by reaching the final.

Back in England on Thursday night, the phone didn't stop. Everyone wanted to go to Barcelona. People you haven't seen for years, people who haven't been to a match for years but are still United fans, were all up for the trip. As long as those who deserve tickets get them, then there's no point anyone being snobbish about who should and shouldn't be there and the 30,000 ticket allocation is over twice as big as the one we got for Rotterdam. Barcelona is a magnificent city, one of the best in the world and the stadium is arguably the finest on the planet making it the perfect venue for the last European Cup final of the century. Victory would provide a perfect end to a glorious Ferguson-inspired decade and if play as we did on that glorious night in Turin, then the trophy should be ours. Until the 26th May, we'd just have to cherish those memories from Turin. They'll certainly do.

Barca...

I got into the ground an hour an a half before kick-off to savour the atmosphere. United had been allocated 30,000 tickets behind the north goal although there were United flags from all over the world spread right around the stadium, over all three tiers. As the temperature cooled and the sun set behind the mountain of Montjuic, the noise level inside the stadium rose with United and Bayern fans out singing each other. The United fans sang classics like 'Land of Hope and Glory', the Bayern fans, backed up by a German pop group, sang songs which sounded like a cross between Chas'n'Dave and E.L.O.

Proceedings then took upon a surreal air as Monserrat Caballee was wheeled out onto the pitch on the back of a Land Rover for strange duet with the deceased Freddie Mercury. All around her were huge inflatable replicas of Barcelona's most famous monuments which looked as if they'd been crafted by Salvador Dali on a bad day. At least the words were rousing: 'Barcelona, it's such a beautiful horizon'. And it was.

By the time the Champions League music was aired as the teams took to the field, the expectation was at its highest. 'Championi, Championi, Ole, Ole, Ole,' roared the United fans in their strange hybrid of Anglo/Italian.

After six minutes. Basler scored. Hearts sunk.

'It's not necessarily a bad thing, this going a goal down, look what happened against Juventus,' said the bloke next to me.

But you knew Bayern would be a different proposition. Once they had gained the lead, they set about defending it for 84 minutes. United, without the midfield foil of Scholes and Keane, looked ordinary. For all the possession they enjoyed, they created painfully few chances and it was Bayern who were in control. The support from the stands did not waiver though. George Best may have left four minutes before the end but the United fans held firm. We could see the European Cup in the stands below, it was dressed in ribbons of Bayerns' colours. It wasn't a pretty sight.

Then Teddy Sheringham scored.

'GOAL' flashed the scoreboard. Like we didn't know. Get in there, get in there, get in there. Teddy, the man who had started just seven games outside the League cup all season, the man had given us a lifeline. We were back in the game. Get in there. 'Oh, Teddy, Teddy, he went to Man United and he won the, erm, TREBLE.'

What happened next will go down as the most dramatic ending to a football match at the highest level in the history of football. It was deep into injury time and United attacked, pumped full of raw adrenalin. The Bayern players were still stunned from the first goal.

Solskjaer scored.

The whole bench charged onto the pitch, ecstatic.

The final whistle blew.

The Bayern players sat, lifeless and drained on the pitch.

Fifty thousand United fans celebrated like never, ever, before.

No word has been invented to describe the feeling, no superlative will ever do that moment justice.

Manchester United were European Champions for the first time since 1968.

The celebrations were the best part of the night. They went on for ages. First, the trophy was lifted. Then, the players did two complete laps of honour. The Bayern fans, so obviously distraught, stayed to salute the team that had just beaten their heroes. That must have been difficult but it was a measure of their sporting nature. The United players then stopped behind the goal where the majority of the travelling reds were. It should have been where all the United fans were put many, many more United fans had purchased seats on the other three sides of the stadium. Perhaps there were 50,000, perhaps even 55,000 inside the stadium. Schmeichel moved forward, European Cup in hand, and appealed for silence. No mater how emotionally or alcoholically intoxicated fans were, there was an immediate silence. He then slowly lifted the European cup above head to huge applause. He did this five more times. All the players followed suit, deservedly milking the moment to it's full. When every red shirt had lifted the trophy, a cry of 'La, la, la, la, la, Keano,' swept around the stadium.

Eventually our Versace suited captain emerged with Paul Scholes from the bowels of the stadium to lift the trophy he has had such an influence in us winning. It capped off the greatest moment I have ever known supporting Manchester United.

Photo: Kenneth Ramsay

QUOTES

Compiled by Eugene Weber -
author of the superb book of Utd quotes, 'Speak of the Devils' (Weber books, P.O.Box 16545, London, SE22 8ZR, £6) - and Barney Chilton

"I'm proud of my heritage tonight. I am proud of my family. I was starting to adjust to defeat near the end. I kept saying to myself: 'keep your dignity and accept it's not your year. I was not going to get myself twisted inside about it because I have got a life to live" Alex Ferguson

"Our Subs Sink Germans" Sun headline

"It would have been Sir Matt Busby's birthday today and I think he was up there doing a lot of kicking"
Alex Ferguson

"To ask how I'm feeling is to ask how God is feeling - on top of the world" Rory Malloy, fan

"I can't believe it. I can't believe it. Football eh? Bloody hell" Alex Ferguson

"This United Treble is football's equivalent of Frankie Dettori winning all seven races at Ascot a couple of years ago...we were over the moon when it looked as if Bayern were going to clinch it and all I can say now is that we are as sick as a parrot" A spokesman for William Hill

"I truly believed the Treble was romance, not reality" Alex Ferguson

"The time was up and I looked round and saw the Cup was on its way down and it had Bayern Munich colours on it. Two minutes later I had it in my own hands" David Beckham

"I can't explain it. I can't explain how we won the game. I just got the feeling that when Teddy Sheringham scored the equaliser that something was going to happen and it did. In a way it was supernatural. It was like nothing I had experienced before" Gary Neville

"The Cup is only six feet away from you at the end of this day. If you lose, you can't even touch it"
Part of Alex Ferguson's half-time pep talk

"I will take it easy - until we lose the first game" Alex Ferguson

"If anyone still wonders why I stayed at Manchester United they can see here why. Team spirit is unbelievable" Ole Gunnar Solskjaer

"People have said it's unbelievable. That word is used too infrequently, too easily - but that was unbelievable" Terry Venables

"When I ran on to the pitch at the end I didn't really say anything to any of them. I just hugged and kissed them. I was slobbering all over them because you can't top that. It's the pinnacle" Alex Ferguson

"Not even Hans Christian Andersen could have written a fairytale like that" Peter Schmeichel

"The Germans were getting flashy. I saw Basler walking over to take a corner waving to his fans. It gave me the hump" Teddy Sheringham

"He's brought me up, he's made my career. He deserves everything he gets and we owe it all to him"
David Beckham on Alex Ferguson

"If you did write that, you'd throw it away" Terry Venables

"Don't you dare come back in here without having done your best" Part of Alex Ferguson's half-time team talk

"I just thought it might be my night. I called one of my friends and told him he better watch the game. I always call him when I have this feeling. The last time I had that feeling I scored against Liverpool in the FA Cup" Ole Gunnar Solskjaer

"Whatever Arsenal or Chelsea or, let's be kind, Liverpool, can conjure up, they will simply be reduced to to being second man on the Moon... In front of a full and noisy front room, I calmly dropped my trousers and pressed my wide screen buttocks against the glass of a 29 inch wide-screen set, which was showing the thunderstruck mug of a yobbo ass Munchen" Danny Baker, journalist

"If this is a bad week, hopefully I'll have a few more of them" Roy Keane

"Oh No! That was bitter! Just unbelievable" German newspaper Bild Zeitung

"To lose it in that way must be terrible. But to win it that way is that much better" Ole Gunnar Solskjaer

"It's been all right saying English football is the healthiest and the best to watch, but you really need to have something to show for it and to win the Champions' League, there's nothing bigger in world club football. I might even have a couple of drinks tonight" Sir Bobby Charlton

"We might have made history but next season we're going to to try to make history of all histories"
Dwight Yorke

"It's difficult to get any higher than this. It's been an amazing thing being part of a team like Manchester United" Peter Schmeichel

"Tactics didn't win that game last night. It was sheer will, maybe luck, too. They never stopped and you have to give them credit for that. For that equaliser we had nine bodies in the box" Alex Ferguson

"After what we've done and the way we played, people have to admire us even if they don't like us" Gary Neville

"With Manchester United, it is never over until the Fat Lady has had a heart attack" Hugh McIlvanney

"Even when we got back in the dressing room and we were almost out of control with delight, I don't think any of us could really take it in. What I remember most was the feeling that what we had done actually meant something, it had affected peoples' lives" Gary Neville

"This team has that continuous drive that certain people have got, whether it's in industry or wherever. You sense from the spirit in there that they won't let us down on Wednesday. They're dying to play now"
Alex Ferguson after the FA Cup Final win

"I can't take it all in to be honest. I really feel for Roy Keane tonight. I watched him and he was gutted"
Alex Ferguson

"What happened after 90 minutes is simply inexplicable" Lothar Matthaus

"I think Sir Matt had wanted to retire for some time, but he knew we wouldn't let him go until we'd won the European Cup in memory of his 'lovely boys' as he always called them. After the Benfica win I didn't say anything to the old man because I didn't need to. I knew exactly what he was thinking and how he was feeling...It was all very, very emotional. How did it feel to be handed the trophy after 10 years? It felt bloody heavy. I was so dehydrated I handed it on to someone else as quickly as possible...that night...the old man got up and sang...What A Wonderful World" Sir Bobby Charlton

"We shall miss Roy Keane in Barcelona but his absence could be the making of some of the young players" Sir Bobby Charlton

"Obviously I'm hurting inside but I'm not going to dwell on it...Manchester United is bigger than any one player, any one man" Roy Keane

"This is the future I dreamed of. It's the reason I came to United" Dwight Yorke

"I first started thinking of the European Cup after we won the Premier League for the first time in 1993. I thought we could get to that level with Eric Cantona in the side. He was our talisman and we should have got to the final when Dortmund beat us...but at least that told us we were not far away" Alex Ferguson

"No, I don't think I'm destined to win the European Cup some time because there's an element of luck in these things" Alex Ferguson speaking before the Inter Milan game

"Solskjaer" Word repeated over again on the whole front page of a Norwegian newspaper

"I want to go out and win it again" Alex Ferguson

"After the first 15 minutes I was beginning to think 'Here we go again'...yet our performance after that was absolutely brilliant. We pulverised them...we showed on Wednesday night that we never give in either. It should be a great final" Gary Neville after the win in Turin

"If ever a club deserves to rewrite the history books this club does. Nobody, no-one, no team will stop us, we don't know what it's like to lose, we won't lose. Winning is inbuilt in this side" Dwight Yorke

"Beat Bayern Munich to help complete the job my father started. He put the heart and soul into Old Trafford" Sandy Busby

"With all the problems I've had this season it's great to come back and shut a few people up" Teddy Sheringham

"We've been at our best only in patches this season. I hope there is more to come" Roy Keane, speaking in February

"We've got to hope Barcelona and Munich cut each other's throats. If they take points off each other while we are playing Brondby, it would be a fantastic opportunity for us" Alex Ferguson's group plans working a treat

"United at Old Trafford were too confident...but now I think they understand...that we will go that final, not them" Juventus midfielder Antonio Conte

"Some people thought I was being hopelessly biased when I said that Manchester United would win the European Cup at the start of the season - but not too many people are laughing behind their hands now" Paddy Crerand

"United are marginally stronger...United to win 2-1" Soothsaying journalist Joe Lovejoy - the only one who got it right

"It would have been far worse if we had drawn either Juventus or Munich. United were third on the list so we are not too unhappy" Inter Milan skipper Giuseppe Bergomi

"I believe it is Bayern Munich's destiny to win the European Cup" Ottmar Hitzfeld, Bayren coach, the weekend before the European Cup Final

"Now we have to go away and come back and win them all again next year - because that is what the boss will demand of us" Nicky Butt

"Whether we can repeat this success is another matter but we can maintain success because the players have got their pride...some players want to go to Blackpool for their holidays, but some want to go to the moon" Alex Ferguson

"I knew immediately after Sheringham scored that

Bayern were beaten. There was certainly the odd hint in their body language...I knew that was it. We couldn't lose after that...I feel a sense of fulfilment I did not feel before...Maybe we were meant to win it. Maybe there was an element of destiny" Alex Ferguson

"What happened in Turin will make them even more determined to make sure they do not lose another game this season" Alex Ferguson

"I was a bit jealous of the United players in the end because they will now be revered for years to come. To say that players from the past, like myself, contributed to that success in Barcelona would be ridiculous. But what was important was to win the league for the first time in 26 years in 1993...I was desperate to win the European Cup" Mark Hughes

"I'm a Manchester United man and I hope they win the lot" Brian Kidd, speaking at the start of May

"It was a fairy tale. You could tell Matt Busby was looking down on me. I said a few weeks ago that I hope there is some meaning to the final being on Matt's birthday and against Bayern Munich" Alex Ferguson

"I hope that 20 years from now, when they talk about the chief characteristic of this team, they will always be remembered for their last-minute goals, for never giving in. The 1968 side were men of their time and now my team cannot be ignored. They are men of their time now" Alex Ferguson

"There was complete euphoria as we ran past German players frozen in shock. Such a great feeling" Jaap Stam

"This is a special season. No matter what happens on the last lap you should enjoy it because you may never see the like again" Alex Ferguson in a message to the fans in April

"The European Cup will not become an albatross around my neck" Alex Ferguson speaking at the start of the season

"We both know the position about yellow cards but I can't change now. I have to be sensible but I have to play my own game" Roy Keane on his and Scholes' situation before Juve

"The last time I went to Old Trafford (with Dortmund) I felt United were too nervous. They were too keen to win the trophy - maybe because Ferguson wanted it too much - and as a result the players were inhibited. That was why we won" Munich's Ottmar Hitzfeld - before the Final

"I can understand why people are talking about destiny this season...there are a lot of coincidences and I hope they all have a meaning when the Final is over" Alex Ferguson

"I am so thrilled for myself...I am actually here" Part of Wilf McGuinness' radio commentary

"I was proud to go to a club with a great tradition built up by Sir Matt. But I wasn't intimidated by it. I've never seen history as an obstacle" Alex Ferguson

"I have nothing but praise for both sets of fans" David Broomfield, British Consol in Barcelona

"The thing that sticks in my mind most about the night is Schmeichel coming up for that corner. I said: 'Can you believe him? There's still three minutes left" Alex Ferguson

"I think I unsettled them - they didn't know what the hell I was doing. I think I got a touch - I definitely contributed to the goal. This is a fantastic finish for me" Peter Schmeichel

"We can rule Europe for ten years!" Alex Ferguson

"On Wednesday night at the Nou Camp I felt that the game was my best chance of ever winning it" Alex Ferguson

"This was a typical game for us! You have to feel sorry for Munich. You just have to imagine yourselves in their situation. But, at the end of the day, that's why football captivates the world - the beauty and the cruelty" Peter Schmeichel

"It seems Alex is touched by God this season. If he kicked a tin can across the street, it would probably land in the net" Gerard Houllier

"I joined in the craic but I can't deny it was disappointing I wasn't out there on the pitch. No one can doubt my appetite for us to do this again" Roy Keane

"I felt we were a passing team so I put David in the middle because he is a great passer. I knew we would miss his crosses but I had to do it" Alex Ferguson

"I have never been sure in the past whether our squad has been big enough to go for all the prizes, but I'm happy now. I think we have the players to do it...the players can handle Turin. The treble is definitely on. We don't have to fear anyone after beating Inter...I think neutrals in Europe would like to see us win the Champions League, we were clapped off the field in Barcelona. People appreciate the way we play. We've attacked in every game and tried to win all our matches. That's the way we'll go about tackling Juventus. Not just believing we can win, but trying to do so in style" Alex Ferguson

"The party for players was in full swing when I left at 4.30am. 65,000 United fans were enjoying their own parties around Barcelona" Sir Bobby Charlton

"Problems? Not one. They are ugly but they are good people"
Catalan newspaper La Vanguardia about the Red Army

"Steve Archibald came to see me on the Tuesday and told me of his experience. He told of being so close to the Cup and not being able to touch it because Barcelona had lost. I wasn't going to say anything to the players because I thought they had the ability to beat Bayern. But at half-time I thought it wouldn't be a bad thing" Alex Ferguson

"Come on, get me on" Teddy Sheringham's shout with 20 minutes to go

"I was gearing up to the question - 'do you think you'll ever win it?'" Alex Ferguson

"I don't want to see out the next three years and, at the end, think that I haven't won anything since Barcelona. That would be a waste of myself and the players. We have to keep setting ourselves new challenges" Alex Ferguson

"We have the arrogance to believe we can win anything" Peter Schmeichel after the Arsenal Cup win

"How did we win that match? Will somebody please tell me, because I'm bloody sure I don't know. We earned it a sight more than they did. But I'm buggered if I know how we did it...There was all that talk about the treble. Month after month of it. Suddenly it's there and you're trying to believe it...You can equal it but you can't top that" Alex Ferguson

"Why do women love German footballers? Because they're on top for 90 minutes and still come second"

The joke was passed on and eventually made it to Germany and changed. "Why are Englishmen such lousy lovers? They'll wait 90 minutes, then put it in twice in the last minute and think they're the world's best lovers!"

EAT HUMBLE PIE...
Charles Bogle

Charles Bogle, author of the acclaimed Secret Diary of Monsieur Cantona (published by Juma...plug, plug!), is 60, a father of seven - dopey, sleepy, bashful, happy, and three others whose names he can't remember - and has neighbours who describe him as a "ranting, frog-faced, odious misfit who wears carpet slippers". Here he describes how the press covered United's epic season and changed their tune. He only wishes he had a much lower IQ so that then he could really enjoy Harry Harris.

Somehow it was destined to be a great season for United the moment Jimmy Greaves slagged off Dwight Yorke. Greaves was undoubtedly a sensational footballer but as an expert pundit he is as thick and shallow as the rest of the SUN team who make such ill-informed comment on United.

For the record, Greaves wrote in September: "Dwight Yorke is good, but he is not that good...he is not the final piece in the jigsaw....a piece that simply does not fit....I question Fergie's judgement...I believe that United are well off the pace that will be set by Arsenal and are no better a team than Chelsea. As for the European Cup, well, let's just say 'Don't put your house on it'...United...duped...Gregory...might just have pulled off the deal of the summer" As it turns out Yorke - and Jaap

Stam who came in for equally over-the-top criticism - were exactly the final pieces in a brilliant jigsaw that ended up revealing a unique treble.

As a fan, watching Arsenal dismantle United 3-0 at Highbury on September 20th, it was possible to see two completely contrasting consequences. On that day, Roy Keane looked out of his depth and unfit and Jesper Blomqvist, Stam and Yorke looked vulnerable. Yet Alex Ferguson must have used the lesson of how United were outplayed - and worst, outfought - that day to drive home how much harder United would have to work to be successful. Of course, United's problems delighted the dimwits of the tabloid Press (the very same ones who fell over themselves to salivate over United after Barcelona).

Even as we entered the New Year, the Press were still wetting themselves over the prospect of Chelsea winning their first title since the days of black and white telly. The incomparably bad Harry Harris should perhaps be reminded that he wrote in January 1999: "I predicted way back in August that Chelsea would be Champions. Chelsea would be wonderful ambassadors for the English game". Um. Yes. P**dophile coach and all.

However it was in Europe that the Press really wanted United to fall flat on their faces. When the original group stages draw was made pitting United in a tough group with Barcelona, Bayern Munich and Brondby, the brain cells of Mr Harris creaked as he penned the following in September: "We could be witnessing the first cracks in the Old Trafford empire...United are in danger of seeing their era suddenly slip away....I said a year ago that United could not win the Champions League unless they had the input of a foreign coach and I've seen nothing to change my mind...United are in danger of being left behind".

This is the same Harry Harris seen later in the year praising United in Barcelona and answering his mobile as "Barcelona H". Harris wasn't alone. Steve Howard wrote in the SUN in March: "There is always the nagging doubt about United in Europe...If they couldn't beat Monaco what price them getting past Inter...they contain enough players...to answer...United" Alan Green, the obese radio commentator, chipped in with: "United's Qtr-Final prospects look a little bleak"

Nigel Clarke Mirror 1997 - "Sadly for Alex Ferguson he may never win the European Cup...Cole wastes too many bread and butter opportunities...Fergie has indicated he may well quit in two years time. It doesn't give him the time he needs to build another side"

Within the United camp - the only place that opinions really count of course - there was undisguised purpose and belief about the chances of European glory. Before playing Barcelona in the group stages, Fergie: "Some people are calling it the group of death but I don't even consider that. These games are what European football is all about."

Ryan Giggs said before Milan: "I think we are better equipped than ever to win the European Cup".

What really turned things round for United fans was putting out two such powerful Italian clubs - and the spirited way in which it was done. Even in a season in which we fought back so splendidly in the FA Cup against Arsenal and Liverpool this was something different. We have put Arsenal and Liverpool to the sword before but never in Italy. The manner in which the team proved

Ferguson right against the Italian team prompted Youri Djorkaeff to say after they had knocked out Milan: "United are now the reference point for the rest of Europe" As Fergie said before Turin: "Juve, that's the biggest game. The biggest because I have a genuine feeling we can do it. When we lost to Dortmund two years ago we should have been in the final. But I was never quite sure that we were ready to go onto win the Cup...now you just feel we are capable of playing against anyone. Juve will try and beat us but we have more control and patience about our game today".

There was a big element of luck about winning all three trophies. The Reds stumbled somewhat nervously and wearily over the line in the title race but once the championship was in the bag you sensed that the two finals were there for the taking.

The FA Cup final was a stroll in the park (and David May has definitely won more medals than the bitter Shearenvy) but the end of the European Cup Final was a fittingly dramatic way to end a season of such high incident. It was also a fitting way to signal the end of Peter Schmeichel's magnificent Old Trafford career. It was a fitting way for David Beckham to crown a mature and significant season of development (although he should dump the royal chair image) and it was even good to see Teddy Teddy stuff those chants down people's throats.

Well, you know what they say...always look on the bright side of life.

FOREVER RED
Ted Nespri

In the beginning there was Denis Irwin. If he seems to have been around forever in the eyes of the new generation of Manchester United fans, then that is the case. When United started their European resurgence under Alex Ferguson in May 1991 by beating Barcelona in the final of the Cup-winners' Cup Irwin was the Reds' right back.

When United defeated Bayern Munich 2-1 in the Champions' League final last May in, appropriately, Barcelona, Irwin was the sole survivor from Rotterdam eight years previously.

To play for United for a decade you have to be a bloody good player and Irwin is that - and more.

Yet when you analyse Irwin he does not possess the sort of qualities that immediately stand out. For example, he does not race down the wing like Tony Dunne 1968 vintage did. He is reliable in the air without being the sort of defender you'd want to put on Niall Quinn at corners.

Irwin's main asset is that he is bad at nothing and very good if not great at everything. His timing in the tackle and his ability to read situations before they occur are second-to-none. His passing is usually spot-on and when it comes to consistency he is in the Roy Keane class (both hail from Cork - it must be something in the water there).

It is difficult going on impossible to recall a bad game by Irwin. Players aren't allowed too many bad games for United or else they soon become someone else's players.

Many Reds believe the biggest favour Leeds ever did United was to sell them Dieu. Fair point but Irwin came to United from Leeds via Oldham so he is a good second in the rare thank-you Leeds list.

Irwin was given a free transfer by L**** (quite enough of that word thank you) and was picked up by Oldham. Tradition has it that players usually leave Manchester, either the Treble Red or First Division Blue corner, and join Oldham.

In 1990 Irwin took the reverse journey and has been a regular ever since. He has clocked up more than 300 league appearances for United and ended 1998/9 with 52 caps for the Republic of Ireland, for who he was the first player to be capped at six different levels (and not a lot of people know that).

Off the field Irwin is a quiet, almost laid-back person who does not seek the headlines but is ever obliging to the growing demands of the media. He is, well, a nice guy. Just about the only people who have a negative word for Irwin are referees. It comes as a surprise to hear that Irwin is accepted as the most vocal of United's players (yes, even more than the other guy from Cork) when it comes to offering opinions to referees but that is the word from the Premiership officials. It is almost a relief to know there is something not 100 per cent about Irwin. Perfection was creeping in.

Irwin's is a fascinating story - a purely football story rather than a Cantona or Beckham story. And there are still a couple of chapters left because at the age of 33 the Corkman has no intentions of resting on his laurels. One more medal will make him Ireland's most successful footballer of all time.

But it nearly all started in tears because when Irwin was released by Leeds he considered returning to Ireland. 'Oldham were a small club,' he said. 'I was glad they came in for me. I learnt a lot there and when the club started to have a couple of good Cup runs my ambitions changed.'

Irwin got a taste of the big time when Oldham played United in the 1990 FA Cup semi finals. The initial game was a 3-3 draw (United never do anything easily) and Oldham lost the replay. 'We [Oldham] should have won,' said Irwin with a smile.

Alex Ferguson was impressed by Irwin in those two games and, looking for a full-back, he looked no further. Year one at Old Trafford saw the Cup-winners' Cup success which Irwin says is a bit of a blur. 'When you're young you don't take it all in as you should. I know how much it meant to United but when I've played in subsequent finals I've savoured them more.'

Irwin's collection of honours is second-to-none at Old Trafford yet such is the professional in him he is upset he does not have more gongs.

'There have been times when we should have won more. The League in 1992 when we let Leeds win - when we did finally win the Championship the following year it was such a huge weight off everyone's shoulders.'

In Irwin's mind the motivation posed by winning and losing is the same. If United have won something he wants more; if they have failed he wants to make amends. Two minutes, no less than that, in his company is enough to make you realise that the Treble has not dulled his appetite.

Pedants may argue that for Irwin it was 'only' the Double because of his suspension from the FA Cup final, but he had done his bit to get United to Wembley so a Treble winner he is.

It will be a hard act to follow and with only a one-year contract Irwin is realistic enough to know that time is running out.

'Barcelona was something else. My wife, my son, my family were all there. European nights are always memorable but this was incredible.

'But you have to have ambitions. A footballer should always want to win more. We have a lot of different characters at United but we are all after the same goal.'

Irwin may be a lesser light media-wise but he remains a valued member of Sir Fergie's squad. The challenge from Phil Neville will become greater. The emergence of Wes Brown will add to the competition in defence but when the day comes that he has to leave United Irwin will do so with his head held high and with the blessing of every true Red. Then, if and when he returns to Old Trafford in whatever colours, a standing ovation will rightly be his. United fans never forget their heroes.

'I realise the manager is always planning ahead,' said Irwin. 'When I'm past my prime I'll move on somewhere else.'

And you can bet the hunger to win will remain the same. That can be taken as red.

Ted Nespri

6. THE PROMISED LAND

THE PROMISED LAND

Bayern Munich 1 - Manchester United 2
European Cup Final
May 26th 1999, Nou Camp, Barcelona
Schmeichel, G.Neville, Irwin, Stam, Johnsen, Beckham,
Butt, Cole, Yorke, Blomqvist, Giggs.
Subs used: Sheringham and Solskjaer
Scorers: Sheringham and Solskjaer
Attendance: 90,000

BARCELONA '99
Dr.Edward Martins

Dr.Edward Martins, who lives in South Manchester, has been a 'Red News' contributor for a number of years. He is young, handsome and intelligent and operates under a pseudonym. His real name is De Niro. A K Stand Season Ticket Holder, Dr.Martins has supported United since birth and only drinks trebles.

How often do you get the chance to be part of an historic occasion? Not just any old historic occasion though, but one where United finally became Champions of Europe again and also clinched an unprecedented treble as part of the deal. Barcelona '99 offered this incredible opportunity and whatever the personal cost to health, finances and relationships it just had to be done. This is one of the many tales of how it was done.

On reflection the 1998-99 season didn't start that well. We wanted our Championship back and we needed to do well in Europe. The shadow of Murdoch hung over us and we hadn't won anything since Eric retired. But then Keano started playing like Keano, only better. The Beckham baiting made him stronger and Murdoch was vanquished. The Championship returned, the reserves won the F.A.Cup and then...

After the epic victory in Turin it quickly became clear that "I'm definitely going" was easier said than done. Personally, I couldn't wait for the trip to the self acclaimed 'Best City in the world' and had checked out some great hotels pre-Juve. However, by Thursday morning, post-Juve, every bloody hotel room in Barcelona had gone and depression took over from euphoria. We didn't expect to pull Easyjet although I knew people that had booked with them in December. I couldn't do this - too superstitious. In previous years I'd booked 'that week' in May off work and made all kinds of arrangements and then blamed myself for the disasters of Dortmund and Monaco. Yes, I know.

A thousand more phone calls, time taken off work to visit every Travel Agent in Manchester and a quote of £800 for a flight only to Barcelona. Now we're really getting silly. Then, someone suggested what appeared to be the perfect solution - driving. Not really. 1,000 miles from Santander to Barcelona after a drive to Plymouth and a lengthy ferry crossing. More gloom. Then, another brilliant suggestion, the train, sleepers please and, surely, it would be cheap. A phone call to those very helpful people at Rail Europe (you should see my phone bill and my work phone bill come to think of it) revealed some very convenient departure and arrival times. There was just one snag - £440 return - fuck you. Following this, packages to Toulouse and Madrid were considered although both were seven hours on an expensive train from Barcelona. It wasn't looking good. Even the club packages were considered. No, we couldn't do that could we? Surely, it wasn't that desperate yet. Some chance. I'd missed Bury at home in the Mickey Mouse Cup when away on holiday and therefore only had 11 of the required 12 tokens so I didn't even qualify. Miss Ellie and Millwest were contacted (phew) before a vision appeared rising like the sun over K Stand. A three night stay in Salou, sixty miles south of Barcelona on the Costa Dorada, flights from Manchester, reasonable prices, well, compared to some of the other ludicrous prices being asked. No tickets but let's worry about that later. Just bloody get there.

Unfortunately, tickets from Old Trafford were still at 12 tokens and the friendly neighbourhood swagmen were asking silly money. It's usually about this time that rumour frenzy kicks in (remember Rotterdam, Porto, Milan). 40,000 tickets for the 'neutral' zones were going on sale in Spain and apparently La Ramblas already resembled Deansgate on a Saturday night. Tales were told of every self-respecting Manc swagman turning Catalonian and flying over to buy up every available ticket. Soon these would be flooding the market back home and spares would be everywhere mate, right? Wrong. None of them came my bloody way, well, not for under £500 that is.

The next big one was that the same 40,000 'spares' were available to any Europeans other than English or Germans by postal application to the Spanish F.A. If you managed this one don't tell me because I wasted an awful lot of time on this without success. Several other minor outbreaks of scare-mongering followed and lots of low-life creatures were grovelled round, all to no avail. The fact of the matter was that Manchester wasn't awash with tickets and we'd have to pick some up over there, preferably on the day, for knock-down prices - simple eh! Then, it happened. The number of tokens was reduced to 11 and most of us were in. My mate didn't have 11 but a Red's got to do what a Red's got to do and there was still Plan A of getting them over there for the ticketless. Anyway, armed with a pocketful of borrowed pesetas and a new pair of shades the time had come to go and watch history being made.

Local radio and the Manchester Evening News ran scare stories of potential chaos at Manchester Airport and advised travellers to arrive an hour earlier than usual. This was a very promising start as, on arrival, the airport was virtually empty and, predictably, the flight was delayed resulting in almost six hours hanging around. The subsequent late arrival at Barcelona airport and coach transfer to our beautiful hotel in sunny Salou meant we were checking in absolutely shattered at about 4.30am. Salou appeared pretty quiet at first but first impressions can be deceptive and as the coach turned into the hotel in total darkness three drunks fell in front of it singing: "Walking down the Warwick Road..." which set the tone nicely for the days ahead.

Salou is described in the holiday brochures as 'lively' and that first night illustrated the point quite graphically.

Being reasonably sober it was easy to be woken by not so sober revellers returning at 7.30am. So, after about an hours sleep it was up for breakfast in the Hotel from Hell. In view of the surroundings you'd expect the food to be spectacularly hideous and it didn't disappoint. Crap hotel. Crap food. Everything was going to plan.

On a sunny day I suppose Salou isn't too bad. Very Costa, very English but basically what you'd expect. When you get off the beaten track there were some pleasant coffee bars and non-coffee bars at reasonable prices but the food still looked a bit dodgy. A definite pattern is beginning to develop here.

WARNING! WARNING! Rumour control calling...

Apparently, either the good people at Munchen and/or the Spanish FA hadn't sold all their tickets depending on who you listened to and thousands would be on sale at the Nou Camp on Tuesday. We have a propensity to believe what we want to and those without tickets definitely believed this. Why not? It sounded plausible and it certainly had to be checked out. Next stop Salou Railway Station with lots of Reds already there who'd heard the same whisper.

The train journey to Barcelona wasn't that bad and was made more interesting by meeting hordes of well informed Irish Reds who proved to be a mine of useful information. I know United's support in Ireland is legendary but was there anyone left there that week? The highlight of this very attractive coastal route into Barcelona occurred when we passed a college about thirty minutes from Barcelona and were swamped by some of the classiest totty I have ever seen all of whom tried to squeeze onto an already crowded train. I've always been a fan of Dutch totty myself, closely followed by the French, however, it was clear that, for me at least, these were already new Champions of Europe, ones that oozed class and an extraordinary level of fitness.

On arrival in Barca (to use the vernacular) we grabbed a taxi up to the Nou Camp and the taxi driver appeared to be waging a personal war against all motorcycle riders, pedestrians and anyone else come to think of it. He got us there, however, and guess what? The rumours were bollocks. It seems there were a few tickets on sale but only to Barca members and not the likes of us. Lots of Reds hanging around though and lots of touts, English and Spanish, with the going rate averaging at 50,000 pts or £200. This was still too much at this stage. Don't panic. Not yet anyway. Time for a few beers and a look round Barca before some more dodgy food. The Catalan capital may be a magnificent city with some truly magnificent women but I wouldn't call it the culinary capital of anywhere at least not at the bottom end of the market where we were scoffing. Still, that's a minor point and I'm sure with more time and effort reasonably priced edible nosh could have been found. With everything else Barca has going for it though it's worth starving for a few days. Look on it as 'The Barca Diet'.

As there was no late train back to Salou we had to get one at 9pm which was preceded by a heated argument with two bastard Scousers in a bar near the station. Some things will never change, although what Mickeys were doing in a classy place like Barca will remain a mystery. By the time we arrived back in Salou it was already rocking as clearly, those who hadn't spent the day searching for tickets had used their time constructively by sitting in the sun

getting totally bladdered. Even more dodgy food in a beach front 'restaurant' (really!) was made more interesting by the regular sight of groups of lads being chased along the front by out of breath restaurant/bar staff after getting off without paying. By midnight the Gardia Civil seemed to be getting a bit twitchy and circulated the centre about every 30 minutes although, to be fair, they didn't actually do very much.

A mighty Keano dominated sing song followed in 'The Parrot' (traditional Catalan bar) and surrounding streets. At about 2.30am, feeling literally legless we retired to the alfresco bar opposite whose name escapes me but was full of extremely sociable (i.e; pissed) Irish Reds. At least this place offered some seats and helped recharge the batteries until alcohol dulled the senses to the extent that mere physical exhaustion didn't matter. When this place closed it was back to 'The Saloon' (another traditional Catalan establishment) where the mental throng spilled out into the street and joined together in a magnificent 45 minute 'We fucking hate Scousers' to the tune of 'Those were the Days' which even prompted a few bemused locals to join in. The street party went on past 5am and I can' really remember very much after that until I was woken by the cleaners at 9am feeling as bad as I've ever felt. Still, this was it, the European Cup Final, half measures were totally unacceptable.

The breakfast from hell in the hotel from the same place didn't help much although it had to be forced down. Then it was time to travel to Barca (let's stick with this vernacular thing shall we?) and start the day that most of us had waited all our lives for. I managed to sleep most of the way which was a bonus but I couldn't really have kept awake if I'd tried. The predictable traffic chaos in the centre of Barca was a pain but being hungover and slowly roasted on a coach seemed unimportant as a tallish, slim man with greying hair, talking on a mobile with his suit jacket slung casually over one shoulder walked right past our coach. The man in question was none other than Arsenal Wenger the well known, er, Arsenal person. Obviously, this brought great joy to a coachload of bored United nutters and the abuse that Mr.Wenger received was spectacular. He did, however, appear to take it in, er, good spirits and offered a cheery wave if not a packet of sweets to his tormentors.

After three circuits of the city centre we disembarked. The coach park was next to the Nou Camp so the first priority was to check out tout prices and see if they'd come down over 24 hours. They hadn't. The average was still about 50,000 pts. The only significant change appeared to be that the Manc touts were conspicuous by their absence and the Catalan touts were taking liberties. We'd arranged to meet all sorts of ne'er-do-wells outside the stadium with a view to ticket transactions but nothing seemed to be happening so there was only one thing left to do - go to La Ramblas and get blasted all over again. Things would look better then.

La Ramblas was kicking and is certainly a beautiful environment for a pre-match piss up. Robbo, Steve Bruce and Foo Foo Lamar were sighted in a hotel bar and the beers began to flow in a convivial atmosphere with further lauding of Saint Roy of Cork helping to pass the time. Heading back to the Nou Camp on the Metro was an, er, experience with about 5,000 drunken Reds squeezing on to every train with even the occasional German, along with scarves tied round wrists, and not a hint of trouble.

The Nou Camp and surrounding area appeared to be a mass of people selling and even a few buying but the prices weren't coming down and panic was beginning to set in. Approximately two hours before kick off things began to get a bit nasty and we saw a number of Spanish touts get rolled with their tickets and money taken. One tout with whom we were 'negotiating' was jumped by four United fans who battered him, took his tickets and left us standing over him when they legged it. Discretion, of course, is definitely the better part of valour and we also legged it just in case the para-militaries thought we'd set him up.

Reds gather around the Ramblas

This was not looking good. We hadn't seen a single person who'd promised to 'sort us out', prices were straying high and touts were getting rolled all over the place. My ticketless mate was going on a downer thinking it wasn't going to happen when guess who should come walking down the main avenue to the Nou Camp? No, not Arsenal Wanger, but my mate Swang from Urmston with something magical in his pocket (once again, not to be confused with Arsenal Wenger). My mate knows a deserving cause when he sees it and produced a £12 ticket for the United end which was available for the princely sum of - £12. This was a very good sign.

A couple more beers were, of course, required to celebrate this good fortune and reference was made to to to the fact that this indicated without doubt that it would be United's night (logical eh?). I had to go into the stadium, after negotiating the crush at the numerous police barricades, through Acceso 4 and agreed to meet the others inside. Unfortunately, this was the entrance where it went off as the para-militaries panicked when a crush that was entirely of their own making developed and prompted them to start lashing out with batons. Having missed the kick off and the Basler goal I found my seat on the top tier occupied but everyone standing up anyway. In view of this chaos I made my way over to the 'Red News Drunks On Tour' banner which proudly adorned the front of the top tier and got down to business. The Nou Camp is a beautiful stadium but by floodlight with three sides full of Reds it is probably the finest football related sight I've ever seen. The authorities claimed to be surprised at the turn

out of Reds but we knew it was going to be massive. Everyone you knew and everyone you spoke to said they were going and the Spanish police estimated our support at 70,000 inside the stadium with another 30,000 outside. Magnifico.

In truth, the match itself was pretty forgettable for 90 minutes although there was no shortage of valiant effort on the pitch or off it. The support for the team in the last five minutes when they were clearly tired was massive and probably kept them going towards that unbelievable finish. Having watched it many times since on video I don't think the enormity and passion of our support came across on television but those present will always cherish the mighty 'Stand Up For The Champions' which saw three-quarters of the biggest stadium in Europe giving it some. I know it's not nit-picking buy you can always justify a dig at the MUFC Board and I'd like them to explain why, if we really are the richest, biggest and now best club in the world, can't we have a stadium like that where we can accommodate Our Martin's Exec's and the majority of our 'real' support. The proposed expansion of Old Trafford will still leave it far too small with little prospect of a further increase in capacity. We all saw what kind of atmosphere 70,000 clued up Reds can create for the team and how they responded to it. Did we give up when all appeared lost? Did the team? Did they fuck.

When the equaliser went in the sight of the mass celebrations in the crowd was one to behold although the front row of the top tier is not the safest place in the world to have a fit. I think we all felt we were going to do it then - but in extra time. Ole's winner was too much to take in and with the game ending about 30 seconds later it didn't really give us time to register the enormity of the achievement. Sometimes I think it still hasn't quite sunk in. Not only the European Cup that we'd coveted for a lifetime but the historic treble. Don't believe all the 'One Nation United' crap because most of our enemies were distraught. Tabloid bollocks trying to whip up an enmity for the German people that doesn't really exist in Manchester and somehow nationalise our victory to let the losers bask in reflected glory. But we can see through it and, thankfully, had nothing to do with it. I know a sheep-shagger who, in an unguarded moment, described it as the worst day of his life. What a shame. It just makes it even more enjoyable you bastard.

No-one wanted the laps of honour to end and we could probably have watched the Champions of Europe (sounds good doesn't it?) messing about with the trophy all night. Some of the immediate post-match events are a bit hazy because something akin to a state of shock must have hit me. I didn't want to leave the stadium and didn't want that fantastic night to be over. Barney commented that: "This will never be bettered" and it's hard to disagree although this does beg the question where do we go from here? Well, seeing as we had so much difficulty in getting hold of it in the first place how about keeping it for a few years? There's also the little matter of The World Club Championship which would be nice but not as exhilarating.

Barca after the match was absolutely kicking and we bumped into Terry Hall (ex Special AKA) who actually looked cheerful. More beers, more madness. 3 hours sleep in 3 days is enough for anyone. The journey home passed without too many problems and we managed to see the victory parade through Manchester with 1,000,000 other Reds who'd travelled up from Milton Keynes just to be there.

The after match activities in general, whilst equally as drunken and mental as those which preceded, somehow seem more blurred and less defined. It may have something to do with the fact that all the preparations, planning, arrangements, travelling, drinking and suffering that represented the build up to Barca '99 were for one specific and easily identifiable purpose. We were going there to do a job which was to make sure our team became Champions of Europe and to not only see history being made but to be part of it. Those who were fortunate enough to be in Barca on that fantastic night will understand.

A SPAIN IN THE NECK
Kevin Jones

Kevin Jones, 31 and from Barnet with a beer gut to be proud of. Kev's love of United is matched only by his love of a beer. You might have seen him asleep in his seat, at grounds across the country, having seriously misjudged the pre-match drink. At the Munich Oktoberfest in 1998, Kev did his best to entertain the whole beerkeller. A very drunk, naked, Kev danced on the tables to the cheers of the crowd, only to be ejected by 8 bouncers wearing rubber gloves. It was only 6pm.

After the Cup Winners Cup win in 1991, Kev had a drawing of the European Cup and Cup Winners Cup tattooed on his forearm bearing the words "MUFC.Champions of Europe". He still has not forgiven Atletico Madrid for knocking us out the following season. Our yearly failure to succeed in Europe has seen him the butt of endless ridicule from opposition fans over the tattoo.But who had the last laugh now?

Since an early age, I've been obsessed with football, and in particular with United. I attended my first United game at Highbury as a spotty schoolkid in 1977, and as a spotty adult have been a season ticket holder at Old Trafford for over 12 years. Between 1985 and 1995 I attended almost every match, including the many Scottish friendlies we played during the European ban of the late 1980s. These acted as a cheap prelude to the trips abroad we have enjoyed since Pecs in 1990. I have now seen United play in 18 different countries, and in all at over 70 different grounds ,at home and abroad.

Not that my obsession is limited just to United. In England I have been to all 92 league grounds (113 including the new stadiums and those which they have replaced). Abroad, I have been to 34 grounds - with or without United - including many fine stadiums such as the Bernebeu, Parc Des Princes, at Ajax and in Rome; which the Reds are yet to grace.

Indeed the game on May 26th was to be my 40th game on the continent. It also completed a notable set of attending: 1) World Cup Final, 2) European Championship Final, 3) European Cup Final, 4) Cup Winners Cup Final, and 5) UEFA Cup Final.

Like thousands of others, the European Cup Final would be the pinnacle of my career as a United fan. In short the greatest day of my life. But I nearly missed out altogether on the experience.

At the end of March I lost my job, which resulted in me missing both the FA Cup semi-finals, and the match in Turin. I had also come to the top of the waiting list to have my tonsils removed. I had considered delaying the operation, but was told that any new date would be sometime in May. This was obviously in the middle of the league run-in, FA Cup Final, and a small matter in Barcelona, none of which were to be jeopardised.

I was advised by the hospital staff that normal recovery time was 2 weeks. Of course in my mind I had already cut this down to 1 week, thereby only missing Leeds away (which I would be able to see on SKY), and back on my feet in time for Villa at home the weekend after. Not only would I not miss a kick, but I would miss the aggravation of the most volatile away match at Elland Road and a ridiculous 11.15am Sunday morning kick-off.

So on Friday 23rd April, off I went to hospital for a minor operation. I was taken into theatre that afternoon, duly knocked out, and came around about 30 minutes later minus my tonsils. As I came around in the recovery room I spat out a mouthful of blood, which I assumed was normal after a throat op. It quickly became apparent that I was wrong. There was nothing normal when I spat out another mouthful, then another seconds later, then another. Panic began to set in when I realised this was not stopping. One and half pints of the red stuff later, and general anaesthetic number.2 was taking effect as the medical men forced their way down my throat to administer several stitches. The pain and the ensuing sleepless night took my mind off not seeing the Leeds match on the box.

Although the hospital had satellite TV, in their haste to knock people out and remove limbs, bladders and tonsils they'd forgotten to subscribe to Murdoch Sports 1. I was later to find out that this was a major flaw in their customer care policy. I was discharged that Sunday afternoon.

Having stayed the next few days at my parents I returned to my own flat the following Thursday. At 2am I was awoken with a cough, quickly realising I had a mouthful of liquid. Red liquid. That looked and tasted like blood. My blood. I ran around the flat in panic, repeatedly shouting "blood" and spitting the stuff into a handily placed breakfast bowl. If the neighbours had heard they could have been excused thinking that Hannibal Lecter had moved in. As the breakfast bowl overflowed it soon was replaced by the washing-up bowl as I awaited my lift back to hospital. Villa at home on the Saturday wasn't looking too promising.

Discharged on Saturday, I was back 12 hours later following a 2am bleed, which was re-lapse number 2. Not only was I back in the same ward, but the same bed I'd only hours earlier left. At this stage I just wanted them to stick my bloody tonsils back in so that things could go back to normal. I was also desperate to see some footy.

Having missed a glorious Bank Holiday weekend, I was discharged again on the Tuesday. I'd already let my ticket go for the Liverpool game but had the offer of one for Middlesbrough (United had knocked back my original application). In reality it was stupid to even consider it and either I bottled it or common sense prevailed. I watched it on SKY again. In hindsight I could have gone but didn't want to jeopardise the fun of the final few games.

By this time Barcelona was booked...a week in Magaluf, flying in for the game and back to Majorca the next day. The trip was paid for and match ticket acquired. All that mattered was that I didn't bleed again. I was getting to learn a few things about my condition and if I were to bleed again I was at maximum risk between 10 and 12 days after the last bleed and a two week recovery period would be needed from that point. If I relapsed again my season could be over. The B word (blood) was banned.

May 12th - the night before Blackburn and I again had my 2am bleed. This time, however, it was only a table spoon full. I decided it wasn't worth telling anyone about, and went back to sleep. A new job started, and the Friday is an early finish, just two days before the final league game of the season. My throat determined that the day

would finish even earlier. The girls in the office weren't too thrilled to see my newly acquired blood spitting ability. I was even less thrilled. I now didn't have a hope in hell of watching us win, or God forbid lose, the league. My chances of the FA Cup Final only about 50/50 and with the Munich game not even in this country, my chances for this were plummeting rapidly.

In hospital that evening I bled twice more. My fourth bleed of the day started at around 10pm and for the first time since the operation it didn't stop. Not after 5 minutes. Not after 30 minutes. In fact, two hours and a pint of blood later, it was still coming out. So just after midnight, it's off to theatre for another new experience. This time I am to be cauterized. It was described to me as a heat-sealant. Judging by the pain of the next few days, it must be the medical equivalent of welding your bodily bits together.

The next days agony was largely numbed out, mainly because I was torturing myself with the realisation that Barcelona was almost certainly out of my grasp. With the main risk of bleeding 10-12 days after the last bleed, the 12th day would be May 26th, matchday to be precise. Add to that the fact that I'd lost over 3 pints of blood and had been given three general anaesthetics in three weeks. It was generally accepted that I wouldn't have the stamina to travel. It wasn't just people telling me it, my body was saying it too. I felt like shit, and if I went to Spain and it all went pearshaped (highly likely) I'd be in the shit too.

To give myself a better chance I rang Easyjet and booked a flight to Palma on the Tuesday before the game. If I made it I could then take up the rest of my 'holiday'.

United won the league against Spurs on the Sunday. I celebrated with a glass of water. I must stress that this is the first and final time that this will happen. One advantage of being in a hospital less than 5 miles from Highbury was that I could set about ribbing the Gooners straight away. If they were sick when they were admitted to hospital, I made sure they were a whole lot sicker after I'd had my fun. For an afternoon Barcelona was forgotten. Up until then I had had Arsenal's Double victory rammed down my throat. This was payback time.

The next day I was discharged yet again, with a lot of thinking to do. I'd realised by now that I shouldn't go. Over the next few days I took advice from a variety of friends, family and fellow Reds. Obviously my Mum came out with: "Your health comes first". My Dad was amazed that I was even considering not going. What surprised me most was that most of the Reds I spoke to actually understood if I didn't go. They were gutted for me, and of course many were very interested that I may have a spare ticket. So in the words of The Clash - Should I Stay Or Should I Go?

The opinion that swung it for me came from my mate Steve, a Spurs fan. I was concerned that United fans generally stand up during away games and I wouldn't have the stamina for this. His logic went something like this. If I went to the game and found that I had to sit down for periods - thereby missing pieces of the action - then at least I would still have been there and seen part of it. Steve then spoilt it by comparing it to the number of games I'd been to, and got so drunk beforehand that I either slept through the match or couldn't remember any of it. But they still counted as going to the game.

Another part of the decision was how could I live with

myself if I didn't go. I don't know what my reaction would have been but I know it would have taken months, possibly years, to get over. I'm not sure I would have had the will to keep on going to football. I considered the consequences of not going to be much greater than the risk of a bit of blood and a night or two in a Spanish hospital. If I went and it all went wrong then at least I'd tried, whereas if I made no effort then I'd be heartbroken. Besides, there was no guarantee that I would relapse again.

The next few days passed without too many problems. I had already sold my FA Cup Final ticket to a mate who had missed out on one. After a couple of sleepless nights the day of reckoning arrived. There had been no sign of blood, and the pain was only intermittent. I knew that medically I was probably unfit to travel - but worth the risk. I flew from Luton to Palma the morning before the game, a nervous wreck.

Theoretically, the flight was uneventful. The only problem occurred when the kid in front of me reclined his seat. The slightest movement, yet I nearly jumped out of mine. In truth I was petrified of what I was doing. Once I landed I was able to relax, knowing that I'd virtually made it.

After a quiet evening, matchday arrived. At Palma airport everyone was panicking which was quite ironic. Our flight to Barcelona was delayed for two hours, which meant we did not get to the city centre until mid-afternoon. Whilst the others saw this as an infringement on their pre-match drinking, I was delighted because it made the day go quicker, rather than sitting in the hotel, clock watching. I had intended to get to the ground early, thereby avoiding the pushing and shoving at the turnstiles which had marked previous European trips, such as the fiasco in Milan and many before.

Having met the others in my group back at their bar, we headed off for the ground in good time. It seemed as though half of Barcelona left for the game at the same time. The tube was absolutely packed, the temperature and jostling of the crowd doing my nerves no good at all.

At the ground the police had taken it upon themselves to display their crowd control abilities. Three cordons of police staggered the flood of people towards the turnstiles. It seemed to work. Whether this was a major slice of luck or a masterpiece on their part we shall never know. From the thousands massing outside, and the later tales of isolated battles between police and frustrated fans, I have my doubts. Certainly we were correct to arrive early for once.

On taking up our seats I began to realise that I'd struck lucky again. The seat was on the front row of the 3rd tier, with a view of the match to behold. It meant that my fears of having to stand for periods of the game (as the two tiers below did for the entire game) were unfounded. I could remain seated, relax and enjoy the game (if only).

The game itself reminded me very much of my first game at Old Trafford, all those years ago. I had spent so much time taking in the occasion, the crowd and the stadium, that the detail of the game eluded me. Indeed it seemed to be over in about 20 minutes. There I was, deliberately sober, and I can't remember much about the game.

I remember Munich getting the early goal, and then having a few chances late on. From early on in the game I had accepted defeat. I didn't even feel upset at that stage.

Then right in front of us Beckham took a corner, with Schmeichel in the area, and moments later Sheringham's goal brought on scenes of utter pandemonium. I managed to restrain myself, remembering not to shout, just jumping up and down in silence.

I have no recollection of how we got the winner, just scenes the like of which I do not have the ability to describe, if such words even exist. My only memory of this was the German players lying strewn across the pitch refusing to get up and re-start the game. The referee had to talk them into taking the kick-off. Utter comedy. Utter joy. Needless to say I sang my head off for the next hour as we danced in one with the players below, parading the trophy.

I know I had been content with defeat, but this was so much better. The risk I had taken had proven justified and the agony of the previous five weeks was soon forgotten.

FLOATING HIGH
Linda Harvey

Born and raised in Salford, Linda Harvey has been Red from birth. A season ticket holder in East Lower, she attends all domestic home and away games with her son. Apart from United, she has one other sporting passion - Salford Rugby League Club. Barcelona was her first Euro away.

It was just after 7.30am, when we set off from Old Trafford for the 27 hour journey to Spain. I have to admit that we did have our doubts about travelling across Europe on a coach, but it actually turned out to be nowhere near as bad as expected! We arrived at Dover in high spirits. Along the way, we had picked up a couple of Irish lads, one of whom was christened "Father Ted", and he looked after our spiritual welfare (hic!) for the rest of the trip. Once in Dover, however, it was realised that we had actually lost a passenger. We had him listed as boarding at Old Trafford, but he was waiting at South Mimms. We were about to miss the ferry and he wasn't very popular! Eventually, it was decided that another coach would go back and pick him up and we would go without him. So it was onto the ferry and a very pleasant crossing to Calais, drinking the bar and the duty free shop dry.

Once on the French side, it was back on the coach for a short journey to a cash-and-carry to buy crates of cheap booze and fags and to wait for our errant passenger. But no-one seemed to mind anymore as the sunshine and the lager worked their magic. We were told that he was French and that his name was something that sounded like vol-au-vent. So Monsieur Vol-au-vent became his name for the rest of the week. When he arrived on the bus looking sheepish, he was met with a barrage of singing and chanting beginning with "He's red, he's late, he couldn't get out of bed". He hurried to the back of the bus brandishing his itinerary, which clearly asked him to be at South Mimms not Old Trafford. Satisfied that it wasn't his fault, the passengers forgave him and spent most of the next 3 days taking the piss! Many United chants were converted for the occasion, the best being "Vol-au-vent, wherever you may be, you're not the king of punctuality".

The evening was spent driving through the French countryside singing United and Vol-au-vent songs, with the SPS guys turning a blind eye to the odd can and fag. We spent the night sleeping in snatches. On one occasion, I woke and looked out of the window and was startled to see a massive Bayern Munich flag on a passing coach, it's owner staring back at me, looking as bleary-eyed as I felt.

We arrived at our hotel in Palamos mid-afternoon and after a shower and a change of clothes it was onto the balcony with a few cans, in the warm sunshine. As the Red Army arrived, flags began to appear over balconies and United songs could be heard all over the hotel. We soon spotted familiar faces from domestic away games and the place was buzzing as the pool filled up with fat (and very white) Manc lads. By 10pm, around 100 Reds had taken over the hotel bar. Every United song ever written was sung that night. Just before midnight, we were shushed into silence as someone counted down the seconds. At precisely 12am we sang "Happy Birthday Sir Matt" and then "The Red Flag" and no-one bothered to hide the tears. We finally gave in to our bodies' demands for sleep at about 3am, whilst some lads were still singing down in the bar below us.

On Wednesday, after an afternoon spent in the Hard Rock Café, we joined the crush on the Metro and were soon walking towards the stadium, in the sunshine, with thousands of other Reds, all singing and laughing in the bright sunshine. After managing to scrape past a kicking police horse, with only a couple of inches to spare, and surviving a rather intrusive search, we were in. We climbed up and up and up, eventually emerging onto the third tier. Many times I have heard people waxing lyrical about the Nou Camp and I must admit, I have usually thought to myself that they must be exaggerating. But they're not. It is an absolutely incredible sight. As I stood there, near the front of the top tier, all I could see was this massive bank of Reds in both directions. United flags and banners were everywhere, including in the Munich end and hanging from all the tiers - I could see the Salford Reds opposite us. As the teams came out onto the pitch, and 60,000 Reds roared a welcome, I looked out across the city and the hills and the darkening sky. The fans around me began to sing "Happy Birthday Sir Matt" and the hairs on the back of my neck stood on end.

The most lasting impression I have of the game itself, is how short it seemed to be! Each half seemed to last about 5 minutes - where did it all go? When Bayern scored, my emotions were all over the place. I felt miserable one minute, hopeful the next. As the minutes ticked by, we said to each other, "We've done it before, we can do it again!" But did we really believe it? We anxiously watched the clock as they had two chances come off the woodwork. I thought of all the times in the last couple of

Steve Bruce mingles with the fans

weeks that I had said I wouldn't mind if we lost this one after such a great season - what a load of bollocks! I minded very much.

It came to the full 90 minutes and the fourth official held up the board - 3 minutes. Then we got a corner and the next thing I knew Peter was in the penalty area. I held my breath and there was a scramble in the goal-mouth. Then suddenly I saw the back of the net bulge. As the subs ran on to envelop Teddy Sheringham I looked at the linesman, preparing for the shattering disappointment of a disallowed goal. But the players were celebrating and the referee was pointing back to the centre circle! At that point I started to scream. I turned to my friend Karen and she was screaming too. We just grabbed each other, jumped up and down and screamed incoherently.

As the game kicked off again, we sang "We shall not be moved" and waited for the final whistle and the start of extra time. But first, we had another corner. The ball came in to Teddy who seemed to head it wide, but Ole stretched out his foot and managed to get a touch on the ball which hit the top of the net at the same moment as 60,000 Reds exploded in ecstasy and disbelief. I was screaming again and the tears were streaming down my face as I hugged and kissed everyone I could get hold of (including Monsieur Vol-au-vent). I couldn't seem to stop screaming at Karen "I can't believe it, we scored! We scored another goal! We've bloody won it!". I found myself telling everyone who would listen that we'd won - just in case they didn't know already! Down on the pitch, Ole had disappeared under a pile of United players, coaches and officials and the German players were just sitting there, in total devastation. Bayern players had to be helped to their feet for the game to kick off again, and there was just time for one last half-hearted attempt at an attack before the final whistle went and Manchester United were Champions of Europe.

How can I express in words what it felt like to be there at that moment? It's impossible, except to say that it was like nothing I have ever felt in my life before, and I never expect to feel anything approaching that feeling again. It was a mixture of relief, joy, incredulity, astonishment.

Even now, weeks later, although I am outwardly back to normal, on the inside I am still floating high above Barcelona on a balmy May evening.

And I don't think I ever will come down. For the rest of my life, there will be some part of me forever floating above the Nou Camp, with a big daft grin on my face, my eyes shining and my heart full to bursting. It was the final incredible note, in an incredible season, and what a game to choose for a first Euro away!

GOOD THINGS COME TO THOSE WHO WAIT
Tony Smith

Tony Smith was born in 1958, and went to his first United match in 1966. As a ticketless 9 year old he watched the 1968 European Cup Final on TV, and resolved to be there the next time. He didn't expect to be the father of four young United supporters before the next time came around. He has missed only a handful of matches at Old Trafford since the days of Frank O'Farrell, and is a regular contributor to Red News.

At the time, I didn't think that United winning the European Cup was such a big deal. I took it in my stride, always sure that we would win. I know that the nation was buzzing, and that the match was taking up more TV airtime than normal, but the way I looked at it, United were a great side, accustomed to winning championships. I knew how important it was, and I understood that it had become a Holy Grail, but I felt it was only natural that we should become European Champions. I expected nothing less, and the morning after a late flurry of goals had given us the crown I skipped along the street singing 'Champions of Europe' as if it were the most natural thing in the world.

But that was in 1968, and I was only nine years old.

Well, perhaps even then I did understand the significance of the achievement, because somehow the European thing had found its way into my blood, and I was to grow up craving the essence of it all. I don't think there has been a day in the last thirty years when I haven't thought about Manchester United, and there have been many, many days when United have consumed my attention and devoured my nerves. I know it's only a game, and that to be so engaged is illogical, but how can an obsession ever stand up to dispassionate examination? I don't want this to get out of perspective, football isn't as important as life itself or the health of our families, but the fact is that United matter to me; always have done and always will.

Having spent my formative years knowing nothing other than glory, and becoming attuned to United's divine right to attain that glory, the next few years were a nightmare. You often hear it said these days that supporting United is an easy option for gloryhunters, and that followers of a team in blue are the real devotees, having suffered for so long. But all I know is that it was hell supporting United in Manchester during the first half of the 1970s, when the enemy not only won things, but took serious delight in our failure. And don't believe the suggestion that the nation's oft-expressed dislike of our team is a function of recent success: in United's darkest days of the 1970s the whole of football lapped it up.

It reached the point when I wondered if we would ever play European football again, and I recall the strange Anglo-Italian Cup matches in 1973, when we were pretending that we still occupied the European stage - just as second division play-off finals are staged to make the participants feel like they are in a proper cup final. Eventually United did play in Europe again, but with little success. It was 1984, an age since I was a young boy taking European triumph for granted, before we reached a semi-final; and we had to wait nine more years to play in the European Cup.

I could never work out why United were so unsuccessful in Europe during the late 70s and early 80s, an era when English sides - and not necessarily auspicious ones - were amassing European trophies. Although United fans were aching for a first league title since 1967, the need (for it was a need) to re-establish ourselves on the Continent was intense. I used to wonder if Benfica and Real Madrid remembered us. So when we won the Cup Winners' Cup on a soggy night in Rotterdam in 1991 I walked out of the ground telling anyone who would listen that this was the greatest night ever. And so it was in a way, though it isn't any more.

Rotterdam proved to be a false dawn over the Continent, and I reached the point of refusing to anticipate victory in any European Cup tie for fear of the disappointment that would follow. Thus I was sadly resigned as Eric Cantona strode from the field, seemingly devastated, after the defeat by Dortmund in 1997. Having failed to meet the supposed destiny of a Munich final in that year I was doubtful about the good omens that were talked of prior to the final in Barcelona in 1999. Instead my genuine hopes of victory in the Nou Camp were founded on the best evidence there is: the proven quality of the team. Already Double winners, United were possessors of an indefatigable spirit and a refusal ever to bow to seemingly inevitable defeat. But no one could have foreseen how the dramatic Cup victories over Liverpool and Arsenal, and the quality combined with guts that overcame Juventus in the European Cup semi-final, would pale in comparison with what was to follow.

Bayern Munich were not short of self-belief either, and their physical and mental toughness gave confidence to their supporters. At my Girona hotel the night before the final I asked a Bayern fan how he thought it might go, and with an expression devoid of humour and emotion he told me straight: 'Ve vill vin - two-von.' End of conversation. For a little time I wondered how I could counter such certainty, but over the next twenty-fours hours I reminded myself of United's class (even without suspended captain Roy Keane), and by the time I was in the ground I began to believe that we could win, then that we would win.

Having heard in the weeks that followed of many fans with genuine tickets being denied access to the Nou Camp because the barcodes would not scan, I'm just glad I got inside the ground. How admission to a match that represents a lifetime's ambition can be dependent on such technology is beyond me. When the barcode scanner fails on a tin of peas in Tesco you go and get another tin, or the checkout operator enters the numeric code. At the European Cup final, you are expected simply to smile and say, "Ah well, just my bad luck. Not to worry." Then be happy to watch the game in a bar.

Admission procedures apart, the Nou Camp stadium

is probably the best football ground in the world, and it was something special to watch it filling up in the hour before kick-off, knowing that the cameras trained on every aspect of the proceedings would transmit their images across the globe. No one on the planet with an interest in football (and that's billions of people - a mind-boggling concept) would fail to be aware of what was about to take place. And it made me feel proud that my football team was the reason for all this. My team that was born in the grime of north Manchester, then laboured to little effect amid the sweat and smoke of Trafford Park for more than half of this century, suddenly to find itself, because of the genius of a man called Busby, the most famous football team in the world. The team whose ground I would walk to as a child, the team that became, I don't know how, as much a part of me as blood and bone; a team that thanks to a latter-day Busby called Ferguson had once again become pre-eminent. That team would be playing before the eyes of the world, on that perfect pitch, for me and for thousands like me: boys from Salford; anonymous people; blurred faces in every crowd in every picture of every match for over three decades. There were those in the high, steep stands that dwarfed the pitch who had bought into the experience, but this was not their night. Because for all the wealth of the young players, and no matter how detached their lives had become from our own, Manchester United would play tonight because of the common people who had breathed air into its lungs for over 120 years, and as the Nou Camp reached capacity it was as a culmination of the passion of millions throughout the club's history.

United fell behind to a free-kick that seems less just every time I watch the replay (I think the expression is 'Played for and won'). This was despite the fact that my stare almost burned through the scorer, Basler, as I willed him to fluff it: "Miss! Miss! Miss!...Oh you bastard!" There was no panic in the stands at this point because we seemed to expect the initial set-back - it's the way United tend to go about things. But the next 85 minutes were a torment, with the Bayern defence seemingly impenetrable. Then, as we prayed for a miracle, two came along at once.

In the split-second after the first, as pandemonium erupted around me I looked at the referee and linesman - it's something I automatically do, always fearing the worst. Later, on the videos, I noticed that Teddy Sheringham looked over his shoulder at the linesman too. Normally you know it's all right when the officials are running back to half-way, but this time they didn't. The linesman, I seem to remember, stood his ground; something wasn't quite right. Perhaps he was simply as stunned as the rest of us, for there came no flag, no whistle. All this was in the time it takes to blink, but I recall the memory and the feeling vividly. The second miracle, surely the reason why a little man called Solskjaer was born on this Earth, sent all normality out of the window. From high up behind the goal I saw the ball in the net and exploded from within. Nothing had prepared any of us for this. The words 'Champions of Europe' flashed across my brain, and I knew we'd won when I saw half of the Bayern team prostrate on the grass, the referee urging them to restart the game in order that he could end it. And when he did the emotional volcano erupted for a third time.

Why did it happen? What made us win like that? We've heard all the spooky theories about fate and about Sir Matt's birthday, and when the improbable happens to such stunning effect it's tempting to put it down to benev-olent forces. It's a nice thought in a way, and I'm loath to reject it, but the kind omens didn't work out in 1997 when we were supposed to win the final in Munich. The fact is that this was not a one-off for this team: apart from the heroics in Turin and in the FA Cup, we'd pinched several injury-time goals in the league, which were ultimately cru-cial to the title success. This team simply does not give up, and that is why many felt an equaliser was still a pos-sibility when the game moved into injury time. So I'd pre-fer to give credit to the team, and credit to the fans who never gave up, whilst acknowledging of course that the spirits of the past were a major part of our refusal to lose.

The long on-pitch celebrations that followed under-lined the strength of this Manchester United. The players shared the euphoria with the fans; there was an under-standing that neither could have experienced this without the other. The spirit of the team, the togetherness, was manifest. That half-hour as they larked about in the penalty area below us was a perfect way to savour the success, and to wash the tensions away. Thirty-odd years of supporting United had been about preparing for those moments.

As the team reluctantly left the scene of their finest hour, an arena to which all our thoughts would return for the rest of our lives, my eyes were on Peter Schmeichel until he finally disappeared from view. The best goalkeep-er I have ever seen would not be playing for us again. I thought back to the early part of the season when his form had dipped, and when a blunder had given Bayern Munich a last minute equaliser in the Champions' League. Some had written him off around that time (though not most United fans), and I had expressed the hope that he would confound them all by retiring from United as a champion. Some Champion!

For a fortnight after the euphoria of Barcelona I dreamed about the place, the journey and the match. It lay just beneath my consciousness, coming to mind on occasions throughout each day then taking over com-pletely as I slept. I can still close my eyes, see it all again, and relive the feeling. It's made me wonder just how awful it would have been had we lost, how deep would have been the emptiness and frustration. Like the FA Cup defeat in 1976, perhaps, when at the age of 17 I was still waiting to see United lift a trophy in my presence. Or the anguish of the summer of 1992, following the loss of the title race when a long chapter of failure had seemed sure to end. Losing to Bayern would have been like both of those occasions, but multiplied a thousand times given the seemingly near-impossibility of even reaching a European Cup final. And the drive back to Manchester would have been lousy too. It may seem odd to dwell on a defeat that didn't happen, but in some way the contem-plation of that horror scenario serves to make me appre-ciate the success all the more. It was simply so important.

Perhaps the most common conclusion that I have heard since the match is that football, supporting United, will never be this good again. It's something I've said myself, and in all probability it is true. Another Treble is as unlikely as the first - so not exactly impossible - but sure-ly it would be impossible to win a Treble in such a fashion again. And could a repeat performance generate the emotion of the first? The thing about football, though, is that you can never be satisfied, for the moment you stop caring you may as well just give up. A new season will bring a new hunger for the fans, and a desire to go back and do it again. After all, the alternative would be a reprise of the early-70s decline, and one of those was enough for me. Who wants to watch others having all the fun? Not the great Sir Alex Ferguson, I'm sure, and with this man in charge Manchester United is in good hands. We've had our moments in recent years, but not all of them yet I hope.

Sitting in the afternoon heat of the Placa de Catalunya a few hours before the European Cup final, the nerves were beginning to jangle as the game drew nearer; the chanting fans around the square were sounding boozier by the minute. But Barcelona is a great city, the sky was blue and the sun was burning down. An older United supporter sat down next to me on the bench; he looked around, sighed, and said, 'This is better than working.'

I looked up and replied, 'If United win tonight it will be better than anything.'

And it was.

A DAY IN THE LIFE -
A LIFE IN A DAY
Paul Windridge

Paul Windridge has knocked up his half century but still retains a healthy mental age of fifteen. Since before his tenth birthday he has been captivated by the Manchester United spirit, hooked for life into a world where the predominant colour is red. He also readily accepts responsibility for the indoctrination of his children with the Manchester United virus, believing that continuity is the key to prolonged and active life.

Barcelona - 26th May 1999 will go down as the most stunning football experience of my entire life. If you could have bottled it you would have to put a health warning on the label it was that potent. But this day meant more than words can express to me because for 31 years I had lived with the fact that due to various circumstances I had missed that epic night at Wembley in 1968. This was a chance to exorcise the ghost.

I was due to fly out from Manchester airport at just after 1 o'clock on the Wednesday morning, but by 8pm on the Tuesday night I was hopping around so much I just had to get out of the house. I said my goodbyes to Karen and the kids and set off to pick up Nigel my travelling companion.

As we arrived at Terminal 1 the others were waiting for us outside. There were five of us who travelled together including my daughter Eliza, her husband Steve and his dad John. We checked in immediately and made our way through the airport past the sign which declared "no trolleys past this point" what, no trolleys at all, but I put a clean pair on this evening especially for the trip!

It was a very strange feeling sitting in the airport amongst a few hundred Reds at midnight drinking a pint of Boddies and waiting to fly out to Barcelona for the European Cup Final. After 31 years we were standing on the threshold once again and Reds from all round the globe had pawned their very lives to be part of the experience.

At just past 1.30 the engines growled into life and Spanair flight JKK 3376 roared down the runway, the boys at the back sang, "here we go, here we go, here we go" and we lifted off into the night sky and on our way to destiny. An hour and fifty minutes later we landed in Barcelona, it was just after 4.20am local time. Some headed straight for the park benches and got their heads down, but we made it our priority to find the Nou Camp and check out the possibilities of tickets as Eliza and Nigel, despite strenuous efforts, were still ticketless.

So there we were very early on a sunny morning walking in a line which spread across the pavement humming the theme to Bonanza on our way to the nearest Metro station. By the time we arrived at the stadium it was around 7am and some of the stalls were already being set up and the touts were out in force. The price of tickets varied between £250 to £750. It just depended how much they thought they could sting you for.

We spent a good three hours or more bargaining, threatening, pleading, anything to persuade those bastards to lower their prices. In the end we gave up and headed back to the town centre. We took the Metro to the Placa de Catalunya and started with a slow wander down La Ramblas.

It seemed that everyone we ever knew from United was there. A couple of minutes after the first encounter we had another and another and another. In twenty minutes we'd gone as many yards, in fact we weren't getting anywhere, the whole place was a rolling sea of red and white.

On to the Hard Rock Cafe where we had arranged to meet a bundle of friends from various parts of this country, that country and every other bloody country. We then we did some Barcelona tourist spots before setting off back to the stadium and this time there was no turning back, get tickets or Eliza and Nigel would have to stay outside with thousands of others.

On our return to the Nou Camp we found the Guardia erecting ticket inspection barriers with orders not to let anyone pass. There was no point arguing with these guys as we'd discovered that morning outside the ticket office while we queued for tickets after an official had told us they would be on sale. Everything is black and white to them - you either do this or we clout you over the head with this long black stick. We had been forced outside their cordon which by now surrounded the stadium and to top the lot we were at the German end. No way to the stadium, no way to get tickets. Hadn't the great ticket god in the sky heard our pleas yet - we'd shouted them loud enough.

We wandered off in a different direction to try and go round the back and eventually found our way to a University building where the United coaches were beginning to amass and drop their cargo. We followed the disgorged passengers into the University buildings where we devised a cunning plan. There were now hundreds of supporters waiting to get through the initial cordon and down to the stadium proper and it was just a matter of being patient and waiting for the right moment to make our play.

When the time came I would go first as I had a small rucksack which the Guardia would want to search. As I went through I would create a diversion to allow Eliza to sneak around the back of me and through. It worked a treat. Nigel would then follow after Steve having to offer his sack for searching and when asked for his ticket would point to me saying I had it. I would already be too far away to be called back. With John following on after him pushing him impatiently and the mass of supporters behind him Nigel was reluctantly allowed through the barrier.

At least we were in business again. Then a minor miracle happened, Eliza asked this Austrian who was wearing a United top whether he knew of any tickets. Bearing in mind we asked everyone we could about tickets anyway, but this bloke was different. He actually had a couple which he only wanted £50 each for. "Take them" we shouted in unison, but the snag was they were in the Bayern end. "Just take the bloody tickets and let's worry about that afterwards" we all shouted again like some male voice quartet impatient for their cue to warble.

They had tickets at last. A huge sigh of relief must have been audible to everyone and immense weight lifted off every pair of shoulders - now the buzz returned. Their job was then to get into the ground and inform a steward of their Red affiliation and be moved to seats in the neutral zone.

There were still two more opportunities for the stadium security to show off their extraordinary powers of compassion and awareness. On the main gate you were subjected to a vigorous body search. I had a flat pack attached round my waist but hidden under my T-shirt. It's where I kept the Passports and money. As the security man ran his hands over me he came across this hard object around the waist area. Now don't start thinking that - I know I was excited but it was really the flat pack! He prodded it as I stood there wondering what he was going to do he prodded it again while mumbling something totally incoherent so I showed him the plastic pack. He then stood back a pace and nervously pointed to it. I

couldn't resist playing on this and opened the pouch very very carefully and motioned for him to come and have a look. He reluctantly stepped forward and peered inside. I wanted to shout "bang" but thought better of it.

He was satisfied and let me go with a wipe of his brow. While all this was going on Steve was suffering similar treatment at the next gate, but after he had been allowed through a little lad fell victim. This lad had a plastic football which the security decided to slice open thus ending it's short life as a football. Why would there really be anything hidden inside a child's football?

After the obligatory barcode check I was inside the ground, it was two hours before kick off. I suddenly remembered I'd had nothing to eat. So with a big pastry thing and a drink on board I could now go and find my seat right behind the goal and smack in the middle on the first tier.

I found myself next to two women who had flown in from Liverpool and I have to admit I was more than a little concerned when I heard the unmistakable tones of the phlegm ridden dialect. Aaaagh, I thought, I'm in the bloody Nou Camp sitting next to two scousers. But as the initial trauma subsided we became best buddies, by the end of the night we definitely were!

After stuffing pastry in my face, with flaky bits everywhere and caster sugar all round my mouth I wandered off in the vain hope of finding Lizzie and Nigel. Steve and his Dad were in the upper tier so there was no chance of seeing them. I walked around the circular route at the back of the stand which takes you all the way round the stadium except for the main stand which was to my right.

I was thinking to myself what a superb experience it was in the Nou Camp for the European Cup Final and was stood there looking out from behind the crowd onto the pitch and probably looking a right jerk with my mouth open gazing in awe at the scene, just taking it all in, when Eliza ran up to me beaming all over her face. We stood there hugging each other like two excited kids. The plan had worked and they'd been given new seats over in the corner to the left of where I was sitting.

By the time I went back to my own seat there were several very entertaining and scantily clad girls who were dancing in front of us. It caused a degree of excitement especially with the male members of the crowd when the beat of the music became stronger and more lively if you get the picture! The girls got a special cheer as they bounced off to be replaced by a slightly heavier Montserrat Caballé who was obviously too overweight to walk and had to be transported everywhere by open top motor vehicle. A disembodied Freddie Mercury appeared on the video screens and they did a duet which crossed the boundaries of life and death as they belted out "Barcelona".

The pre-match entertainment disappeared, the teams came out and we got ready for the game of a lifetime. At this moment we were prepared for anything. Now we were in our own Cup Final and not everyone elses, this was the big one.

The game started and I looked around the stadium. I gazed up at the Reds in the top tier and down at the Reds below and I thought to myself, this is what I have always wanted, this is where I have always wanted to be. Whatever was in store for us I could take and to be honest those first few minutes passed me by, but then destiny reared up and slapped me in the face. Suddenly Bayern were awarded a free kick on the edge of the box. You could see that the United wall was chaotic with Peter unsighted and in truth it was no surprise when the ball ended up in the back of the net.

Shit, I thought, that wasn't supposed to happen. But we'd always made it hard for ourselves especially in Europe, so why shouldn't this be any different. The rest of the half passed by so quickly I nearly blinked and missed it, but at half time I remember saying, "when we score they'll shit themselves and we'll win it."

There was an air of expectancy at the start of that second half, surely the Wizard would change things around, but he hadn't. With about twenty minutes to go he did with first Sheringham and then Solskjaer coming on. The noise was deafening and the sheer emotional turmoil sucked you in and kept you there. I noticed a dragonfly overhead. You don't get this at Old Trafford I thought. Do these creatures only live for a day, or is it a myth? Would I chose this as my day if it was the only one I had? I reserved judgement for the time being.

I was still absolutely convinced we would win even when Bayern hit the woodwork twice, in fact even more so after that. Mind you as the clock ticked relentlessly on a few doubts were creeping in and then...

I hadn't realised we were already in injury time when Becks came over to our right to take the corner. There had been a series of pressure raids on the Bayern goal and we had come very very close to scoring. We all screamed our encouragement as the lad who has become a hero this season ran over and placed the ball by the flag down to my right. Peter came charging downfield and stationed himself in the box, it was now or never and everyone's thoughts turned to the Volgograd game. It couldn't be - could it?

The stadium seemed to go quiet as the ball arced on it's way but what happened between then and it nestling in the back of the net I've no idea, but the noise was unbelievable - a deep throated release of pent up frustration roared forth from the Red Army.

As we tried to re-invent ourselves for however much of the game was left I turned around and found there was a phone on my seat. The phone was switched on and the display lit up. I picked it up, put it to my ear and a voice said, "if you think that was good - watch this." It was a beautifully expressive Scottish voice I'd heard many times.

I turned around and gave the phone back to it's owner who was scrabbling around on the floor under her chair and turned back just as the lads had forced another corner. I can't believe this I thought to myself, but there was an air of inevitability about it. By this time the noise was so loud you could hardly hear it and everyone around was shaking with anticipation. In came the ball again. This time Teddy flicked it on and there was Ole. And there was the ball in the back of the net again.

This time we were out of control. I don't just mean we went mad - we were completely, absolutely and totally out of control. I was screaming, laughing and crying at the same time, jumping up and down on my seat like a demented lunatic. The poor woman next to me got the biggest hug ever and I swear the bridge of her glasses got pushed so far into her nose she'd never have got them off again. I ended up two rows behind before being catapult-ed back to my own seat. I looked behind me where the phone woman was screaming her head off and she just flung herself over the seat and landed in my arms. No-one stopped to breathe. It was the most fantastic feeling - a huge collective orgasm of delight. 60,000 Reds coming together in celebration of a 31 year wait in the wilderness.

The Bayern players were on the ground motionless where they ended up as the ball entered the net. They were so shattered they didn't have the heart to play anymore. The referee had to help them up and encourage them back to the centre circle where they eventually kicked off just in time for the final whistle.

It had been two minutes of supernatural madness which changed the face of the earth for millions of Reds. Two minutes that will live in the memory forever. Two absolutely priceless minutes.

The celebrations on the pitch were the joining together of team and fans choreographed by Superstar. You'd have thought he'd played in the sodding match. I forgot he hadn't! We were in the stands, they were on the pitch but we were together as one - a true bond collectively known as Manchester United. This really was the bright side of life.

As we made our way out of the ground we were all in shock. Thousands piled out together and we were among many who walked back to town, it was a very long walk, but we cared not a jot. We finally made it back to the Ramblas where for most of the time we sat in silence still smiling, intoxicated by the experience.

At 3am our coaches arrived and we left for the airport. We arrived back in England at 6.30 local time and the sun was shining and when I climbed into my bed on the Thursday night I had been awake for 65 hours continuous, I had blisters on my feet after walking over 20 miles but I was exceptionally happy!

ALL ROADS LEAD TO BARCELONA
Guy Parsons

Born 29 years ago in Aldershot, Hants, Guy Parsons left the UK aged 5 months with his folks and lived in Hong Kong, Cyprus and Germany before settling in London where he now works. His obsession with all things United can be blamed on his grandfather who hails from Fallowfield. Guy has had it up to his neck with people trotting out the 'not from Manchester' line and often wishes he is armed when faced with this frankly piss-poor put down.

A quick prologue: myself, Kevin, Dave, and Brian had a bad experience flying back from the quarters in Milan, so we decided to get to the final by ferry (Portsmouth-Bilbao) and road. Eddie was happy to do all the driving and his brother had offered us the use of his car. This promise was rescinded on Friday night - the ferry left on Saturday evening - and Brian went missing the next morning. The landlady at Kevin's local bravely volunteered her wheezing, fourteen year old Sierra for the job and we reached Portsmouth at around six, having stopped en route to catch the action from Wembley. A sheepish-looking Brian was spotted meandering amongst the parked cars below the docked Pride of Bilbao so we were a full complement on boarding for what turned out to be quite a trip...

Once aboard, we chuck our belongings in our cabins and head to the ship's nightclub, where we grab one of the tables closest to the cabaret stage. Eddie, short, aggressive, tattooed, quite possibly clinically insane, had reasoned that he'd get as much booze down his neck as possible on the first night because he'd need to take it easy on the Sunday night as we were docking in Bilbao at dawn on Monday. He wanted to reach Barcelona rather than spend the Wednesday night in a cell being rodgered by Juan's truncheon whilst awaiting the results of his drink drive blood test. Sounded fair enough. Fairly soon, though, the booze begins to get the better of him, the loudness and bravado level increase proportionately and the ferry's security start to take a keen interest in his antics.

Neighbouring tables had begun to empty when one of the muscled uniforms comes over to make friends. He too looks certifiable and, when viewed crouching down next to Eddie, the two of them could be father and son. His kind advice ("Shut it or I'll kill you", perhaps) does the trick though, as Eddie quietens down and the party games start in the cabaret, Butlins-style. One's called 'Gopher' and involves four blokes and four girls having to race around the nightclub collecting whatever the compere shouts out ("Two girls' bras - Go for it!"). Eight chairs are laid out and one is removed after each round meaning that the last back with the wares is eliminated. This is a right laugh until the penultimate round's task when the two remaining contestants - both on a hen cruise, incidentally - have to remove a guys trousers. Cue nervous shuffling.

Suddenly getting the table nearest the stage seemed a distinctly bad idea, made worse when in a blur of flashing lights, music and wild cheering from the 1000 or so people in the ship's club I'm struggling out of my jeans, and she's grabbed them and now she's waving them around her head and my head movements are following the movements of my duds in arcing circles above her head as I just wait for the wrap of posh and wedge of skunk stuffed into my pocket to come flying out and land in some day trippers margarita. I'm ashen, but of course it doesn't happen and I collect my denims from the stage, trying to work out whether I'm more relieved about the pharms staying put in my front bin or the fact that I'd decided, on a whim, to sport pants this evening. I manage a self-conscious bow to the baying masses before staggering to the casino where I discover, to my delight, that the cards (under the guise of Blackjack) have, on our behalf, extracted revenge on Brian's earlier no-show by relieving him of a ton.

Sunday passes without incident and we meet a couple of lads from Sale who managed to get down to Portsmouth for £2.10. Like us, they've no match tickets. I'm surprised there aren't more United fans on board. Presumably everyone's flying, the mad bastards! Never again! We dock at about seven on Monday morning. The route to Barcelona seems pretty straightforward - toll roads virtually all the way via Vitoria, Logrono, Zaragoza, and Lleida, but we manage to take the wrong exit immediately on leaving the port and find ourselves slumming

it on the normal roads. We need to get our arses onto the A68 but instead we find ourselves behind an oil tanker on a dual carriageway winding its way upwards through the Sierra de Gorbea. Eddie had reckoned on 5 hours for the 450 mile journey so we'd arranged to meet an old friend of Dave's, Mar, at 4 o'clock. She lives and works in Barcelona and had managed to sort us out with 4 star hotel accommodation for twenty quid a night each at the Hotel Numerica through her company.

I remember smelling the fumes first and shouting whether someone had dropped a fag, but almost immediately the whole of the inside of the car is engulfed in thick oil smoke. It's pouring in from the pedals underneath Eddie's feet and there's oncoming traffic and no hard shoulder so we can't pull over for another couple of hundred yards. Eddie spots a hostel and restaurant on the left and veers across the road, leaving a great band of smoking oil on the road. We cruise to a halt, jump out and inspect the damage. None of us have really got a clue but we agree on the oil running out thus making the engine overheat. Sounded plausible, if a little simplistic. Solution? More oil. We freewheel to a garage that we'd passed a mile down the road, rip the bonnet open and gesture to a nearby mechanic. He doesn't appear too keen to take a look at first but eventually starts fiddling about and, with a Latin flourish, holds up the dipstick which has become stuck to the oil sump. This has a gaping rusty hole in it. Our dungareed saviour disappears indoors and returns with some silicone filler, telling us to wait 20 minutes for the filler to set. We question him as to the likelihood of the hulking skip making it to Barca and back. He shrugs and quivers his right hand, palm-down. 50-50.

Half an hour later and we've stepped gingerly back into the motor. Eddie guns it into life and we're off on the steep climb again. Two minutes up the road and we make out the slick we left and are just admiring its size when...smoke starts pumping in again. It's happened in exactly the same spot. We bisect our earlier line of oil and park up. It's been gearbox oil all along. The car's going no further. We decamp to the restaurant, order drinks and put our heads together. Its midday Monday and we're 400 miles short. Still plenty of time. Kevin phones Kay at The Three Sisters to break the bad news and discovers that there's more, as she's not registered with AA. The car's worth £300 top whack and we consider flogging it to the garage but decide to get a move on. A call to Avis informs us that they can't deliver a hire car and that we need to get to one of their offices in order to hire a replacement. Forty minutes later and we're on our way to Vitoria in a couple of taxis, the car abandoned - minus plates but plus 24 cans of Fosters. It's probably still there now. If you're interested it's the white Sierra, the one with the rear suspension shot to bits, the wheel arches that look like a shanty town after 20 years of continual acid rain and the exhaust that does a passable imitation of a smashed up piece of driftwood. It's a fucking disgrace. It's about 600 metres above the valley at a place called Alto de Barazar, overlooked by the Pena Gorbea. Take it, its yours. You're welcome to it.

We get dropped in Vitoria and head to the nearest bar. It's siesta time so there's no chance of hiring transport until 4. We reckon on spending the night in Vitoria, so Dave decides to phone Mar and the hotel. I rummage in my bag for the mobile and realise almost immediately that I've left it in the cab. I leg it over to the station where we were dropped and dive in and out of the traffic, frantically approaching every cab in view before I spot my man serenely cruising past, waving a Nokia out of the window in an approximation of the royal wave. Dave cancels the hotel for the night and we book in to a guesthouse in the centre of town. Vitoria's not the most lively of places but the people we meet in the bars are friendly and we spend a thankfully uneventful night on a crawl before somehow winding up in a backstreet bar with an American who works locally and his ghastly looking Cuban girlfriend.

We rise early on Tuesday and whilst I look after the bags the others troop off to the Avis garage. An hour passes and I begin to realise all is not well. Thirty minutes later and they return explaining that, because Eddie doesn't have a credit card, and because those that do don't have valid driving licenses, we can't hire a car. It has to be in the same name for insurance purposes. I call Avis in UK. Apparently it's down to the managers' discretion. Faced with four sunburnt, dishevelled English football fans who need a car for 2 days to reach Barcelona and who want to leave it at Bilbao, rather than Vitoria, I'd have done the same. If I was Spanish. Football fans? English? QED! Hooligans! What a lovely reputation we've got abroad...Dave phones Mar again. She must think we're a real bunch of losers. All our plans are disintegrating rapidly - we should have been there yesterday and were hopeful of sorting the ticket situation by Tuesday afternoon which would give us time to relax and go for it in the leisure 'n' booze stakes. The train (journey time 9 hours) isn't an option as the return doesn't connect with our ferry in time and we've been quoted 100,000 pesetas each way for a cab. We decide to give Europcar a bash, more in hope than expectation and they say, yeah, no problem. Now? OK. Leave it in Bilbao? Sure. The car will be ready at 4pm. We're ecstatic.

We've a couple of hours to kill so we pull up some chairs outside a bar in the Town Square and discuss the game on Wednesday, which we've hardly done since Saturday. I'm insistent that Johnsen will partner Nicky Butt in the centre of the park, with David May slotting alongside Jaap at the back, Ryan and Becks on the flanks as normal, and Teddy getting the nod over Coley up front with Dwight. There's concern over Sheringham's lack of pace and Eddie reminds me that he's the slowest we've had since old concrete boots himself, Neil Webb, but I argue that Matthaus is hardly Mr Agility is he? Dave and Brian are convinced that Giggsy will start centre midfield with Blomqvist on the left. I hope not. He tries, Jesper, we're all aware of that - but the way he grips his sleeves with his fingers over his palms makes him look like some angst-ridden, fey indie guitarist. Get stuck in, ya poof! Eddie puts Becks forward as Butt's partner after Saturday's masterclass at Wembley and goes for the tried and tested Yorke-Cole axis. Kev remains in the bar.

We head off to Europcar and collect the keys to our Golf. It looks small, but it's the only thing they had so we stash the bags in the boot and hop in. I assume map-reading duties and we approach the first toll road without any mishaps, driving into a spaghetti-western landscape, quite barren for long stretches, with the odd bit of vegetation fighting for prominence against patches of scorched earth. The road, incredibly, is virtually empty so we bomb along for a good five minutes before seeing another vehicle. It's an HGV and, with the speed Eddie's doing it's approaching rapidly. He pulls out to overtake at the last moment and, the car being left hand drive, I catch site of its rear mudguard flash past my window no more than ten centimetres away. This scenario repeats itself continually - he's overtaking in the same lane sometimes and the car's tyres are hitting the sound-grooved white edges and broken centre lines of the road sending an intermittent low humming through the car, but I resist the temptation to check the speedo, and instead grip the armrest tightly, trying to stop myself conjuring up different scenarios which invariably end with the same conclusion: we'll all die. My palms are swimming with sweat and I resort to closing my eyes whenever we overtake. Eddie later informs me that he'd hit 200km/h on a downhill stretch of road. This in a no-frills 1.4L Golf containing 5 out of condition geezers plus luggage. Their advertising's too modest.

We whizz past Zaragoza in no time, stop for some grub in Lleida and descend upon Barcelona at around nine. We head towards the port, get lost and decide to hail a taxi to act as our tug which we can follow to the hotel. It's a balmy evening and we're all desperate to check in and then check out the atmosphere. The hotel's a twenty minute stroll from the Nou Camp and it appears to be where most of the media are staying. We have a brief chat to Lou Macari on the way out and clock monkey-man Richard Keys from Sky Sports loitering with intent at reception. Probably after a mower for his back. We hear a rumour that the Germans haven't sold their allocation. Promising. We hail a couple of cabs and head for the centre, expecting to pass legions of fans en route but, whilst we spot a smattering of both reds and Munich followers, its nowhere near the scale we thought it would be. It's around 10.30pm when our cabs swing round a bend and pull over at the entrance to a wide, tree-lined street. The reason why we haven't passed anyone is staring us in the face: they're all here. We pile into the nearest bar, order drinks and set about getting the low down on the ticket front. One guy reckons that yesterday they were asking £300 but by this morning (Tuesday) he'd been offered a pair at £200 each. He's bravely planning to hold out 'til the price drops to £100, but I wonder whether his resolve will last if he's still ticketless at 7o'clock tomorrow. He's heard the rumour about the German tickets, too - he claims their unsold portion number around 7000, which I can scarcely believe - and warns us of forgeries. We've yet to see a ticket - genuine or otherwise - so God knows how we'll tell...We move outside and mingle amongst the crowds, speaking to people who have travelled from everywhere to be here, all parts of UK, South Africa, Ireland, Scandinavia. Many had been at Wembley on Saturday so we catch up on the gossip and bore a few with anecdotes about our troubled journey. I can hear sporadic singing and chanting from further down the road as I chat to a couple of Germans from Mannheim, who express doubt over the (by now ferocious) rumours regarding the surplus tickets. They've come over on an unofficial tour but have got tickets from Bayern. The rep on their coach had warned them about forgeries, so I grab a look at the real thing and try to commit it to memory. The last thing I want is to be metaphorically shagged up the fire exit by some tout's worthless piece of photocopied trash.

We go wandering and end up in a bar just off the street where we were before. Its rammed and there's a fair sprinkling of Spaniards in, so we again enquire after tickets, and they tell us to walk up to the ground tomorrow morning where, apparently, many of Barca's season ticket holders are going to get rid of theirs. There's a bit of a commotion going on outside after one of the residents in the flats above the bar empties a bucket of water over one of the outside tables. They've presumably called the police too, because they arrive almost immediately and set about closing the bar. There's no trouble. We move on and decide to call it a night after a further half-hour spent talking in another bar to the fantastically named Hannibal who's flown from Bergen in Norway via Frankfurt to be here.

Wednesday we rise early and head up to the ground. It's around ten-ish, hot, and there's already quite a lot of activity. I look for the telltale signs of two or three people clustered around a furtive-looking wide boy, and spot a group outside a bar on Travessera de les Corts. Some tosser from home is trying to knock them out for £300 a throw, so we move inside the bar and look pleadingly at the locals. The barman gestures to us to go further up the road nearer the ground so we take his advice and, sure enough, we come across some Barca fans looking to line their pockets. They're cheaper, but not much, at 60000 pesetas a time. Kevin has a nailed on plan not to buy until an hour and a half before kick-off when, he reasons, the price will be nearer a hundred quid. This course of action served him well during the World Cup in Marseille last year, but Brian and I want to get it sorted so we can relax. Dave has arranged to meet Mar at a bar near Tarragona Metro at midday so we arrange to meet Kevin and Eddie later on at a music bar next to our hotel and Brian and I accompany him.

The locals in the bar look suitably astonished that the hooligans (well, we are English) actually know a Catalan and we're just leaving to collect her daughter from her babysitter in the nearby Parc de Joan Miro when the owner shouts across to her and they engage in some rapid fire conversation. Mar turns to us and explains that he knows someone who may have tickets. We grin idiotically at each other as he reaches for the phone. He replaces the receiver a minute later and looks up, shrugging his shoulders. False alarm. He says he'll ask around on our behalf; Mar gives him her mobile number and he tells us to return at three if he hasn't been in touch. We cross over to the park where Dave gets all paternal with Mar junior as Brian and I await the call that never comes. Three o'clock and we're back in the bar where our man introduces us to a suit at a corner table. He speaks English and tells us that lots of his friends were selling their tickets for the equivalent of £50 on Monday. I feel sick. We would have been here then. Probably right here, in this bar. That fucking car. He reckons we've got a good chance and writes a phone number down, telling us to phone it at 4pm.

By quarter past four I've been passed around the houses and end up calling a Jordi Anglarill. He's got one ticket and he wants 100000 pesetas for it. By this time Dave, Brian and myself had agreed that it was every man for himself in the ticket stakes, so Jordi and I begin ten minutes worth of frenzied bartering and settle on 40000. £160. Bargain. I write his address down and half an hour

later am hurtling across Barcelona in a taxi to his office, semi-convinced that he's a tout and I'm going to be dropped at some run down deserted cowshed, standing on tiptoe looking through a crack in a boarded up window at a single phone in the centre of the room ringing continuously. The cab pulls up outside number 429, Avda Diagonal. The building is immense, marble frontiered, with a sign - 'Gaesco' - above tinted glass swing doors. A doorman beckons me through and, after I announce myself at the reception desk (Jordi's left my name there - by this time I'm actually beginning to feel rather important) I settle down to wait. A tanned, confident, immaculate Spaniard approaches after a while. Its Jordi and I can't help but think of Patrick Bateman from the novel American Psycho. He can sense my unease over the validity of the ticket, so he shows me his Barca membership card and map of the stadium, explaining exactly where the seat is. I'm convinced, we do the deal, and I feel a surge of euphoria rush through me. Now for the game.

It's a couple of hours before kick-off when we hook up with Eddie and Kevin and head to the ground. Almost immediately Brian strikes gold and gets a ticket off a Maltese for £80. Fantastic. We split up, arranging to meet at midnight back at the music club for the drive back to Bilbao. Whilst the others search for tickets, Brian and I nip in to a bar for a couple of looseners. We're in different parts of the ground, so we part and I begin queuing. Its painfully slow and all I can see is a sea of people in front of me, to the left, to the right, as I pass through the first police cordon and get caught in the bottleneck outside entrance 2. I look back in a vain attempt to spot a familiar face amongst a mass of colour as hoards of fans descend on the ground.

Eventually I'm near the front of the outside perimeter. We can all hear the crowd inside and impatience is running high. A push starts from way back and the police try to force us back, but it's useless as there are too many people congregating around a tiny opening. Horses enter the fray as the police try to create a pathway in front of the gates, but a couple of lads at the front have no option but to encroach upon it and pay the penalty as the police begin to lash out. I'm thinking Porto all over again. Everyone's incensed, we're not looking for trouble, we're trying to get into the ground for fuck's sake. We catch sight of several reds in tears going coming our way, away from the ground. They've paid £400 for forgeries, and explain that there's a bar code reader at the turnstile so they stood no chance. It's fucking terrible. We've been queuing for at least an hour. A few people catch the brutality on film which puts the police right on the edge.

I eventually get past this second cordon and into the inner perimeter. I'm searched and pointed towards gate 63. I'm sure my heart stops for a couple of seconds whilst my ticket is scanned, but then I'm in. The game's already kicked off but so what, I'm in. I've got a crap view in the lower tier opposite the grandstand, but so what, I'm in.

You've all seen the game. The frustration is almost drowning me as their gargantuan, meathead centre backs stroll around hoovering up everything being thrown in their direction. We can see the lads straining, chasing, harrying, but there's no spark. It's looking bad. Fuck it, we've done the double for Christ's sake. We'll be back. Word spreads that the fans of the losing team will get kept back for an hour. I can't miss our rendezvous. There's

88 minutes on the clock as I squeeze past people and head up the steps, pausing halfway for a final glance around. I descend the steps and go down the tunnel towards the turnstile. There's three or four people following behind. I feel utterly deflated as I exit the stadium and begin to walk around towards the perimeter gates, reliving the past four days in my head, the high jinks on the ferry, the breakdown, the hassle with the hire car, the terrifying cross country dash, last night's booze jaunt, today's ticket scramble...suddenly I hear the most incredible roar and I stop and stare at one of the other fans. We spin round towards the stadium and catch sight of a policeman with a radio to his ear. He's pointing excitedly at us and then towards the stadium, shouting "Manchester, Manchester" and raising his index finger. We bolt back the way we came with the policeman in tow and hurtle down the steps again towards the turnstile. It only moves one way, but the policeman motions for us to go underneath. He shoves us all through and we fly up the steps to the top row of seats of the lower tier. It's manic and I dive into a frenzied crowd, screaming and punching the air for what seems like an eternity. The feeling is indescribable. I pick myself off the floor and am just getting the description of the equaliser when we get a corner. Becks' right foot, Teddy's flick-on, Ole's stab. Bedlam.

FROM `68 to `99
Maz

May '68. Age - 5 and-a-half. Location - front room in sunny Margate with my family who were making such a fuss over Best, Charlton, Kidd and Matt Busby and his Babes, instead of me, their baby boy!

May '99. 31 years on, still dreaming of an event not in my control, but in my heart a passion of obsession. On my way to Barca to see if dreams really do come true and having to pinch myself with nervous apprehension.

Front row, 3rd tier, block 455 at the Nou Camp. It is really happening with Fergie's babes.

With 90 minutes played on the clock, 1-0 down, still hoping, praying, holding my head up with my hands. My life began to flash back in time in my mind thinking the worst.

Then Teddy struck home! Looking at the ref and linesmen. Extra time again on Sir Matt's 90th birthday! Yes! Fate maybe!

Ole! I went into fanatical shock. My whole life started to flash forward with a great feeling of such a natural high that I've never felt before and probably never to feel again. Who knows?

That present moment of magic, remembering what a fuss my family made 31 years ago - fantastic buzz - tremendous treble to top it all! Life is complete...

United always and forever!

A EUROPEAN FAIRY TALE
- with some grim bits
Sue Simpson

Sue Simpson, 43 and a half, and mother of two first saw United in the year that they became Champions of Europe and lost 3-0 away to Arsenal in the league. No not 1999 but 1968. She travelled through the 70's with two friends whom she still goes to games with today. Enjoys the annoyance caused to fellow rail passengers when then come to sit down next to what appear to be three respectable middle aged women, only to find themselves subsequently surrounded by Red travellers who are perhaps slightly less than respectable. Employed as a University senior lecturer, she has been known to fail Scousers and give match-going Reds a First (allegedly).

It's hard to believe, when writing about being a United fan, that a fairy tale format seems appropriate, but that is the only description capable of describing my story of a long European odyssey. Not for me, I am afraid, the tales of drunken exploits across Europe spanning decades, for I went to Barcelona a Euro-Virgin (so to speak), my previous experiences of euro-aways being totally via TV, radio, or in the old days a very crackly wireless. This is a tale of a little girl who grew up with a dream; and how that dream finally came true, in a manner that is beyond even the wildest imaginings.

In 1968 I was 12 years old, fervently in love with George Best, with a growing love of the football team he played for. One fine day in May (we know a song about that) , Georgie's team were playing, so I was told, their most important match, ever. I knew the story of the team that had perished in Munich 10 years before, because my Gran had told me, so as I sat down in our front room to watch the European Cup Final I knew the significance of the game. We drew the curtains to plunge the room into darkness as on a black and white TV it was almost impossible to see the ball in the bright evening light. The first half was really quite boring, and Georgie was not playing well. As extra time approached, Stepney had to deal with Eusebio, and I had to deal with my mum. Would she let me stay up late for extra time? Yes, well, it was half term.

At the end of the game, the emotion of it all was clearly apparent, as George hugged Sir Matt, and tears were shed. Oh, I wish I could have been there I said. Well, said mum, perhaps you and Alison can go together next time. I think she probably thought the final was always played at Wembley! Alison, being my best friend, and of course a Red.

United were spread all over the papers the next day, but not in glorious technicolour, rather a variety of grainy greys, so I was so thrilled the following week when I went to the pictures, and on the Pathe News were shown the goals IN COLOUR. The next time I saw United in colour was 6 months later, when having nagged my father mercilessly, he agreed as a Christmas treat to take me to a game. My affections by this time having turned to the youngest member of the team, a fine young man called Brian Kidd. I was mesmerised by the experience of being at the match, and I can remember to this day standing on my seat at half time, just wanting to shout out to the world that I was a Red, and having to be told to get down by my dad! I didn't know then, but the decline of my team had begun, but to me they were just the best, the Champions of Europe. That season I hoped, and hoped for another final even though I knew I wouldn't be able to go, as it was in Madrid, but in the semi-final the ref (allegedly) saw to it that AC Milan were in the final, and not my beloved Reds.

If I had been told then, that it would be so many years before another European Cup campaign would be mounted, that my own son would be the same age as I was in 1968, I really wouldn't have believed it. My devoted home and away days, were during the really dire time of the early 70's, not a sniff of qualifying for even the old Fairs Cup. The best we could hope for being to avoid relegation. Of course in 74 we didn't, and we were reduced to chanting Champions of Europe rather ironically at such mighty teams as Oxford and York. Although we came back up on a glorious Red tide, time was passing me by alarmingly fast. As the team were promoted, I "graduated" from the Stretford End to be a LMTB holder in K stand, and bought my first manufactured scarf. I'd always knitted my own before.

By the time we made it back into Europe in '76, my teens were gone, and I had started on the road to doing grown up things, like get married, having babies, working weekends, and being worried about having no money, so euro-aways were not an option.

Fast forwarding quite a bit of my life, and United's history, through Sexton and Atkinson, and the early Fergie, I didn't even make it to Rotterdam as I was too busy being a single mother. When we finally won the league in '93, with my old love Kiddo back in the United fold, my thoughts were, now for the big one. However even with my '94 dream team, included in which was Eric the only player who has ever meant as much to me as George, it was not to be. When we made it out of the group stages in '96 and '97 I carefully organised my students' timetable so that I would be free for the 3 days over the date of the European Cup Final, but all that gave me in the end were some free days to catch up with my paperwork! So I did the same again this year, always believing, and finally we were there.

The utter frenzy of the next couple of weeks led most people to think that I had completely lost my grip. It involved; panics with a token sheet that had only 11 tokens, passport photocopies, running a two car relay to get the token sheet to the person who was going to queue for tickets, ringing for flights, trying to get accommodation, giving up and going for a package trip, having arguments with the agent when we went to collect the plane tickets, finding the long term car park at the airport full, arriving at Gerona to find no one had heard of our hotel, being taken to a different hotel, in a resort we didn't think we were going to, who oddly were expecting us, and finally, we were there. So just like my mum had predicted, the next time United were in the European Cup Final I went with my best friend Alison. An awful lot of pounds have been put on, O & A levels and degrees obtained, husbands obtained and discarded, and children given birth to, but there we were on the 26th May next to each other in the Nou Camp. Me still wearing my 1975 vintage scarf. My only sadness being that I knew Kiddo wasn't there. Alison and I had already seen some of the most fantastic

games ever during the season, and achieved one of our most cherished ambitions, watching United win the title at home, so could we really expect even more?

It seemed not, as the team had saved one of their worst performances of the season, and certainly the worst in Europe, for the final. My thoughts wandered to the '76 Cup Final so eagerly awaited as my first ever trip to Wembley to see United, where I watched them lose, as they gave their worst display for ages. But this was the '99 United, so I hadn't completely given up as the clock ticked to 45 minutes. However I have to confess that my thoughts when Schmeichel came up for the corner were that Bayern were bound to clear the ball, and poor Schmikes would finish his Red career looking a right tosser. In fact as the ball went out of the area I was transfixed with horror, and when it came back in, well, I have never gone from one extreme of an emotion to another in a millisecond before, pausing only for a brief glance at the linesman. I came back to earth when Bayern kicked off again, and for a moment the '79 Cup Final loomed large, but what happened next is a feeling I know I will never feel again. Pure unadulterated, no holds barred joy; ringing the bell at the top of the Richter scale, ecstasy. It was different to '68, there the joy was tinged with such sadness, this was a pure celebration, a celebration of Sir Matt's life, a celebration of everything it means to be a Red. We sang "We are the Champions, Champions of Europe" for the first time in 30 years, and really meant it. Only those who were in the stadium that night could possibly understand the feeling of togetherness the massed Red Army had with the lads on the pitch. After the cameras had gone, the level of intimacy was indescribable, for that brief moment in time, they weren't highly paid players, they were fans like us, having the party of a lifetime. They seemed to be saying to us, 'We have achieved this together'. That above all else is what I will always remember. I was jumping up and down on my seat, singing to the world the joy of being a Red, and this time no one was going to tell me to get down.

Emotional exhaustion seemed to hit many people as we came out of the ground. The chant of "Now you've got to believe us, we've won the ****ing lot", was sung, not with arrogance, but with an air of utter disbelief. It was so difficult to believe what we had just witnessed. I saw hardened fans with tears in their eyes, others seemed to be in a state of shock. One I know well walked passed me with a completely fixed expression of utter amazement, the only way he could communicate being with a little Tele-tubby like wave, as he went off into Las Ramblas night. Then we all got our second wind, and suddenly we were all kids again.

We didn't need to drink that much, we were drunk on our own adrenalin. There I was walking down a Spanish beach showing complete strangers headlines in a German newspaper! Spotting people who had been in the Nou Camp by the bruises on the backs of their legs, caused by jumping up and down against seats that don't tip up. Trying to teach strangers, who are now my friends, songs in a bar, when owing to all the excitement and a lot of gin, they had the attention span of a goldfish. Finding the yo-yos in the newsagents that played Ole, Ole, and almost seeing a riot start because there were about 15 people who wanted them, and there were only 8 in the window. Thankfully the owner had another box in store. Recreating the goals on the beach with a blonde 10 year old playing a very realistic role as Ole Solskjaer. Walking around a town where at every bar, there were people raising glasses, flower vases, urns or even nothing at all into the air to be greeted by a loud roar, as we all played at being David May.

Sadly the party had to end and we had to go home, with lots of new friends, and a feeling which if it could be bottled would save the NHS millions. As I nodded off to sleep on the plane, the hum of the engines seemed to turn into the roar of the Nou Camp, and it was singing Champione, Champione...and so thanks to a Teddy and a fair haired Munchkin, they all lived happily ever...well, for quite along time anyway.

A MARRIAGE OF TRUE MINDS
Roger Brierley

Roger Brierley has all the wrong qualifications for a Red. Brought up in Bramhall (posh git), became a chartered accountant (bleedin' suit), left Manchester to become an actor (show biz glory hunter) and used to sit in G Stand (wanker). Also teetotal, hates standing, drinks coffee from a Thermos at half time, finds some of the songs offensive, and admits to (occasional) buying at the Megastore. Is also so old he doesn't give a toss what anyone thinks.

For a few seconds after the ball flicked off Ole's right boot almost vertically into the roof of the Bayern net, I swear there was total silence in the Nou Camp. The silence between a flash of lightning and the crash of thunder. Time to swivel to check that the linesman hadn't raised his flag, swivel back to see the ref pointing to the centre. Then the explosion of 50,000 triumphant voices. In those silent seconds, the players had become immortals and WE WERE THERE. A moment the players, Alex and the fans will forever share. The greatest moment in my 52 years watching United.

Later, standing in that beautiful stadium as the celebrations died down, desperate to stay forever in the arena where history had just been made, I wondered how I could have got this lucky. How did I get here?

It all began a long time ago. Only a torn, faded programme is witness to the beginning of a lifelong love affair. United versus Leeds, April 7th 1947. Childish pencil records 'United 3 Leeds 1'. It wasn't instant romance, because I continued to watch my local team, Stockport County, until the sensational 1948 Cup Final, when United beat Blackpool, after looking dead and buried a goal down and not long to go. Sound familiar?

I was smitten but not, to be honest, devoted. Difficult to believe now, but in the late 40s and early 50s, although United played exciting and creative football, they weren't THAT different from other top teams. Support was no more passionate, as I dimly remember it, than for City or Wolves or Newcastle. Bill Nicholson's Spurs also played beautiful football. Crowds were massive everywhere. Television was still only for the well off and there wasn't much entertainment competition. It was, truly, in the current vogue phrase, The People's Game.

To me, a schoolboy, Johnny Carey's team were heroes, fascinating but remote, akin to Hollywood film stars. Then, dramatically, against Huddersfield Town in 1953, Matt replaced half the team, many of my heroes were gone, and, in their place, mere boys. Kids my own age. Duncan Edwards was a year younger than I was. The Babes were not only a revelation, but signpost to the youth revolution of the Sixties. No one suggested United would win nothing with kids. Even the cautious Busby thought that they would soon be "too good for anything else" in the League. By this time, I loved the game to distraction.

Indeed, I fancied myself as, in the jargon of the time, a 'scheming' inside left. I was, in fact, hopeless, co-ordination and dexterity not being my strong suits, but I could, at least, now identify with United's young team. Just a bit more talent, I kidded myself, and I could have been a Babe.

When so many of them died at Munich in 1958, it was like losing a brother or a friend. Everyone in Manchester felt it; they were our children, our neighbours. And in that awful moment at Munich's Riem airport, United became more than just a football team. It became the embodiment of Manchester's spirit, part of my generation's lives. Eight players had gone, others would never play again. But the handful who did carried on Matt's vision.

So we, the fans, had a duty to the dead and the survivors to ensure their memory never dimmed. And to promote Matt's beliefs in creative football, humanity in dealings with players, and in a Manchester United as a beacon of excellence. Independent and proud of it. I can't pretend I ever consciously said, or even thought it in those terms at the time, it happened osmotically over the years. A romance had become a serious relationship.

Ten years on and only Bobby and Bill Foulkes of the Babes made it to the '68 European Cup Final, but Matt had fashioned another charismatic side. I had just moved, nervously, to London, and my only ticket contact rang the morning of the Final to say he'd failed to get one. So I squatted in front of the black and white television pictures in my attic garret, ludicrously waving my rattle, with as many Man U fans as I could muster in North London at the time viz two...

I can still feel the intense excitement, not so much because it was the European Cup Final as such, but because everyone knew it meant so much to Matt and the survivors of Munich. I think it was George Best who said 'We did it for Matt'. Not given to weeping, I blubbed freely as the post match embraces were shown, and still go misty-eyed every time I see the tape again. It was the culmination of a decade of yearning.

Historically, the 4 - 1 score looks overwhelming. Easy to forget, then, that, in normal time, the Wembley 68 Final was just as tense as Barca '99. When Bayern hit the woodwork twice, minutes from the end of the 90, we were a few millimetres from oblivion. This mirrored the heart-in-the-mouth moment in '68 when Eusebio strode through our defence just before the 90 minutes were up, with only another Alex to beat. Stepney's save turned the match, as surely as did Peter Schmeichel's nonchalant gathering of the ball as it rebounded from the post as though he had thrown it against the woodwork for fun. At that moment, Bayern must have had at least an intimation that it wasn't all over.

After '68, when Matt's knighthood was followed by retirement, I certainly had no inkling that things could go seriously wrong. No experience of what it was like NOT to have a great manager. To follow one is usually the managerial equivalent of the 'hospital pass', and, with the exception of Liverpool's Boot Room, I can't recall any club which has produced two great managers in succession.

The 70s and early 80s managers were, with one exception, worthy, but, for various reasons, couldn't recapture the Busby spirit. Ironically, Tommy Docherty, who few would describe as worthy, came closest to producing the required magic.

But there was a saving grace in this gloomy period. The fans. They became the keepers of the passion and never-say-die spirit of the Busby era. Other clubs were gobsmacked that United continued to fill grounds home and away whatever the team's league position or, indeed, whatever division they were in. A slice of the debt owed to Matt, the Babes and the other players was repaid. The Gods, I like to think, smiled on this faith and eventually sent us another genius of a manager from a tough Scottish community.

But during this period other things were stirring, out of the fans' sight. A few, including the derided Michael Knighton, realised the club could expand with monies from non-pitch activity. The club got the message and, in 1991, offered 2,597,404 shares to the public. Many fans were horrified at the idea of the Club as a plc and relatively few fans took them up. Big mistake. Other fans realised it was already a business and that having shares

at least allowed you a voice, albeit small, in the club's affairs, when previously we had none.

I bought a modest hundred shares, partly for the sentiment of having the certificate framed on the wall, but also because it was a chance to put my bit into the Club we all loved. I was now not just an onlooker, but a participant. A tiny bit of United was mine and, although I had no idea at the time, seven years on it gave me a chance to fight for United's independence.

My relationship with United had moved on. I felt it was now more of a partnership.

The share certificate never got framed, was stuffed in a drawer and forgotten because 1992/3 was here and glory beckoned. At last, the Championship. In the emptying Barca stadium on May 26th, I remembered the last time I had felt so emotionally drained after a United match. It was another sunny May day. May 3rd 1993. Then, it wasn't just excitement, but overwhelming relief.

The bandwagon started to roll. We howled when Hughesy, Ince and Kanchelskis went, complained when United bought no stars in '95/6 and showed unpardonable lack of faith in the Wizard's choice of Jaap and Dwight. The future was bright, the future was Red. But, inevitably, given United's burgeoning success, others were thinking of United very differently. As a can of baked beans. Golden baked beans. A top class product with limitless worldwide potential, they were saying behind City doors.

On Sunday, September 6th 1998, it happened. A friend rang to ask if I'd seen the Sunday Telegraph, which carried the leaked story of BSkyB's proposed bid for United. Even though, with hindsight, I should have realised it had to come, I was stunned. And outraged. This was MY club, not some businessman's cash cow.

My United supporting life so far had been simple. I assumed the Club was on the side of the angels and only got worked up about the team, the manager, the winning, the losing, the fatuous but inevitable debates about Eric versus George, would the '93/4 side have won the European cup but for the asinine UEFA 'foreigners' rule, etc. Now all this was threatened by a company whose Managing Director hadn't bothered to find out that Denis Irwin was our left back

Two things were obvious. If Rupert Murdoch took over the Club, United, as an independent organisation, was finished, relegated to a footnote in BSkyB's multinational accounts, safe from any shareholder scrutiny, since there would no longer be any United shareholders, only BSkyB shareholders. Any manager would be at the mercy of the multinational's global needs.

Secondly, BSkyB needed United, but United did not need BSkyB. The only coherent reason the Board ever gave for recommending the offer was that BSkyB's coffers would enable United to compete in the new global football environment, though no such promise was ever made by BSkyB. Some less than alert fans and some journos who should have known better (and probably did), but didn't want to upset the Club, peddled the nonsense that the bid money was going to be available to buy Ronaldo, Zidane, etc. In the event, we managed quite well without them, thank you, but the £623.4M was never offered to the Club, only to shareholders, to persuade them to give up their interest in the Club. Shamefully, the Board accepted the bid without any discussion with individual shareholders or fans.

The truth is that United, already the richest football club in the world, have no problems financing future expansion. A business which last year earned nearly £90M and made a near 30% profit is hardly going to find the bank manager's door shut. More likely he'll be doing some very serious grovelling, nose deep in the carpet pile, pleading to shovel money in United's direction.

That September Sunday was one of those moments when you know you have to do something, or you'll never be able to live with yourself. But what? Naturally, as a middle class Mancunian, I fired off a protest letter to the (ex-Manchester) Guardian. On the Monday, another shareholder fan, Michael Crick, fronted a BBC Newsnight programme on the proposed takeover. I spent a frantic few hours tracing him. Suddenly, I was part of SUAM (Shareholders United Against Murdoch) and, for 8 months it took over my life. IMUSA had anticipated a bid and were ready. After a week, we had a dozen people and not even the price of a stamp to protest to anyone. Then an anonymous donor paid for a mailing to all 28,000 shareholders and we were on our way.

IMUSA and SUAM's campaigns and the Government's eventual rejection of the bid have been well documented, but the overriding lesson is that United are an emotional part of so many lives that woe betide anyone who messes about with something they don't understand. For the present, United is independent. But the story isn't over. The Murdoch bid threatened a divorce, but the marriage survived. Fans, via IMUSA, and shareholder fans, via SUAM's successor, Shareholders United, now have to find a way to structure the Club so its independence is never again threatened. Why Chief Executive Martin Edwards insists on being painted a villain when, by putting his shareholding into a controlling Trust, as C.P.Scott did at The Guardian, he could be a local hero, the latest in a distinguished line of great Manchester benefactors, is a mystery.

All this happened as United were gathering pace for the impossible dream, the Treble. I was so involved with the struggle to defeat Rupert Murdoch, that, for the first time as a fan, some games became less important than a press release or a mailing to shareholders. Happily, the blocking of the bid came just in time for us to all get back to the reason for all our passion, the football. Came the unbelievable Juventus game and the FA Cup Semi-final replay, the Match Which Had It All, and, at last, Barcelona beckoned.

From the moment we left the White Cliffs of Dover on the Monday morning, it was as if United had invaded Europe. The Calais ferry had been taken over by IMUSA, the Gare du Nord and Gare d'Austerlitz rang with United songs and the corridors of the overnight Paris - Barcelona train debated Fergie's likely line up. At Port Bou, where we changed trains, by 9.00am the platform was littered with fans already stripped to catch the Mediterranean sun. No beds in Barcelona, so we stayed in Llafranc, a beautiful village on the coast. In the evening, walking round the headland to Calella, even before the village appeared, the silence was broken by that old Spanish gypsy song 'Glory, Glory, Man United.' and, sure enough, another bit of Spain was in our hands.

And Barcelona was something else. No Arndale Centre to numb the senses. Fantastic architecture and the Ramblas, one of the great meeting places of Europe, overrun with Bayern and United supporters at alternate tables, though United outnumbered Bayern by about 2 - 1. Brilliant sunshine, no animosity (after all, Bayern fans helpfully brought a STOP MURDOCH banner to the Old Trafford tie), just anticipation you could almost touch. United noisy and extrovert, Bayern more introspective, but both making Spanish brewers very happy.

I knew this trip was something special; every minute to be savoured. But, as we all know, nothing to do with following United goes smoothly for long. The problems started when we, along with the rest of the ticket holders and the estimated 15,000 without tickets, tried to get to the stadium. Metro carriages were rush hour packed and each station brought more fans throwing themselves, in bunches, at those already on. Not the place for someone 6'5" and ancient. My legs were in a different part of the carriage to the rest of my body. I had visions of never getting to the match, of my two halves being swept up by the cleaners next morning.

Never have I been as glad to reach a destination as Maria Cristina station. Now for the Nou Camp. Whey - hey, here we come. Bought the T-Shirts. Grabbed bottles of water and turned into the wide road leading to our end of the Nou Camp. More problems. Barca's crowd planning seemed minimal. Only when the vast numbers funnelling into the narrowing road jammed did the police act. Vans were driven into the crowd to separate fans into narrow streams. Fans promptly climbed onto the vans. The vans gave up and drove off, fans clinging to them in the hope of getting nearer to the stadium gates. Only half an hour to kick off and a sea of people in front of us. The tall narrow steel gates into the stadium were closed.

The huge crowd pressed forward. Suddenly, that frightening moment in a crowd when pushing from behind leaves you with no control of where you're going started to cause panic. A few people were getting in, but progress slowed as forged ticket holders were turfed out and thrown bodily back into the crowd trying to get in. Chaos was close. Suddenly a line of police appeared, and forced their way into the crowd to relieve the forward pressure. Right idea, almost too late. The police were very young and were trying, unsuccessfully, to look less worried than we were. A boy in a blue shirt, weeping uncontrollably from being ejected from the ground, pleaded with the officer in charge of the police to let him in. It didn't work, his picture appeared on the front page of 'el Periodico' the next morning

We were now too close to kick off for comfort and the crowd was getting angry. Someone shouted 'Leppings Lane'. Dramatically, half a dozen mounted police appeared from nowhere and rode into the crowd, batons swishing. Near panic set in, a horse reared only a few feet from me. But the police action worked. No one actually got whacked - the police, to be fair, were careful just to make a lot of sound and fury, hitting trees and whirling batons in the air. Then, suddenly we were through. At last, the promised land.

The game is already just a blur until the Sheringham and Solskjaer strikes. United didn't play as they can. As we all saw, the 3 matches which actually won the Treble were ordinary, Barca injury time excepting. United, though, achieved three Holy Grails. They won the Champions League. They won the Treble. And they have achieved something no other United side has done. Creativity AND consistency. The ultimate Holy Grail. Sir Alex's gift to the future.

POSTSCRIPT
Being a United fan started, appropriately, as a slim thread running through my life, just as Granny Brierley started winding cotton in Stockport's Vernon Mill at the age of 10. The thread has thickened over the years to become a rope. It's not too fanciful to say it has become a lifeline in times of difficulty, a comfort when unhappiness strikes, a source of excitement and intense pleasure, alternating with the necessary gloom of defeat. Most importantly, my son understands and shares the same belief and passion.

LOCK OUT
Sid the ******

Sid, from Manchester, doesn't want his real name used so that his reputation (!) at Old Trafford can remain secure without the pisstaking that the knowledge of his writing this article would undoubtedly bring. He is a United Road regular - standing there in full ski hat mode ever since he was 12 in 1985 - and still standing there in spirit since United made the disgraceful decision to remove the terrace and he had to move to Old Trafford pastures new in the North Stand, or whatever it's called. He will be found on most matchdays in a Salford Quays bar or two re-living his 'Karma United Road' memories...

How much has changed at Old Trafford in such a short space of time. No, I'm not on about the glory and the infinitely pleasurable success that Alex Ferguson (don't think there will be so much of that Tinkerbell stuff after May 26th now somehow) finally brought with him but the aestetic changes that have gone on at the club many of us grew up in. School was supposed to be for learning (certainly not mine - taking the piss out of Bitters and bunking mainly), but it was on the terraces of United (and United Road!) that the real education came from.

Passing acquaintances became friends, became mates for life - mates who you went to games with on a Saturday and you now travel thousands of miles with to see the Reds play. Not a family, better, yet as many young Mancunians brought up in perhaps the last great Old Trafford dynasty - the 80s - will testify - United changed off the pitch, and not for the better. I'm not one of these 'stand on the streets and sign a petition against it all' Reds - I go to Old Trafford to get away from that shit - but nonetheless I question the validity of the support of the executives - or whatever evil incarnation is thought up next - and how Red many actually are.

United were always the biggest club in the country, we knew that, and so deep down did the Scousers. But to get amongst the big boys on a greater stage than Britain we had to quantify it - and once the trophies started to come everything changed. And so it is that where we usually had one European away trip a season to look forward to (and that usually involved some crappy sort of bizarre penalty elimination in Russia) now we have more games on the continent than we used to play in the 1980s in the FA and League Cups combined.

So supporting United has - and I'm not joking here - become a full-time profession, bad enough for those lucky enough to be Red bread winners but a full blown calamity if you're not working. Fair enough people will argue that it is a job fitting in all the different games, affording them, getting to them and getting enough work holiday to take off to see the games but it's a lot bloody worse when there is no money in the pot.

I'm not going to turn into a bleeting Scouser and plead my case but safe to say that without any sort of work last season but the most menial and demeaning jobs paying less money than an Indonesian sweat factory - getting to games outside of Old Trafford were few and far between. So it was that things have to give - and how it killed me to choose going to the Sunday FA Cup semi (big mob!) and be unable to go to the Wednesday one. Yeah, great choice.

A bit can always be made here and there but even that didn't allow for purchases of the Fulham, Bury, Lodz and Notts Forest vouchers in their Cup ties and it was those home Cup games where I had decided to save £80 that was to see me lose out on so much more later on in the season.

The result - a truly stunning performance that should not be lost in the mists of last season's many achievements - in Turin paved way for the mass of immediate thoughts of Barca and how to get there. By the weekend as many of my mates were planning their many contingency plans for Elland Road, I was seeking confirmation of plans for further afield. What would we do? How would we get there? And perhaps, most importantly, how much would it cost and what about the tickets?

The case for who deserved and who didn't get over European Cup Final tickets will go on for some time and can get very boring, emotional and angry to those affected, but like it or not, because of those missed home Cup games I was not required when tickets finally went on sale at Old Trafford.

Some of the richer establishment amongst our group opted for the luxurious coastal trips, and others struggling with time had the desperately tragic decision of opting for Millwest - but more of that later.

I, and two others, opted for the less grand but equally satisfying train service. Heavy on the body but so light on the wallet. People may say the telephone and all that crap when asked what their favourite invention is of this century but I go hook, line and sinker for the laser copier - a great contraption whereby we could buy off another Red, inter-rails which were perhaps better than the originals! Well, desperate measures and all that. Courtesy of a bizarre meeting in Cockney twat land on the Saturday with a group of Scandinavian Reds who had somehow lost a number of their party I managed to overcome Cup Final ticket obstacle No.1 of 2 - all for face value and a couple of beers. This was getting too easy.

What's that about speaking too soon.

The trip down was full of the usual stories. Quite a number of Reds, as expected, some taking advantage of my favourite invention of the 20th Century and others from cheap travel agent deals. Whatever, there was no hassles and a good bon homie - a few cities came and went, the draw was being smoked a bit quicker than our stock had anticipated and if living on the cheap and avoiding hotels on the way down had some advantages - financial - it certainly did not relieve the situation when one of our group pulled a stunning French local and then lost the script as he walked her home (don't worry - she'd already told him that there was to be "no sex, no sex, no sex, no sex" - and still declined even when he offered to wear his Eric Cantona face mask) and did his chances no good whatsoever when Mr Vomit decided to visit. "But I'll walk you to your taxi then" were the last words he spoke to her and the dribbling bits on his shins and shoes certainly added to his aroma during the dreadful night's stay in the station as we both, pissing ourselves, moved further and further away from him.

Through a haze the sing-songs and great pre-match celebrations in Barca came and went. I'll never forget some of those sights, even if tickets were scarcer than a smiling Scouser in Liverpool that week. Everytime it was suggested - and again I ask do you blame us here, these little young shits were taking liberties with us all - that we relieve the Spanish students who seemed to have most of their club's allocation of tickets someone else beat us, or should I say them, to it. And sometimes the dibble got there first. Work this one out - if they catch you in the act of buying off a tout, you get nicked and the tout gets let off!

Things were looking bleak, and as our mates who travelled on Millwest joined us, things got worse. Some really bad stories were emerging. How could they let them down like this - one had travelled with them all over the place and couldn't believe he'd been blown away for the big one. Out of order.

So there were more than anticipated without briefs on the day of the game. Some paid over the odds, some like me simply didn't have it. It was - as is the case in these things - the luck of the draw. Keep jibbing and many will get in. Many won't of course, or will be caught. I knew which category I wanted and had to fall in later.

I am of the belief that you will always have a chance to get in whatever the occasion, wherever it will be. One of our group had got into the World Cup Final last year. The blag performed at its best can be an artform, and through many of the gates one last steward rumbled him and was about to destroy all the pre-planning and work with a shout to his colleagues. What happened next? Well I'll leave it to your imagination.

This time it was a bit of a nightmare, in a chaotic sense. Nobody seemed to have a clue what was going on - and add to this a crush developing at many of the turnstiles and it soon got out of hand. I know some people will look down on all this talk but I've been to over 400 United games - I think I had quite a good right to be in that ground with everyone else but was being forced out of it by Spanish students and touts. All I wanted was the opportunity of jumping a turnstile or two - all those that got in said there was room enough to fit us all in. You might not understand but as kick-off time approached chances were decreasing and the thought of being so close to the greatest day of my life yet being so far away from it was tearing me up. Looking at the increasingly desperate attempts by those without tickets to get in was mad.

Maybe it was because many of those without briefs were not the barmies and gloryhunters that I'd at first thought would be there. These were genuine. People who

had been betrayed or let down by companies - a coach with old people in it from that bankrupt one who were unable to get in - and people just like me or you. Red to the core but, because of whatever circumstances, unable to get in.

First came a chance when a young Spanish bloke had a few tickets pinched off him. He started shouting and pointing to the police - what for you twat! - but the young Red was off before you could say anything. But being a bit adept I nipped in and followed. I didn't know what I was going to say or if he'd even sort me out (I wonder if he would have...) but before all that, somehow and out of nowhere, the dibble got him.

A couple of our group got through fairly easily. One when there was a surprising lack of police on the front line and got through when a surge erupted and another jumping over the barcode turnstile because the bloke doing it was the only thing stopping him from the stadium itself and he was obviously not going to leave his post and delight the rest of us outside! But another got through obstacle no.1 before being nabbed and unceremoniously thrown back out into the melee.

I'll refute forever that those without tickets were causing the crushes, this was simple incompetence, but as kick-off approached so did the realisation that it wasn't going to happen. Finally the dibble arrived at most of the turnstiles just before kick-off and and the hard (I'd already been manhandled back three times...losing it) was just about to become the impossible. The look on the Red's faces who were watching those go through into the ground will live with me for a long time. There wasn't bad feeling - those in deserved it, but was it that much to ask that we join in or get in as well? As usual rumours grew - 'there is a gap here, 'a bloke will take a bung at the gate here', 'they'll let those without in here', but they were just a frantic rush around different parts of the outside perimeter to delay and deny the inevitable.

Worst of all was seeing the people with legit briefs turned away by some crappy computer system. What would I have felt like then. It was a terrible sight.

I was now alone - all but three of us got in but unable to locate each other - and at the lowest point in my life. To be so close, to hear it all and literally feel inside the ground but know you are not actually in is something I can't really describe. Whereby getting through the police ticket check had been a doddle there was now an acceptance that nothing was going to happen - and it was a choice of wait and desperately see if anything will miraculously appear or go to somewhere showing the game. I chose to stay by the ground - and try and find out what was going on from various points around the ground, each time as different people tried to herd me away.

Resigned and disconsolate - and that's before we've found out we're 1-0 down. I was told that the game went quickly but for me it seemed an eternity, and without any super skunk because it was back in the left luggage. Shit - when plans go wrong they go wrong big time!

My situation was perhaps put into better perspective when I met a middle-aged bloke who had been screwed getting here by the travel company and then paid for one of those copied tickets only to find out that £300 hadn't guaranteed him a legitimate one. Knowingly selling a false brief was out of order. Also a bloke who had been mugged on his way here by a Spanish pick-pocket could barely talk he was so upset - and later we were to hear of the people who were turned away when they had legit tickets but the barcode was fucked. Gutted, not knowing the right words and looking all the time to see if one of the coppers is going to change how all this was going and say we could go in, yeah, as if!

Anyway, the game neared its end and what happened, happened. There was no happy ending outside for yours truly. One story goes that a gate was opened for Reds and those around it all got in to see the second goal - my tormentors were having none of it, apart from those baffling few who had left early and obviously had not read the script from many of the great games this season but still got back in. But the celebrations outside the ground when the second went in (and it had been confirmed!) by those remaining outside were perhaps equal in some part to those in - and as it finally dawned on me that we'd done it it became less about my personal fuck-up and more about the collective euphoria and joy. I tried to hide my own feelings and to replace it with the buzz - well, how was I supposed to feel? I didn't know what to feel but knew it would be stupid to let it all get to me and not cherish the bigger event going on courtesy of the team nearby. It was wild outside and I was soon to be at least fortunate enough to discover the wild, wild post match celebrations as we finally were allowed in. All was not lost. Well, nothing was!

'All that way for nothing' was the cry when I got back by the pisstaking lightweights. And so it may be, but if there is part of me that now knows to buy the vouchers for whatever crappy matches at Old Trafford from here on in, equally - however gutted I feel about missing out on the final fence - I still count myself as being part of it all. I was there In Barca, on the 26th May.

But next time - and believe me there will be, to do it all again for those of us who didn't get in - nothing and nobody will stop me from getting in and seeing the bloody European Cup Final.

THE END OF THE WORLD AS WE KNOW IT
Stephen Ryan

Stephen Ryan,36, saw his first game at Old Trafford at home to West Ham In 1970 and soon gained himself the reputation as something of a jinx. Forever on the ball,the sales of Whiteside and McGrath convinced him enough was enough; always a keen supporter of the 'Fergie Out' movement he declared United would never win anything as long as that man remained in charge and promised not to return until Fergie had gone. He packed his bags and removed himself to Japan and made another promise:- he could never leave Japan until United played the World Club Championship there.

It wasn't just the unbelievable climax to the most glorious season any English club has ever known; it wasn't just one of the most dramatic endings ever seen at any sporting contest; it was quite simply the end of the world as we know it. Things can never be the same again.

The 'we' I am referring to, are the fans born in the shadow of the '68 triumph and the world we knew was one of constant failure and disappointment as United strove to reach that peak again. Like some aboriginal dreamtime, 1968 lurked in the backs of our minds and our 'walkabout' would never be over until the European Cup was back in Manchester. Winning the European Cup was at the heart of our folklore; all the roads on the way up led to Wembley and Benfica; all the roads down could be traced from that point. Any subsequent achievements our teams made were bound to remain in the shadows of black and white photographs of a sweat-drenched Bobby Charlton and a beaming Matt Busby holding that impossibly large trophy.

Everyone will have taken slightly different paths to Barcelona, will have arrived there by different routes and different means, for what it is worth I am going to share the story of my road to Barcelona. The first thing that comes to mind is just how long that road was, just how far we have travelled. To hear it told today you would think that there was some inevitability about United's return to the top of the tree, that it was only a matter of time before the European Cup was claimed again. For the first thirty years of my life the European Cup was a dream too far, just one league championship was all I wanted. For most of that time I really believed I would never live to see even that.

September 29th 1976 was when my own European campaign began. United's first post-Busby tie in Europe, at home to Ajax, the recently dethroned kings of Europe. A comfortable win which allowed us to burst into song, "When the Reds go on to win the UEFA Cup..." well I certainly didn't believe European glory was beckoning that year, but it was nice to be mixing in that sort of company again. In fact, I remember there being quite a good deal of confusion surrounding the pronunciation of 'UEFA'; one version went, "When the Reds go on to win the 'Yoo-fah' Cup..." and the other had it, "When the Reds go on to win the Yoo-ay-fah Cup..." We didn't need to trouble ourselves unduly as Juventus were our next opponents, and after a game of 'miss-the-sitter' at Old Trafford they put us firmly in our place in Turin. We were out but the European bug had bitten a new generation.

On the field those pre-Heysel years were largely undistinguished, and that is putting a very favourable light on it. There was, of course, the odd great night littered here and there but we were only competing for semi-final places in the minor tournaments. Off the field things were different. Ajax was the start of a new phenomenon; it was the beginning of the Euro away. I don't begrudge the over-50's their tall tales of Gornik in '68, we've all stretched the truth a little here and there, but I still don't believe most of them. However, I clearly remember talking with my little pals at that Ajax game in awed tones of friends of friends of big brothers who had been to Amsterdam. At the time I don't think that I knew anybody who had been abroad in peacetime so the idea of people really going to a foreign country to see United was something that belonged in the Sunday papers, like wife-swapping and orgies - it was nice to read about but I knew it never really happened. Foreign travel was not for the likes of you and me, most people had never even seen a passport. Mine, and probably many other people's, European adventure began with a team a million miles from being contenders and in an age when mass foreign travel was not an option. The idea that one day we would see United lift the European Cup in Barcelona was not even worth starting to dream about, and besides I wouldn't have known where Barcelona was.

Twenty three years on and I knew where Barcelona was, but it seemed almost as distant. The omen's were not good. The end to the previous season had been disastrous, had United collapsed like that in another era, the manager's job would have been on the line. We all knew the team wasn't what it had been; we were not very exciting to watch and we weren't even winners anymore; there was a big hole in our hearts once filled by Eric Cantona; and we all knew that there was no place at Manchester United for the likes of Teddy Sheringham. If the team was bad the club was worse. 'Football Club' was removed from the badge and obscene amounts of money were being made as the club moved further away from anything that it once stood for, and the Murdoch bid seemed to spell the end for the Manchester United I had grown up with.

I started the season with a familiar promise. It wasn't going to take over my life this year, I was finally going to grow up. And the outlook was fine as I started the campaign on a beach in Hawaii, as far removed from European football as you can get. Not a word of it on the television, nor in any of the papers, it was exactly the start to the season I had promised myself. All the expense, the stress, the sleepless nights that supporting United had brought my way would be behind me; my only worry was what to do with all this extra free time and money. The beaches in Hawaii had given me a few ideas. I started the 1998/99 season just not in the mood for football and I don't think I was the only one. Then word of the Barcelona game filtered through.

Anybody who can be bothered to read this will be more than familiar with the games leading to the European Cup Final, there is no need for me to go over familiar ground. My involvement really started with the quarter finals. My map tells me that I live about 9540 km from Old Trafford (it doesn't give it in miles) so trips are thin on the ground. I had to pick my games carefully. Inter Milan tempted me no end and I knew I could make the trip, but what if United went and won? I could only make two of the next three rounds. The previous season I had gambled on a victory over Monaco and had very expensive flight tickets booked and paid for, guaranteed to get me into Ringway for about 6.00pm on the day of the semi-final. As it turned out Monaco's win saved everyone another case of air-rage as the flight was to turn out three hour's late. My choice was simple; I could go for Inter Milan, or I could gamble on them getting to the final and skip Milan. The choice was made for me, as a few days before the Milan game I slipped discs in my neck and my tickets were passed on to a deserving cause.

Everybody knows the tale of that game, at the time it seemed like the greatest triumph in all my years of supporting United now it merits barely a footnote in this story. I was a little apprehensive about Juventus, but if truth be told they were the opponents I fancied. My main concern was that it was a home leg first; this was after consulting the flight schedules from Tokyo to the other cities; as long as it wasn't Kiev away. I made the trip to Manchester for the Juventus game, and it was a long, long flight back. Our pretensions had been showed in

their true light, it had been men against boys, just like in 1976. A thirteen hour flight gives you a lot of time for reflection and by the time I went through customs at the other end I had convinced myself that a 1-1 draw was actually better than a win. At least now our tactics were clear; we had to go to Turin and win. And we did!

It was in the early hours of the morning over here, late night for you, when the military style planning began. Match tickets were going to be a problem but nothing like the headache getting into Barcelona would be. Travel agent after travel agent provided the same response: 'a flight to Europe no problem but no way into Barcelona'. 'Don't understand, is something happening?' It is difficult to describe the feeling of helplessness being 6542 miles away (Tokyo - Barcelona), all your dreams about to come true but no hope of a flight. At one point there seemed to be a chance of going via Moscow but that meant arriving on matchday and relying on the famed punctuality of Aeroflot; Tokyo - Kuala Lumpur - Rome - Barcelona was another option and the airtime involved in that would have entitled me to some senior rank in the RAF.

The early weeks of May 1999 were amongst the worst in my life. The closing weeks to the league season were singularly unpleasant, I didn't speak to anyone who enjoyed the run-in to the season. For me, the fixture pile-up meant lots of games played at 4.00 am; permanent tiredness without the slightest hint of enjoyment. (The Arsenal semi excepted.) A typical day might have gone something like this: 6:30 get up, leave for work at 7:40 and then get home 9:30 at night. Have something to eat and then spend the hours 11 - 1 making calls and faxes to Europe about tickets. 1:00 am go to bed, lie there for a couple of hours worrying about the game ahead then get up around 3:30 to watch it. Game finishes around 5:30 - 5:30 - 6:30 free. The next day, more of the same.

It wouldn't have been so bad if any of the games had been any good, or if the chances of getting to Barcelona were a little higher. The longer it went on, the less likely it looked. I also had the added headache of branch members to worry about. Since I am involved in the running of the Tokyo branch of the Supporters Club, quite a few people were looking to me for help. I knew some would drop out but we were left with a stubborn twelve, and I knew there was no way I could accommodate them all. Of course, I took the bull by the horns, 'Don't worry, as soon as I get any news you'll be the first to know. It's looking good.' I lied

No match tickets, no flight tickets and no hotels, and not much hope; it was with mixed feelings that I watched United win the league. I tried to kid myself, and others, that the league was the really big one, that Europe was just icing on the cake. But it was if Andy Cole's half-time substitution changed not only United's fortunes. The next morning people started dropping out, a fax from Old Trafford and a message on my answering machine from a travel agent.

I was now down to a party of six, I could manage that now United had exceeded my wildest hopes. The travel agent was offering a nice little package of flight, hotel, match ticket and grand prix, all for the price of house around Maine Road. I said,'Could I just have the flight and hotel, and make it the same price as for someone coming from England?' He said he'd think about it. He then got back to me and asked if could he buy a pair of FA Cup

Final tickets for a 1,000 each. I did have access to a pair, and that is the kind of money that makes me corruptible, but I declined and just asked him again,'Could I just have the flight and hotel, and make it the same price as someone coming from England?' This time he said OK.

I couldn't believe it. Within the space of a day United had won the league, and I had got my tickets. I really would be there.

I don't think that I ever really believed I would go, but there I was on a sunny spring morning at Tokyo's Narita airport. I was still waiting for something to go wrong but all seemed fine with the inside of the plane. A long flight so I settled down to the in-flight entertainment, Enemy of the State was the film, it had to be an omen; I had seen it both coming and going for the Juventus game. All was going smoothly ...too smoothly as they might say - in Enemy of the State.

The flight from Tokyo to Zurich was totally without big match atmosphere, there were only two of us on the flight that had ever heard of the European Cup. It was exactly what I expected but I was a little disappointed when we arrived in Zurich: no signs that the end of the world was nigh there either. Then it happened. After about three hours hanging around Zurich airport there was another body going to the game, albeit an aging body in freshly pressed jeans and a T-shirt straight out of its megastore wrapping. It was a sign that the Red Army was on the move, the clans were gathering and within an hour there were another 200 at the gate for the flight to Barcelona.

Arriving in Barcelona at about eleven o'clock the night before the game, I had never felt so pleased with myself; I had not only got myself there, five other people would be owing me the rest of their lives. The airport was buzzing but it was a mild kind of buzz, even the 'student' touts were pretty half-hearted. I got on the bus and started a conversation with my neighbour, 'Just come in from Manchester ?' he inquired with the look of someone who had come much further and wanted to let everyone know about it. Well, I knew I would win any of these 'I've come further than you' games so I just said, 'No, Tokyo actually' and he looked really impressed. He then started going on about something he had read in the paper about someone coming to the game to Barcelona from Tokyo. I thought it might be me so I asked could I see but he wanted proof of my ID. Eventually he let me see a half page piece in The Times, the newspaper of record, 'Stephen Ryan, 36, is flying 13,084 miles...' - I was an official freak and this man on the bus was in awe of me.

Getting into my hotel I felt at home. The next few hours I couldn't stop bumping into people I hadn't seen for years, there were messages from all over the world, it was as near to This is Your Life as I would ever come. A few drinks in the bar and it was soon 3 in the morning, 11 in the morning Japan Standard Time, time for bed but my jet-lag had me up again at 6.30. If you'd been in the centre of Barcelona at eight in the morning, and I assume you weren't, then you would have seen nothing but Germans, not just Germans but very big Germans. This took me aback as I had been expecting Red domination, but I was forgetting the jet-lag. Anyway, by sometime around midday normal service had been resumed.

There's no need to go into too much detail about the day itself, as I am sure my day was exactly like yours; meeting up with lots of old faces and missing out on a lot more; calling international to catch somebody on a mobile 20 yards down the street. (At one point I had run out of change for the phone, none of the Reds slumped in the street had any either so I asked a familiar looking face walking towards me. Sure enough, he had what I needed but it meant taking money off Mark Lawrenson.)

There's something about sunshine and beer, I love them on their own but as a team they always catch me out. It still seemed very early but I was getting the call to go to the game, a friendly barman seemed happy to supply me with a few cans for the taxi; I thought he'd overdone it but he knew better than me exactly how long that taxi was going to take. Beer, sunshine, a European Cup Final and an endless traffic jam. Eventually we got out and walked, it was then that I realised I had put one of the open cans in my pocket, the wet patch shows on beige. As I approached the ground I felt my bladder giving way, and this was all I could think of as I approached the ground. I should have been soaking up the sights, the atmosphere, the noise and the smells, I was just concerned with how long it would be before I could release the flood. Everyone told me to just piss myself, since it already looked like I had, but a good upbringing prevented me from doing so. The news was not good; we were going to have to do one lap of the ground before we could get in, by way of a diversion through some surrounding suburbs. I had forgotten about the game, my bladder was all I could think about. The pain was searching out unknown nerves in my teeth and every time a promising opening in the concourse appeared so did one of Barcelona's finest on horseback. I didn't want to be 'Stephen Ryan, 36, travelled 13,084 miles to get arrested for indecent exposure before the European Cup Final.'

Finally we got into the ground and relief was instant. We missed all the opera singing, we just got in as the Bayern fans waved their pink cards. What seats we had! A little far back but right on the halfway line, any offsides just ask me. An empty bladder but still a little numbness around the cheeks as the game kicked off. Bayern get a break and a free kick, no problem as I saw the referee indicate indirect. I let everyone around me know this jewel of information, 'Just let it in Peter.' I helpfully suggested. My voice must have carried 460 rows and I looked on smugly as the Bayern players celebrated, little did they know it had been disallowed. Then it sunk in, the numbness vanished from my cheeks, I was as sober as anyone in the ground.

One thing everyone at the game agreed upon was just how quickly the match passed, I have never known a game of football go by so quickly. The clocks at both ends dominated. Half time came and went, and so did my optimism; from feeling that we were bound to put it together sooner or later I started consoling myself that it was only a one-off game and the result didn't really matter. The important thing was that we were all together at the European Cup Final. I had come to terms with losing, at one point when one of their players bowed to the crowd I told myself that kind of crowd pleasing never goes unpunished, but we just hadn't got started. Then IT happened. There is no way that the mere combination of a human mind and the English language can get near to describing what happened, I would not presume to try. You have your version, I have mine.

The celebrations after the game were strangely subdued, I spoke to a hundred strangers and they said to me, 'I can't believe it.' I carefully considered the implications of what they had said, thought long and hard how I should construct my reply, then interjected, 'I can't believe it.' This was a scene I saw being replayed throughout the night. The next day I was drained and the weather seemed to be telling us it was all over. I had a plane to catch and 'Enemy of the State' was waiting for me for the fourth time in two months. Before 'Enemy of the State' started there was a programme on the plane 'World Sports Round Up', not a word of the European Cup. I knew I was on my way back to Japan; the land that football forgot.

I am writing this almost exactly a month after the game. I still haven't got over what happened, I know my life will never be the same. I will still follow United but there can never be the same drive about it, all my dreams came true in one day; they weren't just my dreams. There were around 40,000 other people sharing exactly the same experience. I consider myself a pretty open-minded type; if someone told me the second-coming was happening tomorrow just after Teletubbies, I'd at least ask what side it was on; if someone told me that the world was flat after all I'd hear them out and tell them I'd take it into account the next time I planned a world cruise. But, if someone told me I will ever experience such concentrated, uninhibited joy as occurred on 26th May 1999, I would laugh in their face.

FOOTBALL, BLOODY FOOTBALL
Richard Connolly

Richard Connolly "Conno", 29, was baptised at Old Trafford in 1974. He nearly never lived to see that day as he ruined his dads prized collection of United autographs from the 50s and 60s. He is married with a child aged 2. His wife agreed to call the baby Keano if it was a boy until somebody told her it was named after a United player. Thankfully, it was a girl and christened Georgina, after another United legend? He goes to see United play whenever he can, but nowhere near as often as he would like.

After spending a night in Biarritz and then Zaragossa we finally arrived in Barcelona at around 11.00am. Our priority was to find somewhere to park close to La Ramblas and to start drinking. Finding accommodation was the last thing on our minds as we knew there would be nothing available in the city.

The afternoon was spent in The Robin Hood drinking, singing and discussing what line up we thought Fergie would use and generally preparing for the European Cup Final, yes, the European Cup final. Yet, just 10 years ago the prospect of seeing my team win the Football League, as it was then, seemed a long way off, and here I was a few hours away from watching them in the European Cup Final. Everyone we spoke to was extremely confident, even though we were missing Keane and Scholes. The talk was not if we would win, but by how many. Were we being over confident?

It was now 7.45pm, 90 years since the birth of Sir

Matt, 1 hour to the start of United's biggest game in the past 31 years. This was our destiny. We decided to forgo another drink near the Nou Camp as the crowds began surge past us. After coming this far we didn't was to miss the kick off.

We could see that the police had set up cordons in order to search people, check tickets and generally stop huge numbers of fans rushing to the gates. After 10 minutes of pushing and shoving we eventually got through and now we just had to get through the turnstile. By this time I could only see Wal about ten yards in front of me, I had lost the other five from our car at the first cordon. It was now about 20 minutes to kick off and numbers were swelling as we tried to get through our turnstile. About 5 yards to my left a girl fainted through lack of air and exhaustion, her boyfriend shouted for help while everybody gave her room. People were screaming and banging on the gate to get the attention of the police, but they did nothing except stand and stare or bang the gates with their batons. Before she could get any worse I told the boyfriend we had to get her inside immediately as she may need medical attention, I grabbed her legs while her boyfriend took her arms and the sea of red in front of us parted as we carried her into the stadium. At this moment nobody thought about the game ahead, just for the safety of this girl.

I stayed with them for a few minutes until I was certain she would be okay. I'm sure she will never forget how she got into the Nou Camp.

As I went up the steps and entered the second tier the size of the place just hit me. Even though I had been before in 1994, it was still amazing, it seemed to be twice the size as I remembered. I found my seat and met up with the rest of the guys, although the lads from our car were not in yet. The Red Army were everywhere, all over the ground, no other club would have this sort of following, 50-60,000 Reds in the ground and thousand more locked outside. The rest of the lads arrived as the teams came out to deafening roars.

Peter came down to the United end for the last time in his glittering career and the teams kicked off. I just gazed around the ground, to the tiers above and below me taking in the atmosphere and looking at flags from all over the world. I couldn't believe we were here. Suddenly Bayern were awarded a free kick on the edge of our area from which they duly scored. Why do we always seem to concede early goals in Europe, haven't we learned yet?

Bayern had got what they wanted, an early goal and now all they needed to do was get men behind the ball and try and spoil United's pattern. It wasn't until midway through the half that United managed to gain control of the game, but for all our possession we were not creating any clear cut chances as the Soul Brothers were getting marked out of the game.

The second half started in much the same way the first ended, plenty of United possession and our players being taken out, notably Cole and Giggs. With half an hour remaining Sheringham came on for Blomqvist. This enabled Giggs to move out to the left and Beckham to the right as Sheringham slotted in behind the front two. The side now looked more balanced and the crowd sensed we would surely soon score.

As United pressed forward in search of the equaliser I dreaded the thought of a German counter attack. The inevitable happened and Bayern hit the post when they looked certain to score. Ole came on for Cole with 15 minutes left and with what seemed like his first touched forced a good save from their keeper. Ole's going to score tonight, I could feel it, he always scores, doesn't he?

Peter pulled off another great save to keep us in the game, and then Bayern hit the bar. With 5 minutes to go we were getting desperate, but we never stopped singing and willing our team on, it seemed as if the Bayern fans were already celebrating their win. Desperate times call for desperate measures, as we sang The Red Flag I looked to the sky, wanting Sir Matt to give our lads guidance and at the same time I gave my lucky pants one last rub. They rarely fail me.

For some reason I took a photo of the scoreboard at the Bayern end, Manchester United 0 - 1 Bayern Munchen 45 mins. We were into injury time and the big Dane was coming up a corner, this must be our last chance. The Germans couldn't clear the ball and the next thing I knew it was in the back of the net. Que pandemonium, the whole place erupted, the noise was unbelievable, we just went absolutely mental. In amongst all that I managed to take another photo of the scoreboard, GOAL 45 mins. "We shall not be moved" echoed around the ground

By the time I had come to my senses and got back to my seat we had forced another corner. I remember this so clearly and it seemed to happen in slow motion, Teddy flicked it on and Ole stuck out a boot. If the whole of Barcelona had heard the first roar, then we had just woken the rest of Spain with the second. In the space of two minutes within injury time we had just won the European Cup. The final whistle went and the Bayern players just sunk to their knees while three quarters of the ground went into mass hysteria, the players, the dugout, everybody. We shouted, screamed and sang louder and louder, as we weren't going to be moved.

The Cup was presented and the players did their lap of honour and partied on the pitch while we partied in the stands. The players brought the cup down to where we were behind the goal and took it in turn raising it aloft as the crowd roared. We shouted for Keano and Scholes, the players formed a guard of honour as they, along with Berg, went and lifted the cup.

After about 45 minutes the players left the pitch, we sat around thinking what we had just achieved. We waited for the crowd to thin out a bit and then left the stadium, still in a state of shock.

We made our way back to La Rambla and that's where the party began.

Conno

Block 247, Row 03 seat 0016

FINALLY ARRIVING IN THE PROMISED LAND
Phil Williams

Phil, 33, assures us he has aged considerably more than the two years since IF THE REDS was published. Following United is still a way of life and Phil managed all seven Euro aways on the road to EUROPEAN GLORY in Barcelona. As most may agree, there is very little left to do

watching United after the memorable 1998-99 season. Even if United manage to win every match from now until eternity, nothing will compare to the feeling of those last 3 minutes of the season and the glory it brought with it. The trip to Barcelona is described below, mind you, putting some of the feelings and emotions into words was a difficult task.

Being born in 1965 meant I was too young to remember the 1968 triumph, and since then it has almost been a lifetime's ambition to see the Reds win the European Cup or Champions League as it is now known. It is ironic that we only qualified for the Champions League in 98-99 as runners up, our previous five attempts since '68 had all ended in various levels of failure.

If there is one place in Europe where you would want to play a European Cup Final, surely Barcelona is that place, a huge stadium and city with a massive drinking potential. Also with the final being held in late May, the weather should also be fitting for the occasion.

I've always liked a bit of a gamble, so when we overcame the might of Milan in the Quarter-Final, three of us decided to book the cheapest flight available to Barcelona hoping we would overcome them other Italians in the semi. This £98 Easyjet option soon became a masterstroke as our second 'Italian Job' was completed. It soon became clear after the victory in Turin that flights to Barcelona and accommodation in the city itself were either going to be very rare or very expensive.

In the time between the Turin victory and the impending departure to Barcelona, it was apparent that although we had been allocated, eventually, just over 30,000 tickets there was lucky to be anything upwards of 50,000 travelling over to Barca and the resorts in close proximity. This was truly going to be a massive invasion from the Red Army.

Also in the time between the semi and the final we had the small matter of the title run-in and the FA Cup Final. Basically football had taken over my life completely like never before. It was very important that we won at least one trophy before we set off for Spain to at least have something to show for the season's monumental efforts. The title was very important as it showed the nation that we were the best this season and also stopped Arsenal from winning anything. The FA Cup Final proved to be a stroll in the sun as we pissed all over the Geordies and sent them back to the land that time forgot empty handed yet again. All in all another double and a week in sunny Spain to look forward to - not a bad end to the season!

On Monday the FA Cup Final hangover had only just subsided when at 1.30am myself and two other battle hardened Reds (Nigel and Lee) set off for what was to be a trip of a lifetime. As we had plumped for the cheap and cheerful Easyjet option, it meant a drive down to Luton. This isn't an airport I've used before so this was another notch on the airports of Europe bedpost!

At that time in the morning it was a quick three hour drive and we arrived at a very busy airport well in time for the 7.15am flight with it clear that the Barcelona flight was going to be made up of 99% Reds - the other 1% being the pilot and crew. A few familiar faces including Drunken Dave who was actually sober - mind you it was 7am. A quiet flight during which I managed to avoid all types of alcohol - a first on a Euro away, remember this was a special occasion!

We landed in a warm and sunny Barcelona at 10am and the airport was already buzzing with Reds, so let the fun commence. Our five days in Spain was to be a mini-tour of the Spanish coast, and one thing was for sure it was going to Costa-packet. The first destination was to be Salou, a resort about 60 miles south of Barcelona. This was chosen because a good number of lads we knew were staying there for the week and I had visited there the year before on a family holiday and thought it would be ideal for a relaxing couple of days in the sun before the bedlam of Barcelona set in.

We took a train from the airport to Salou via Barcelona Sants Station. A beautiful journey down the coast arriving in Salou via a taxi ride from hell from nearby Tarragona. We had not booked anything beforehand and therefore were in need of a hotel or apartment, although we did have the not so mouth watering prospect of two nights on a hard apartment floor if we were desperate. I've got to say however that I'm getting too old for that sort of thing.

Our first port of call was, as you might have guessed, a bar, but it did have rooms above it for rent - unfortunately some other Reds just beat us to the last room. As we arrived at siesta time the tourist office was closed, so it was a case of wandering around until we found something. Thankfully it was a case of third time lucky as we checked into the Hotel Monaco at the far end of the promenade. A nice two star abode costing just £13 per night each. A walk on Salou beach and we all thought 'what a life, what a view, what a week we have in store'. Surprisingly whilst walking along the beach we met a few familiar faces who were giving their beer bellies a good airing. At that time I hadn't exposed my ample features to the sun and most of the beach sighed with relief!

As we all know, too much sun is not good for you, so we heeded this sound advice and headed to a nearby watering hole. Salou is cheap for both food and drink with beer £1 a pint and after a much needed rest - constituting only an hour unfortunately - it was time to get ready again.

The choice of bars was pretty impressive so it was a difficult choice of which area to head for. We headed for a pub called Flower of Scotland where we meet up with Harry from Preston who was on a two week break with his family taking the match in as well. Sadly this would be the last time I would see Harry as he tragically passed away a week later whilst still in Spain. Harry was a hardcore Red and will be missed by many and I'm only glad that he managed to fit the greatest night ever watching United into his shortened lifetime. He was 41 when he died.

From the Flower of Scotland we had a quick food break in a nearby Indian - when in Spain do as you do on a Friday night after all. We had a slight lingo problem however and ended up with one chicken madras and a naan bread between the three of us!

A bar called Kiss Kiss was well mobbed with Reds and a full sing-song was about to start. On leaving we were approached by a Spanish news crew who asked if we would like to do an interview. We agreed thinking they would ask about the match. We should have known better as the first question was: "How many hooligans will follow Manchester in Spain?". We tried to put them right but that didn't make the headlines they wanted so each ques-

tion they asked veered towards trouble and hooligans - we nearly cracked and said we were going to wreck the place! We just walked off to the next bar.

We met up with the rest of the lads on the week long 'here we go' holiday. They were sitting outside the lively Parrot Inn but unfortunately the police thought so to and were keeping a very close eye on proceedings and we decided to move on. We headed up to Charlie Chaplins, a bar with a female singer who looked, sung and danced like the roadrunner but as her name was Kelly Brook thought it was worth a look! It was a disco bar so decided to stay for a while and as there were a few females in the single lads were happy although they should draw the line at girls young enough to be Graham Rix's girlfriend! And Scousers at that...you know who you are. At this stage Dermott is on heat and thinks the world is going to end in the next five hours so he makes an attempt to pack in a lifetime's smoothtalking into that time - top lad.

We eventually force our way out and headed back to the disco at the Flower of Scotland. You wouldn't believe it was the same bar from earlier, and it was even more lively after two cocktails. Another bar mobbed with Reds and by 3.30am it was time to leave as we were all fucked as we had been up for something like 26 hours at this stage.

Tuesday was the start of another day in paradise. The sun is shining, the head is a bit muzzy but two of us manage to make the breakfast deadline of 10am - it was 9.59.30. Lee the lazy bastard would have been lucky to make tea never mind breakfast. Persuading him to move his arse so we could get to the beach was a problem, he can sleep and snore for Britain and eventually we persuaded him that he could sleep on the beach and this seemed to make all the difference.

We head to find the other lads, with directions given by Stevie Wonder and get there after an hour to find that they'd already left. We stop off for a snack and I order a small ham salad and the chef comes back with a bowl the size of a tractor tyre. Half an hour later enough was enough with this monstrosity and the beach called loudly.

Settling down for a bit of sunworship - not a normal hobby of mind but in these conditions it had to be done - was made slightly more interesting when two babes from Eindhoven who liked to bare their chests came and sat by us. I didn't bother to chat them up, just asked them if there was any chance of tickets if we ever play PSV - it was a good intro!

We bump into a few Reds who we knew, you could tell them a mile off as they all had United shorts on and red lobster bodies. Our chums finally turn up with one missing as the red wine from the previous night was still causing him a few problems. Lee had taken up the offer of a sleep on the beach but unfortunately was using Factor 4 instead of 28 and as a result he turned a very bright red and earned the nickname Lee the Lobster for the rest of the trip. His nose was glowing brighter than the great Peter Schmeichel himself.

Our bodies were about to be barbecued so we decided to leave this lovely arena, and head for a meal before getting ready. A three course meal with drinks, enough to feed a pack of hungry wolves for under a tenner. The sight of the mixed grill would have been enough to kill a vegetarian stone dead. Even I struggled to finish it and thankfully needed the exercise of the mile walk back to the hotel.

It was soon evident that there were a lot more Reds here tonight, someone estimated that in excess of 5,000 were staying in Salou alone. The din of distant singing could be heard all night, but with no real hint of trouble. Some bars were offering tickets for £400 and as you can imagine there weren't many takers.

We decided to try a few different bars first of all for a change. Lee having turned into a lobster was also suffering from mild sunstroke and this meant drink was a no-no, only coke poor lad. We met up with a few more Reds including Mick from Blackpool who was on his best behaviour as his wife Judith was keeping him firmly in hand. He told us that he'd been up to Barca that day to see if he could purchase any tickets for his friends. When he arrived, the tickets were only on sale to Spaniards who were buying them for £12 and then going outside and trying to flog them for £400 to waiting United fans. This was all done under the not so watchful eye of the local police - what a bloody disgrace. Needless to say that the end result was that Mick returned with zero tickets.

Back to the karaoke bar. As we were leaving we got wind that the most unlikely singer in the Western hemisphere, Carl, was going to do a turn so we couldn't leave. His first number was 'Oh Carol' and with our vociferous vocal backing went down a storm. He then went for 'We Are The Champions' which, as you can imagine, was extremely popular in the ranks. As it was going to be a long and tiring matchday a reasonably early night was called for. We had decided to get an 8am train into Barca in order to beat the charge and it was to bed by 4am.

Worryingly yet again I didn't have a hangover and we're all up straight away at 7am, even Lee. Mind you he's had enough sleep for the three of us. The railway station is around the corner and thinking we would be one of the first out was a sad misconception. By 8am the platform was filling up and by departure time it was clear the train would be packed. Strange who you should meet, but early morning, thousands of miles from home, there were three lads from my home town who I haven't seen for years, either in my town or at United. And I bump into them at Salou Station. It's a small world.

Once again it's a stunning ride and it was to be the start of a truly memorable 24 hours. At 10am we're in and already the concourse was filling up with both sets of fans. We joined the ever increasing taxi queue and finally get one to our abode for the night, the Hotel Campanile on the outskirts of the city. This was also the meeting point for the rest of our crew, some who'd travelled via the South of France and some the whole way by coach - poor sods!

We chilled out for an hour or two, had a couple of beers and then headed back to the Olympic Harbour area, an idyllic setting to pass the time away before the most important match in my lifetime. The port area is a square mile of restaurants, bars and cafes which was more than adequate for the thousands of Reds in the vicinity. There was something conspicuous by its absence - 'the lesser spotted German fan'. In the whole afternoon I think I only saw 6 Bayern fans, were the hell where they all? After all, they'd supposedly sold upwards of 30,000 tickets. It was clear again, as the song goes, that Barcelona was being "taken over" by the Red Army.

What a life! A large jug of sangria, food on request, the sun cracking the pavement, good company and the prospect of the European Cup Final to come. What more can you ask of in life? During the afternoon it appeared that the whole of the United reserve teams, under-19s and 17s and anyone else who could find a Utd blazer was walking up and down the port side. Unfortunately for them they were not allowed any alcohol. This was a stark contrast to former United legend Bryan Robson and his sidekick Viv Anderson. They were certainly making the most of the local Spanish hospitality.

It had been decided that as it was the European Cup Final we would head to the ground nice and early for a change. Four of us were lucky enough to find a taxi by the harbour so off we went. Unfortunately the traffic was extremely heavy and it seemed to take hours to get anywhere near the Nou Camp, mind you I did have a quiet snooze in the front of the cab by all accounts. In the end we disembarked about a mile from the ground and made the rest of the way on foot via a couple of bars. Both of which had run out of beer.

We then headed towards the stadium as there was less than an hour until kick off. As we approached the vast arena there were already thousands and thousands queuing to get near the ground. The police cordon was a good idea in theory but in practice it just didn't work as the numbers of people involved were just too great and it led to severe congestion. Yet again this could have been a disaster in the making but for the overall common sense of the majority of United fans. Once through this cordon it was then a case of looking for your entrance gate. In my case this was No.4, yet another queue! Once I had passed all the hurdles it was a sigh of relief as it was always in the back of my mind that something could go wrong. For some lads, it did go wrong, as a couple I know were pickpocketed and another one refused entry for being too pissed. As these lads were hardcore Reds it must have been a traumatic experience, one which I can't imagine and glad I didn't have to endure.

Once in the ground there wasn't a lot to do but wait for the match to begin. It was clear even though there were 30 minutes to go that the ground was less than half full and most Reds were still struggling to get in (lucky what happened at the end of the game wasn't at the start of it!). However the German fans were as efficient as ever and had their towels on their seats hours before we had even thought of moving to the ground. By 8.30pm the atmosphere was really building although I did notice a hint of nervousness in the crowd and I hoped this wouldn't be conveyed to the team.

The teams came out to a massive fanfare, the Red Army welcoming their heroes from three sides of the ground. Bayern seemed to be supported by just one end with around 25,000 accommodated in it. The rest was Utd - what a following and still thousands more outside.

The game kicked off in a crescendo of noise as the stadium erupted. Here I was in the Nou Camp, one of the finest sporting arenas in the world, watching a game I had waited for all my life. Unfortunately I was still brought down to earth with their goal...after only 9 minutes. It looked all too similar to a goal we had conceded last time we played in Barcelona in November. Let's hope we score three!

In the first half we managed very little in the way of goalscoring opportunities and the Germans were almost controlling the game. We weren't strong enough in midfield therefore we weren't getting hold of the ball enough. I thought the decision to play Blomqvist was misconceived instead playing Johnsen in midfield and pushing Becks wide. Mind you, it's easy to say sitting high up in the stands.

Despite being 1-0 down at half-time the mood was pretty upbeat as everyone was thinking that we couldn't really play that badly in the second half. It started pretty much in the same vein though, Utd having a little bit more of the ball but not managing to create the chances. Yet as the half progressed we had more and more of the ball but still no goal bound efforts. It wasn't until Fergie changed it around and brought on Ole and Teddy that our prospects improved. Suddenly the odd chance came our way, but to no avail. Time was desperately running out and it looked as though the dream was over, so near and yet so far away!

I looked across with five minutes remaining at the giant electronic scoreboard with BAYERN MUNICH! MANCHESTER UNITED 0 shining ever brighter in the night sky. At that precise moment I felt as low as I had ever felt watching United. All those matches, all the effort, commitment and money over the years. Could I really pick myself up and do it all again? Could the team? At that moment the prospect of either doing it were pretty remote.

Into injury time and it's getting desperate. We manage to get a corner. Up comes Peter. Can it be Volgograd, please God make it Volgograd! The corner sears into the box towards Peter (does he get a touch...), confusion reigns, the ball comes out to Ryan on the edge of the box. He half hits a volley goalwards and King Teddy manages to steer it in. First instinct is to look at the linesman (imagine if he'd put the flag up!) to check the goal is allowed - YES! Que absolute delirium. We're back, we're back in it, we can do it, how did we pull that off?

We try and compose ourselves if that was humanly possible under the circumstances. It was clear that the Germans had gone, they were stunned. We all knew that in extra time the game would be ours for the taking. Little did we know what was in store. We managed to force another corner, this time Peter stayed put! The ball floated over once again, Teddy rose and flicked it on, then Ole flicked it into the top corner, writing this down is sending a shiver down my whole body! What followed was the celebration to beat all celebrations! How many thought that Ole's goal against the Scousers could be beaten? How many thought Ryan's goal against the Arse could be beaten? How many thought Coley's against Juve could be beaten - nobody I guess! But this was truly unbelievable. If I live to be 100 years of age I don't think I will ever witness anything quite like it. In the space of just over two minutes we had gone from utter despair to uncontrollable celebration. There were bodies flying everywhere, grown men hugging and crying, these were very emotional moments. We had won the European Cup, our Holy Grail, 31 years after Sir Matt had led another great United team to victory.

The German team lay on the floor stunned, they couldn't understand what had happened to them. Their fans sat silent in the distance trying to come to terms with what had just taken place. Within another 60 seconds it was over, we had done it! The final whistle blew to ignite more chaotic scenes on and off the pitch. The sheer enormity of the occasion is impossible to describe.

It seemed to take an age for the presentations to start but nobody cared, it could have taken all year. When finally they did get started, the Germans somehow managed to pick themselves up and went first to pick up their runners up medals. Wasn't it nice to see the look of utter dejection on the face of Lothar Matthaus - I've never liked him! Looking over at the German end of the stadium, all credit, their fans had stayed behind to applaud both teams. That must have been hard to do, as I am bloody sure that if the boot was on the other foot I'd have been on the first flight home by then!

Next up were the EUROPEAN CHAMPIONS - Manchester United. This was a tantalizing presentation as the last player up hailed the trophy. The roar that greeted Peter lifting that trophy could probably have been heard back in Manchester. The lap - or laps - of honour went on for ages with the whole team really going over the top on the celebrations. It was great to see Fergie, Keane and Scholes join in, as they all deserved to be milking the moment as much as anyone. It was such a great pleasure to see that the whole team wanted to win it as much as the fans. I only hope the desire continues on both parts well into the next century.

After all sorts of barmy celebrations on and off the pitch I eventually left the ground at somewhere near midnight, still not believing what had happened. Our plan was to meet at a nearby bar and then to our usual haunt of the Velvet Club. The bar had run out of beer and closed and the metro had been closed by the police so it was a long walk back into the city. We managed to stop at a couple of bars on the way and whet the appetite for the session to follow. The atmosphere was that of total amazement.

Eventually we found a taxi and we head to the club, amazingly it was only 200 years from where we got in the taxi. The driver looked amazed that we got in and told him where we wanted, we not realising, mind you he charged us £2 for the privilege! On arrival the club was fairly quiet apart from a few Germans who actually came over and shook everyone's hand and congratulated us on our deserved victory, honestly they did! I wonder if we would have been so sporting if we had lost in the same manner?

Within an hour the club was rocking with all the usual pissheads we knew in attendance. The beer and champagne was flowing rather well and I imagine the takings here would break all records that night. The DJ was superb, playing everything we requested including SIT DOWN and the most fitting of the night, We Are The Champions. What a night, what a celebration. The club eventually kicked us out at 6.30am, too early for most of us so we went in search of another drink, although Rob Jones slopped off home early yet again on a Euro away. Rob - you lightweight!

We were supposed to vacate our room by midday but there was little chance of that even though the hotel staff insisted on knocking on the door every 20 minutes just to remind us. We eventually surfaced at 2pm and packed our gear and off we went to our next destination - Stiges. The weather was poor and we arrived at around 4pm and headed to a very posh hotel where some mates were staying. This was over our budget (£100 a night!) so we head down the road and find a comfortable hotel for a lot less!

We wondered why the hotel was full of enormous men until we realised that the Barcelona Dragons American Football team were staying here. Apparently earlier in the week a Utd fan had picked a fight with one of these giants.

A group of about 50 of us had arranged to have a meal whilst watching the homecoming on SKY live. This turned into a nightmare as they could only cope with 4 at a time and eventually moved to the pool area and relaxed whilst some splashed about fully clothed in the pool. Although a gay resort usually the place was buzzing with Reds but we were struggling to find a late drink after 4am. However we did have the master drinker Phil Holt on board and he insisted on another drink. As he explained earlier he found a driver of a battered old car when we are lost in the middle of nowhere and the bloke drove us there although the bet wasn't paid as there was a time dispute!

Our last day in paradise started just before midday and we packed our bags and chilled on the beach and it was soon time to depart. The airport was packed with departing Reds all with great memories of a truly memorable occasion. The flight home gave me time to recollect on a monumental week. Soon I would be back to reality and literally back down to earth.

Let's hope the future can bring even more occasions like this and even greater success for the team. It will take some beating but I am sure with Sir Alex Ferguson at the helm we can move onto even greater success. I certainly hope so!

NEVER TO BE FORGOTTEN
Mark Southee

Mark, 37, started going to OT regularly in the dark days of Division 2. Apart from a break when some idiot decided he was good enough to play non league football (didn't last long!) he has been going ever since. Was heavily involved in the IMUSA campaign against BSkyB, and was responsible for unfurling the Stop Murdoch Banner at the San Siro after the Inter game. Also responsible for making sure that his mate Duncan gets to the ground before half time.

Our party for Barca comprised of Duncan, myself (it seems we are stuck with the 'joined at the hip', moniker) and three friends of mine - Jim, Wendy and Donna who were all ticketless, hotelless and couldn't care less, they just had to be there.

We were travelling from Luton on Monday evening, and to avoid any Turin type cock-ups, left plenty of travelling time, which was just as well as we drove in a storm that would have had Noah nervously hunting for the Black and Decker!

With no further problems we reached Nice at 11:30pm and picked up our battle bus to take us on to Spain. Apart from Donna's inability to locate the bucket with the toll money we had an easy drive through the night, and were parked up on La Ramblas at 7:30am. This was the only time we were to see the place empty.

Our first priority was to find a hotel for the waifs and strays, so we found the tourist info place at the top of La Ramblas and got them in a hotel not too far away. With them taking the bus round to their hotel, Dunc and I went off to find the IMUSA Hilton. We located it with it's stunning views of the St Joseph market and building site with the associated noises and smells that fully justified the vast amount we were being charged. Having cleared the shower room of some wildlife, it wasn't too bad, and having showered and grabbed a bit of kip we greeted the rest of the inmates as they arrived.

The rest of the day was spent soaking up the atmosphere that was already building up and trying to suss out the spare ticket situation for the rest. We got talking to someone that evening and with prices not dropping below £200 and with a mass of forgeries flying around the others were not too optimistic. Dunc, Mick Meade and myself decide to finish the evening off with a visit to the Michael Collins bar where we bump into Nick Clay. We make it back to our beds at about 3:00 am.

On match day we decide to stay at the hostel and ease our way into things gently. I think the nerves were already starting to kick in, as well as having to contend with the vicious head cold, which despite copious amounts of black medicine consumed before and after Wembley, I'd failed to shift.

A phone call to Mr Leeming (Red Devils e.mail list meister) confirmed that everyone was gathering at the Hard Rock. So we made our way up there, with Dunc joining the cue to get in, whilst I did a raid on McDonalds for some Big Macs which had to be smuggled in to the Hard Rock under my jacket!

We see Barry, and Bill and I go and say hello to Richard and Hazel, my banner carrying friends from the San Siro. Linda and the Son and heir then appear, followed by a bloke carrying a huge bag plus rucksack, who turns out to be Mr Hennesey (Boston Red head honcho and another of the Red Devils e.list meisters). Soon Jim, Wendy and Donna (aka the other 3) appear and a great afternoon is spent talking about all our Red experiences. I also kept looking at the scene in the square which was now a mass of people all making a great deal of noise.

All too soon it is time to get closer to the ground. We take Sean back to our place so he can dump his bags for the evening. The other 3 decide to try and find some friends in the Robin Hood. We head for a heaving Metro station and make for Kitty O'Sheas near the ground, alas we get there to find none of our crew left, so we have a quick pint and a Jamesons (the largest single I've ever seen!) and then up to the ground. We say our goodbyes to Sean and try and make our way past all the checks.

Having to show my ticket so many times before I'd got near the ground made me very nervous (as if I needed any more tension!). I could just see someone making a grab for it, so I held on tight and hid my hand up the sleeve of my jacket. As we got close to the final entrance, we see this Spanish copper on a horse completely lose it, charging around, swinging his baton around like he was trying to swat flies. With so many kids about it was amazing we saw no one seriously hurt. It takes ages to get into the ground, and you can imagine my horror to find that the Germans have scored already! We say a quick hello to Pat Jennings, Sid, The Sausage man and girlfriend who are sat near us and try to take in the atmosphere.

We also seem to have been planted in the middle of some people who didn't seem to care less that we were one-nil down in a European Cup final! All my life I've dreamed of cheering on the Shirts in such a game, yet I see one guy a few rows down reading his hotel guide halfway through the first half! An honourable exception goes to the guy I'm stood next to, and the few of us who really cared tried to drum up some support. This extended to me singing 'Stand Up, when 'Sit Down' came on at half time.

In the second half it is clear to me that although we have more than our fare share of possession, Bayern are coping easily. When they hit the woodwork for the second time, my new found friend says to me "If we win this I'm going to shag those goal posts". I laugh, but I doubted whether the honour of the posts was going to be compromised, as I couldn't see us scoring.

We had, I'd convinced myself, used up all the lady luck at our disposal this season, and I was just preparing for the inevitable when that "we shall not be moved" attitude of the Delle Alpi, Villa Park, and the Scousers cup game showed up once again. If Teddy's equaliser sent us mad with delight, Ole's goal seemed to stun me into shock for about 30 seconds, then cue pandemonium. I didn't see the final whistle go as everyone is hugging, kissing and crying. Just incredible!

The celebrations after the game will never be forgotten. I reminded my friend of his date with the woodwork, but he said it would have to wait until he got home. So if you see reports of someone getting arrested at Hough End for performing a "lewd act", that'll be him!

After the players had been literally dragged off the pitch we made our merry way out of the ground. Pat, Sid, Dunc and I grab a beer near their hotel to relieve the vocal chords. Dunc and I then make our way to the IMUSA party at another bar, where Champagne (sort of) cost about three quid a go. With events off the pitch occupying hearts and minds for most of the season it was a long and emotional celebration. We then made the long walk back to town in the most amazing fashion, hoisting a huge banner we had above our heads and marching back to the hostel. It was half the width of the road wide and god knows how long, but we somehow got it and us back in one piece.

I woke up on Thursday morning to find that everything ached. From my vocal chords to my feet I was a bit of a mess. We got to the breakfast bar Andy had recommended in the market to find that everyone else had been long gone.

We make our way to the other 3's hotel to find out they had had quite a night too. By the time they got to the Metro the Spanish had given up trying to force people to pay and to a chorus of 'it's free on the underground' (to Go West) they made their way to the ground. They are wandering around desperately trying to find somewhere with a tele but give up and decide just to get near the action. They find themselves outside the Bayern end when they spot a burger bar with a colour tv (and cold beers to boot) - result! They attract some others and soon there are 50 Reds around this bar. Jimmy gets handed a large, top quality banner with Macclesfield Reds on it and a huge club crest which they put up. He tries to give it back afterwards but he is told he can keep it!

Having walked for ages beforehand they weren't in the mood to walk back, so Donna spots a big black English reg Merc with only the driver on board so she knocks on the window and asks for a lift, and gets it! He drops them off within a mile of their hotel, lucky sods.

We decide to pack the bus up and pay a visit to the Porto Olympico, where we have the worst paella served by the dimmest waitresses known to man. The fact they were wearing next to nothing didn't quite make up for it! We then make it back to the Nou Camp and pick up programmes and other goodies.

We then start the drive back to Nice. Dunc decides to revive the new song competition he started on the way back from the Villa Park replay. Jimmy, who spent some time in the eighties trying seriously to get a band off the ground joins in and for some reason we settle on Bazza big nose's Copacabana as the tune. I am unable to join in due to my vocal chords having packed in completely, not that I get much sympathy. Amazingly this manages to entertain us all the way back to Nice.

The plane is full of Reds in a similar state to ourselves, and I even manage to sleep for the majority of the flight, a rare occurence for yours truly. We arrive back at Luton at about 8:30 am and head back up the M1.

If I've missed any body out please accept my apologies. With so much to remember from this season of seasons, I'll never remember everything!

THIS IS A MAN'S WORLD
Emma Dodd

Emma, 23, was born in Salford into the legacy that is Manchester United, laid down by her J Stand attending father. A 'sales person', she can usually be found on Sir Matt Busby Way shouting 'Red News' and when pushed the odd obscenity, ever attempting to help the cause and supplementing her football and alcohol addictions. An avid K Stander, she finds her way to the 'odd pub' before, after and sometimes during away games - drunkenly and somewhat poorly fighting the cause for female Reds

How can I put into words something that I have only ever dreamed about? An experience so immense that the thought of it still makes the tears for the millionth time well up in my eyes, the feelings are still as
intense as they were on that barmy night in Barcelona.

Everyone has their own experiences of the European Cup final 1999, memories that will go with them to their grave, all as unique as they are incomparable. My angle on this is my journey to the European Cup final, not just physically but metaphorically. How I as a female red travelled from my first game as a bewildered five years old to the European Cup final in Barcelona, unquestionably the greatest moment of my life.

Writing this, I feel as if I have won it myself and I am sure that I am not alone. I was lucky enough to be one of the fifty thousand who 'won' the Cup that night. In fact I do not think that I could have been more proud or privileged had I actually scored the winner myself. Being a female who loves Man United has meant treading a different path to that of the majority, with perhaps a steeper hill to climb. I cannot say that it has been an easy road but I also would not change any of it. United fans have always been a diverse bunch of people and female supporters are one growing element to this diversity. I think that you have to be a woman who goes consistently over a number of years to know how you get treated differently. It is not always negative, I am well looked after when it 'goes off' and the banter is usually light hearted. But just sometimes the comments and attitude are cutting.

I have made a great many friends through supporting Man United and have been fortunate in the experiences that have taken me so far and wide. I look forward to many more in the future. But I have endured a number of prejudices just because of my sex and feel that I have gone through a lot in my simple quest to follow the team that I carry in my heart.

You need an ability to laugh at yourself and over come prejudice in any walk of life, but for me it has become imperative. However, I have accepted that having to prove myself is part and parcel of going to watch United and having to do so is a challenge that I have loved undertaking over the years. The thing that I do find infuriating is the fact that I have to do it in the first place.

I have been going to watch United for a few years now. At 23 I have had a season ticket for ten years and have been going regularly for a few more on top of that. Since my first games at the age of five, I knew that United were special. The atmosphere was magical and I was immediately captivated by it all. Of course at five years of age I was frightened to death of the people around me as they celebrated, ironically now I fear it is the other way around.

Even my Dad was sceptical the day I told him that I was going to start going on the Stretford End. Even more so when he learned that this meant getting to the ground at about eleven and waiting for four hours for the pleasure of watching the sheer class of Ralph Milne. To me though it was everything. Nothing gave me greater pleasure than getting to the ground early and queuing up to be the first in, the challenge of getting a barrier to stand behind to ensure survival. Of course I soon discovered the demon drink and five to three is deemed early for arrival at the ground these days.

As for my Dad, the scepticism soon turned into regret at the fact that the 'Dad, can I just borrow £500 for Rotterdam/Barcelona/Dortmund' was all his fault. There it started and was destined to continue. From my first game to the age of fourteen it became consistently more important to me, Man United becoming a bigger part of my life every day. It was at this point that we got to the The European Cup Winners Cup final. I was too young to go out there alone and as no suitable chaperone was found so I was not allowed to go. I went to Wembley that year but it was not the same knowing what I was about to miss out on. It was on that day I promised myself that as far as the Magic of European Football was concerned nothing would stop me from missing a game like that again. Man United was my life and I should have been there. So when it came to the European Cup final, I felt all the more fortunate to have been a part of it. Nothing could give me the void that missing Rotterdam had given me. Win or lose, we were in the European Cup Final and I would be there.

So it was a week by the coast that would be our base for the biggest game of our lives. The experiences of that trip to Barcelona seemed to sum up everything about being a United fan. The biggest low, the biggest high, the spirit, the atmosphere, everything. On a personal level it also epitomised the highs, lows and hurdles that it is necessary to overcome being a girl who loves football.

Whenever United play in Europe you can rest assured that in whichever airport, hotel, bar or stadium I will always get asked the same question, 'How did you get a ticket'. Sometimes it is said with spite, sometimes with respect but sometimes it is downright patronising. Why should I not have a ticket? The answer is an obvious one, simply because I am female. It was no different in Barcelona, worse in fact as I was asked more than ever, how I as a simple female had got a ticket when they, were without. My well practiced answer of I have a ticket because I go to every game, every year is well worth the response. I did once try to add a little variety to this retort by adding 'you misogynistic bastard' but the answer of 'what's a soginist then?' made me realise that it really was not worth it.

An obscenely early start on Tuesday to the 'classy' resort of Lloret de Mar was where our trip started. Being three girls, my sister Louise, Charlotte and I knew that we were leaving ourselves open to no end of abuse but being fully seasoned football fans ourselves we felt that we would be fully able to handle it, after all we had well and truly earned our right to be there and had long since got used to the abuse. It was at Bryan Robson's Testimonial that 1,000 or so Celtic fans sang 'get your tits out for the lads'. As a fourteen year old I was delighted, but it has since become really quite tedious.

Why as a female have I always been made to feel second best at football? I truly love Man United, I love football, I drink too much, swear too much, shout too much, if the topic of conversation takes on a vulgar undertone I have usually initiated it and I cause offence. In short, I behave exactly the same as any of the blokes that I travel home and away with. So what is it? I do everything else that a man does,but perhaps it will probably save any remnants of a reputation that I have if I do not actually go there. However, looking at all of those waiting to get on the plane at the airport I thought we are all the same, we all have the same dream and we all love United.

Once on the plane, we dared for the first time to talk about the game itself. As we took off, the reality started to set in. We were actually on our way to the European Cup final. The realisation seemed to come over in waves. It was difficult enough to come to terms with being there, actually winning it was a thought too incredible to begin to contemplate. So we spent the rest of our journey regaling each other with stories of 'Euro Aways' past and what potentially lay in store for us in the week ahead.

The biggest fear for us was the prospect of a liver battering unparalleled by any other occasion in our lives. I think that I was about fifteen when I first realised that I had a talent for drinking and with the words of 'if you have a talent, you should develop it' still ringing in my ears from School, I felt that I owed it to myself to nurture my ability and make it great. Eight years on I feel as though I am getting there and it does have to be said that I like a drink. Seeing as the majority of my football friends are also partial to a tipple or twenty, most post game sessions tend to end as most normal people are venturing out for the morning papers. Euro aways' are legendary in the drinking stakes and carry on regardless I will always be out on the piss until the very end. So with this in mind, the prospect of what lay ahead, win or lose, left me worrying as to whether my E111 would cover me for self induced liver failure.

We thought that Lloret was the best choice for our destination. At a Euro away, sometime you just to concede that it is a man's world. Being a minority on such trips, I have developed a fantastic ability to avert my eyes as I have probably been into more strip clubs than your average pervert in the pursuit of a late drink in more than a few European Cities. At times like this, you just have to conform or have an early night, conforming and getting a late drink is more my style. But we thought that we would be safe in Lloret and with one of our party already lost to a liaison with her boyfriend in Barcelona we headed into the night and to the nearest beer.

Stopping at every bar on the way, we found the main square and with it about 2,000 United fans. There were no real faces there, but nevertheless it was packed with Reds going barmy and dancing all over the place. I was kept amused by continual comments from various people as they apologised for 'being rowdy' and that they hoped that it was not 'ruining my holiday'. I am not quite sure what I found more insulting, the fact that because I was female I could not be a football fan, or the fact that in my right mind I had chosen Lloret De Mar as a holiday destination. One bloke even came up and said to me 'There is a game on here tomorrow you know' - no shit.

By now we were well and truly hammered and decided it was time for a sing song. As the only person up for instigating the singing and with a lot of coaxing from Charlotte, I stood on my seat and started regaling the bar with my repertoire, pulling out some really old classics. I had a captivated audience and if proving myself as as loyal a fan as anyone else there was part of the bargain, I made my point. I even got a standing ovation for my rendition of 'Denis Irwin's Barmy Army'. This was all the encouragement I needed to lead the singing in the next two bars.

Walking back to the hotel later, the police presence had mounted and bewildered fans were being rounded up, we were so drunk by this point that we were capable only of crawling to the Wimpy and collapsed

in front of a trough of food, barely looking up from our food to register that we were only yards away from a mental baton charge by the riot police, our 'dirty sex with Peter Schmeichel with or with or without the leather gloves' debate far more interesting - I know that I complain about the abuse I get for being a woman fan, but I am only human after all.

Entering the fray to get back to our hotel and the police forced us on a massive detour. It was rather fortunate for me that the local constabulary did not understand the words 'do you not have anything better to do, twat'. On occasions it is beneficial to be a female, this was actually one of them as I was well and truly given the benefit of the doubt. I am sure that had I been male, I would have most definitely been carted away. The evening ended in perfect fashion with me announcing that we were 'well lost', whilst standing directly outside our hotel and being told 'go to bed, English girls' by a most pissed off night porter as we spent hours trying to tell him that 'we only love Man United'.

A weird atmosphere surrounded us when we woke the next morning. Apart from the hangover, the tension was already there - the day ahead was not going to be an easy one. Charlotte managed to astound me with the volume she managed for breakfast as I struggled with the bile and remnants of last nights drink binge.

A remarkably painless trip to Barcelona followed and we were instantly grateful for the foresight to book a hotel in Barcelona three months ago. It was comforting to be surrounded by United fans again and in such a huge volume but the nervous feelings made the day somehow unreal and difficult to enjoy. I just wanted to go to the ground but was glad that I spent some time soaking up the atmosphere on La Ramblas. There was just a sea of red and the police visibly relaxed as the day went on, a tribute to the impeccable behaviour of our fans. It was a weird feeling though, there was a party atmosphere that I just did not fully feel a part of, even a meet with all the familiar faces was strange. The atmosphere was tense almost to the point of subdued. If earlier I had forced myself to be philosophical about the game, now I knew that to all of us there, it was everything.

The tube ride to the ground was horrific, no extra trains seemed to have been laid on and my nerves turned to panic as we were crushed into the already full train. The bloke stood behind me apologised for the fact that he was so close and I am convinced that I did not have that much physical contact when I lost my virginity.

If I thought that the train was bad, getting into the ground was to prove much, much worse. The police were forcing us into a bottleneck leading up to the north goal end of the ground. All we wanted was to get into the ground yet every barrier was in place to ensure that this was not possible. We finally got to our seats with about thirty minutes to go before kick off. The atmosphere was incredible and the sea of red was again quite amazing. We were lucky to know quite a few of the people around us, people we were going to share the most amazing experience of our lives with. Time and time again I have sat next to people who have ignored me but immediately struck up a conversation with the person stranger sitting on their other side.

The first half to me just passed in a daze, the atmosphere of the occasion was simply draining and the shock of going one down so early on had left everyone stunned. The belief was always there but tempers were visibly fraying with the frustration as the game had seemingly been killed off. We all felt the same with one minute to go. I will openly admit that I thought we would never score that night. I had that feeling that I had when we failed to win the league at West Ham in 1995. The whole crowd were singing 'we'll never die', one song that never fails to have a massive effect on me and it was being sung with more passion and pride than I have ever known.

United fans are tremendously proud and in defeat and compared to other fans (in particular Scousers at Old Trafford last year, or Geordies every year) it is rare to see someone cry. As the last seconds of the game ticked agonisingly away, there were still no tears, no bitterness just sheer and unadulterated pride. The bottom had just fallen out of my dreams and I was dejected but nothing would ever be as strong as the immense feeling of honour that I felt towards my team and even in the face of such tormenting defeat I felt lucky to support United.

So what happened next was just breath taking. The desperation was apparent as Schmeichel came charging up field and the world seemed to come to a standstill as the ball seemed to fumble in off Teddy's shin. The reaction was overwhelming and the relief was like the weight of the world had just been lifted off our shoulders, we were given a lifeline and it was as if the belief had never died. I can't remember who or how many I hugged, but I remember that everyone was just telling everyone else 'we're back in it', as if to stop reassuring one another would stop it from being true.

The next two minutes just passed in a haze, it was as if there was a delay from what I was feeling in my heart to what I was registering in my brain. I was still trying to make sense of the first goal when I saw the ball once again hit the back of the net. I did not know where it came from and frankly I did not care. I turned to my sister for reassurance that it had really happened and she just looked at me and said 'we've done it'. It is a moment I will never forget until the day I die. It was only then that I began to comprehend that we had done it, we had actually won the European Cup. I could not move, speak nor even breathe. The wave of emotion that followed was so intense that I thought I was going to die there and then.

I can't remember ever crying like that as I clung uselessly to everyone and anyone. Everyone was crying though. Not just tears of joy, but pure unadulterated heavy sobs. It may seem odd to some people to see old and young, male and female, people from all walks of life in fact, just crying and embracing, but to all of us there it just seemed like the most natural thing in the world. We may defy our disappointment and be proud in defeat but in the most triumphant of victories the floodgates opened. Suddenly it no longer mattered whether I was male, female or somewhere between the two. We were witnessing the greatest moment of our lives and for a time there we were all just people who shared a love of Man United.

Of course after the game normality reigned once more and a new angle of 'get your tits out for the European Champions' was the latest ploy to entice us. Some things will never change.

My life feels complete, I know that throughout the rest of my days I will never experience anything that will come close to what I felt in that stadium, that night. A line from Trainspotting comes closer than I ever could to capturing the moment:

"Take the best orgasm you have ever had, multiply it by a thousand and you are still nowhere near it".

It is the unique experience of being forced to feel so many different emotions in such a short space of time. A sense of disappointment so nauseating that you cannot think straight to the most intense exhilaration in the same breath. Only Man United can do this to me. On that night in Barcelona however, this went far beyond anything that I have ever felt or will feel again. I heard one person put it on a par with the birth of their son. That is something that I have not yet experienced but surely it cannot be as painful.

So that is how it felt to me that night. Everything. To feel that I have achieved this by the age of 23 should be depressing but I just do not care. I travelled far and wide to get there that night. Not just in terms of distance but in gaining the respect from people that I still have to earn every time I make a new acquaintance at football.

I have seen many female fans fall by the wayside. The abuse, the patronising and the inability to gain respect proving that little bit too much. I persevered and I was

there. Nobody can take that away from me. For about a week after I got home I was just telling everyone 'we won it, we won the European Cup'. The postman, the bus conductor, the bloke in the off license and various random strangers did not share my euphoria. In fact I think that they were probably quite scared. Cart me away, put me in a padded cell for the rest of me days, I'll probably end up there one day anyway.

Failing this, I will still be there next season, next decade, in fifty years time. I think that I have proved that I am here to stay and people have finally got used to it. I love Man United and that will never change. I am just extremely fortunate to have been born into it and what do I really have to complain about? After all some people go their whole lives without seeing their team win everything and we have seen it all.

The greatest flag that I have ever seen was hanging from a balcony on La Ramblas - it sums it all up...

"Sent to me from heaven, MUFC you are my world".

ODE TO JOY
Ricky

Ricky, 33, a Royal Box steward at Wembley Stadium, has been a United fan for all his life. The highlight of this was seeing United lift the European Cup. All that is now left for him is to die happy in a wank booth in Amsterdam.

Oh the joy of it all. For so many years now I have been waiting - no praying - for this moment to arrive. Travelling up and down the country, week after week, across Europe, year after year, spending all the money I earn. Some good times, some bad, but always a great laugh. Seeing my marriage disintegrate in the process, United helping me through it all - boy oh boy has it been worth it.

It really can't get any grander than this. I am on such a constant high, a high I never want to come down from. You can take any drug you want, but you won't ever experience such a feeling like this. The season may start afresh but this party is going to go on and on.

To win the Championship and FA Cup Double again (especially shutting up Wenger) was special, but to take the European Cup and clinch the treble and in such dramatic circumstances is only something dreams are made of - and pretty stupid ones at that. And to be the first English club to have achieved this feat - it could only be our United.

As a child a good league position or maybe an FA Cup win was as good as it got. As the years passed I came to expect mediocrity. Gordon Hill and Stevie Coppell were my childhood heroes. Racing down the wings, swinging in wonderful crosses. Sammy Mac controlling the midfield. Great players on their day, but only on their day. Unlike this truly great team of 1999 who consistently turn in great performances, week in, week out. I really never thought I would see a United team so thoroughly complete.

I first started travelling to watch United in the late seventies, by car and coach, home and away with my hat and scarf. As the years passed this behaviour was replaced with trains, drink, sex, no colours - getting to know everyone, the real hard core Reds, was the next natural progression.

The more you go, the more you travel, the more clued up people you meet and the more wiser you become - travelling to a game and straight back afterwards were no longer enough. Socialising before, after and on non-matchdays became the norm. Over the years many friend-ships have grown and there is a deep bond between the loyal and ever present from all over the country who are always there, home, away or in Mandalay. They know who they are.

My first Euro away was a friendly match in Amsterdam in 1986. For a young lad on his first Euro away to find him-self in a place like Amsterdam was the ultimate pleasure. A wonderfully colourful city, full of the most perverse establishments you couldn't possibly find in any other city. You could shag or wank until your heart was content. A truly pleasurable city. Oh, and I nearly forgot, with a rather dull and meaningless game of football in between.

Banned from Europe for five years because of some rather smelly people, pre-season Euro friendly matches became our only contact with the outside world. With only these meaningless matches, football became just one of the reasons for travelling abroad. For me, pornography became a very big factor, certainly in my earlier days. As you may remember with my Barcelona tales in the book IF THE REDS, bless me father for I have sinned, repeatedly, for I am a pervert.

A trip to Amsterdam was always Number.1 on the list, whether we were playing in Holland or not - or just pass-ing through on the way to Madrid - eh!

But wherever United played we would always seem to end up in the red light districts of these wonderful European cities. Not only the sleaze calls the Reds, but you are always guaranteed a late drink. My idea of heav-en. After all, the locals are certainly not interested in pulling beer swilling, United pot bellies, and I hear the local 'women' of Barca were rubbing their hands at the thought of 60,000 or so Red willies in town. Disgusting...

But no thoughts of porn on this special trip to Barca, this the most serious day ever to be experienced by myself and thousands of others alike. The week had start-ed better than I could ever describe - a little exclusive fact that the first United hands to clasp the winners medals of the FA Cup Final after the win against Newcastle was yours truly as he got them ready for the team as I worked in the Royal Box and said good luck to Fergie and came within touching distance of the Cup courtesy of an awe-some United side on the crest of a wave and a lacklustre set of Geordies. Touching the United winners' medals - could it get any better than this?

In Barca it was great to see faces I've not seen for years. People who have done their bit, travelled, but now have family commitments. The true Red may not go to every game, but they will be there, when it matters, year after year.

United is in you. It starts as early as you can remem-ber and stays there. I have often wondered what it must have felt like to have experienced that great night of 1968. If it was anything like as good as in Barca, those lucky people to have seen both must be in some cloud of cele-bration at the moment.

In looking back at the win on May 26th it is hard not to put it into context with all that you have seen with United - all those travels, all those wonderful times.

From my experiences Amsterdam is my favourite - for porn! Without doubt the porn capital (wank booths my personal favourite) and there really is something for everyone with the best city for bars Barcelona itself - far too many to mention but the David Lynch inspired Velvet standing out. Nice is stunning and for its wonderful Cuban bars and most German bars are all up there, although if I'm honest any establishment serving alcohol, no matter where it is, will do.

The strangest bar on these bizarre and incomparable travels is in Vienna. We think it was actually someone's front room. Instead of having the usual pain of searching for an open bar in the centre whilst the police close them down we headed to an obscure district on the metro and ended up in what we thought was the entrance to a bar. We entered the front door to discover a number of local youths sitting down at tables playing board and comput-er games whilst drinking under the watchful eye of what looked like someone's parents. They didn't seem to mind us intruding though and at only £1 for a large bottle of beer we weren't complaining, even if walking to the toilet really did raise doubts that the back of this bar was in fact a house!

The strangest people I have ever come across (in a bar of course) was in Dortmund. The establishment was appropriately called the Hotel Bender. It was full of very odd looking transvestites alongside people who had obvi-ously been in the same position at the bar for 80 odd years. The barmaid was 70 going on 145 and every so often would put on an old German SS helmet whilst lifting her top and serving beers between her breasts - a very strange, and entertaining bar.

The most beautiful women would be found in liberal Copenhagen and - on a tangent - the best stadium has to be the Nou Camp. It has great views from all levels of the ground - and when, as I've seen twice with United, 100 odd thousand people are in it, there is an atmosphere not matched anywhere in Europe - with no fencing or netting behind the goals. It beats the San Siro hands down. The worst ground was Lodz in Poland. This was like an old 3rd Division ground - crumbling terraces, very small ends but surprisingly good food and an easy entrance system!

My easiest jib (and I'm getting too old for this as my efforts to get into BCM club in Magaluf after the Final showed - I didn't even get further than 5 yards!) into a ground would be the Olympia Stadion in Munich. I walked around the perimeter fence, picked my spot and climbed over, cutting my hand in the process. No problem. I was in. I didn't realise until I was inside however that I actually had a ticket for the match in my back pocket. I could be excused though as I came straight from the mental Oktoberfest. Most European aways are pretty much the same for getting in.

Best city for transport has to be any city with trams. The most direct and quickest way of travelling by far and the great local authorities always make them free!

And so on. These memories from so many places flood in as I think of May 26th. Whatever we are on the outside - be it old, young, or differing outlook on life (and porn!) - we all shared the feeling on the inside when that goal went in. 60,000 cosmopolitan, diverse people - coming together (to paraphrase Primal Scream) as one.

And so it ends as it began. The best city for culture and sights is the one where we had the best night of all.

And, of course, my favourite airport - Bahrain. Nothing to do with football or United - but who cares - we've won the bloody European Cup. And my favourite all the same.

HERE WE GO GATHERING CUPS IN MAY
Julian Smith

A blithering dribbler reports on what he can remember of it all.

As May began, United were still involved in all three major trophies. Spurs had already won the Worthington Cup and their fans were amongst many to remind us we hadn't won anything yet. So several fans around Old Trafford were nervous as the season came to a close, remembering '95, '92 and other near misses. Every game was vital and SKY conspired to make things more exciting (and more difficult for the travelling supporters) by spreading matches over the whole of the final week.

After we coped with the Scousers winning the World Cup against us and putting in our application for the European Cup Final - a three day trip with the club which we hoped we'd get on as filling in all the forms was like an examination - we wait with no news on Barcelona which worries us. On the Monday Spurs draw 2-2 with Chelsea. This puts them out of the Championship race when I thought they were out of it ages ago. On Tuesday I did not watch as Arsenal travel to Leeds. So much crap had been spoken about Leeds not wanting to win it was pitiful. I keep flicking the radio off and on, half-time 0-0, Leeds miss a penalty and after everything is switched off for ten minutes the radio goes back on, 1-0, but four minutes to be added on. So off it goes again and eventually it is confirmed. We are equal on points but we have a game in hand.

So to Blackburn, with only the end bits standing and singing (this is the corporate boxes away trip) and a poor game, ending 0-0, Blackburn are down and we are one point clear with one game left. All we need to do is match Arsenal on Sunday.

To the next morning and we had some kind of response from United suggestion we were on the official trip but I rang to confirm. Yes we are on. It's all action now. The Dog is boisterous for the Sunday, Utd fans in good voice but some nervous faces - Terry dismissing it all with his 'been there, done that' attitude. He just wants the European Cup.

As the tension mounts we can't sit on the grass outside the Scoreboard as the building work has begun. We get my wish as we kick into the Scoreboard first half. This means big Peter will spend the second half joining in the singing with us and clowning around for the last time at Old Trafford. I will miss him orchestrating - whether it be the fans or his defence. The people around reveal their plans for the next few games.

So this is it. Three games. Three trophies at stake.

As this match finishes we are deafened by 'We Are The Champions' by Queen, come on lads think about it. We have eight minutes whilst they make the podium. Schmikes is leading the dancing as "Always Look On The

Bright Side" blasts out. The team disappear for a few moments as the plane declaring MUFC Premiership Champions 1998-99 flies overhead. I later discover this is an official plane sponsored by SKY/CARLING, not, as I'd assumed, some bloke who phones his mate 10 minutes before kick-off and tells him to start the engine.

As is traditional on Fa Cup Final day - Mum coming down on the Thursday - we have the photos taken in the garden with the flag. We meet up with everyone in McGlynn's, have a few pints and decide on meeting at 3.15am for the Barcelona trip!

Mum and I then leave for Kings Cross to get the tube. It's full of gobshite Geordies. As soon as we go down they are at it. Munich songs galore which caught me out, they don't sing that at their own hovel. At the ground a few Geordies are still doing their songs behind us. However they are so clued up they miss Posh Spice and the opportunity to abuse her. In the ground there are even Geordies in there. Not in our section thankfully. Inside however the Geordies fail to get behind their side as we dominate the game. Our best moves were cheered as each player touched the ball. The team stayed on the pitch after the Cup, dancing and larking around. Giggs collected a Welsh flag and others had scarves. Where was Brian McClair's silly wig? After the match I manage to pick up a couple of Double winners' badges.

Monday was the early night as we prepared for an early start. But we were finally on our way. The match tickets were being given out so we queued up for them. They were in named envelopes but you needed no ID to collect them! We had £28 tickets together.

We finally arrive and it's hot and sunny. The hotel is enormous, the flags are on display and unlike the plane there are a few shirts and familiar faces. The Tuesday night is very pleasant and we stay up for a few songs, beers and to sample the duty free vodka.

The coach leaves for the ground late at 1.30. It's a good atmosphere but we are all (Mum, John, John and myself) a little nervous until we have a few beers. We arrive and park at the ground. Toilets and programmes are sought and then its on to the underground for La Ramblas.

La Ramblas is one big mass of noise, colour and sound. In the main square fans are mixed and share beers, waters and lots of tall tales! A great atmosphere before we head off very early for the ground.

On the train the lads are in fine voice but there is the feeling that far too many corporates are amongst us. Songs such as "Do you go week in, week out" come out. Still, everyone is happy. We get the free Manchester Evening News paper and look at the t-shirts before heading to the ground. After various rumours, it's confirmed that United will play in Red but several of us have the white ECWC Final shirts on. Even guys I've never seen in colours before have shirts on.

There are several police blocks and they do a full search which requires you to show your ticket - which I'd kept well hidden - and also remove your hat! Finally we approach the ground itself. Tickets are shown to get through and the end portion is ripped off. We are then into a sort of inner area where they sell more t-shirts and scarves, sweets and, somewhat bizarrely, cigars. We then enter the ground itself which is where your ticket is barcoded. All clear. Inside we see Diane who has a complete ticket neither torn nor barcoded. We can see the crowds building outside.

They sell non-alcoholic beer inside which is an improvement on Old Trafford which sells nothing for European games. The players are on the pitch in suits. The team is announced slowly between records and we discover that Blomqvist will start with Johnsen in defence. This means Giggs will play right and Beckham in the middle.

I have a pretend beer and as people pile in they say it is getting silly outside. This is one hour before kick-off. It seems if your ticket doesn't get through the scanner you are left in the outer area, so people keep trying different barriers. I have a quiet time to myself wishing, as ever, that my Dad was here to see this. He sat through all the rubbish served up by Sexton and right through the late 80s before passing away in 1990 just before the trophies started mounting up.

I've put the flag up as best I can as the others arrive and we take our seats for the match. The dancing girls are out and some massive inflatables are on the pitch. What was all that about? It's obvious we are hearing different music from the Germans as they have just been bouncing up and down for a couple of minutes going bonkers. Why do we not have any upbeat songs. Sit Down by James is fine but let's have some more. Sham 69s If The Kids Are United was good in its time. Let's sort a few new songs out.

The teams come on but there is so much going on that it's hard to make anything out. The game starts without much of a warm-up with United defending our end. The singing is a bit strained as our area is so large there are often two or three songs going on at the same time. We are at the back of the lower tier and it's pretty dark. I was sure when Johnsen pulled Janker down that it was indirect, but so 1-0 down and a familiar story. The fans couldn't seem to get the singing going and we all seemed to be getting at each other a bit. After weeks of saving, planning the trip, worrying about flights, tickets and more, here we were failing to enjoy it and get behind our team. Sure we were playing poorly and failing to create much but this was the biggest game of our lives and we should enjoy it more than this. Thankfully we improve on the field and the Calypso gets going on the terraces.

Half-time and its all been a little disappointing. Various substitutions are suggested, almost all of which are based on taking Blomqvist off and putting Giggs on the left. Beckham is playing really well and running the game but he needs more outlets.

There are no substitutions. We now have a major problem as an enormous banner has been draped over the second tier obscuring our view of half the

pitch. There is much grumbling as we try to get the stewards to radio up, they are useless so we climb over seats to the front to attract the attention of those above. Never easy as they assume we are just trying to get the singing going. Eventually we get through to them and the banner is lifted a little. Not perfect but most of us are now out of our own seats and we move down a little and see all the pitch.

Eventually Sheringham replaces Blomqvist. He back-heels to no-one, they break with the best move of the match but thankfully Peter saves Effenberg's effort. So we are making noise, creating chances and leaving gaping holes in defence. Pretty much the story of the season. Thankfully we are generally also scoring hatfuls.

As a last throw of the dice we take off Cole and put on Solskjaer. They hit the post then the bar. Hell, we only need one goal. Gary crosses low, Teddy can't reach it, Ole leaves it, Yorke misses it...time is running out. Still we sing and hope. Everyone is desperate. Thankfully we can barely see our watches as it's so dark. I can't see the fourth official. We are chasing everything and win a corner. Schmikes is up there so can't be long left. He rises high and I'm sure he gets a touch to it. Giggs shoots and Sheringham puts it in. Bedlam. Is it allowed, it is! We are back in it. Like thousands of others I have no idea what happened next. Where are we? Madness. We prepared for extra-time, the dreaded golden goal. We have a corner. We never score from corners! It's a decent one. Ole's scored. I shouted something along the lines of "We've done it" as I did a demented dance with Mum and anyone else who cared to join in.

The Bayern players were gone. I'm sure no-one knew how long was left. Mum by now could not see as when the whistle blew she asked if that was it. It was! We have won. Mass choruses of "We shall not be moved" and 'Running round Barca with our willies hanging out". I think Mum went down the front. I think I went and stood on a chair. We waited an eternity as the podium was made. The players did not seem to know what to do. Eventually Schmeichel went up in the wrong order and collected the giant trophy. A dream come true.

The team stayed on for ages dancing and lapping the applause. Keane and Scholes were called on to join in the

celebrations. They were clearly embarrassed but the Cup would not have been won without them. Several players just sat and stared at the Cup in disbelief. A great night. A night to remember.

Somehow we leave the ground as the players leave the pitch. It is now 11.15. We finally make it to the coach where a clever driver has stacked up on ice cold beers which he sells from the front of the coach. This results in everyone trying to get on our coach but we squeeze past acquiring a few free beers as we go. The coach leaves at 12.15 with a few extras - everyone is too stunned and drained to sing much.

The bar is open on our return so the beer flows, continuing to drink and sing in the outside bar until 4am. Thursday was an early start to the airport. Our flight was due at 11.15am but delays meant we actually left at around 8pm. We were now very tired but happy. We arrived back home around 3am. I managed to get to bed and as Tracey woke me I could still speak. "We won" is all I managed before falling back to sleep. This doesn't even happen in your dreams!

DESTINY:- DOOM, FATE, FORTUNE, KARMA, KISMET, LUCK, PROVIDENCE.
Mick Burgess

Do you believe in Ghosts? Do you believe in Fairies? Do you believe in God (not just Eric)? Do you believe in Father Christmas? Do you believe in Destiny? If you can categorically say no to all of the above then you are definitely not a Manchester United supporter.

Most people in life come to accept that some things go right for you, some things go wrong for you, but all in all most things balance themselves out at the end of the day. I know that this might be a little hard to swallow if you come from one side of North London or Bavaria but really lads you never stood a chance. I'll explain.

Whenever you embark on a journey to the unknown you will perhaps have a rough idea of your chances of achieving your aims, both with a bit of luck or without. It is only when you have commenced your journey and suffered adversity but still kept going that you begin to think, nothing can stop me, I am going to get there, do not even think of defeat. I am destined to do this.

This is not to say that you can travel the course with wanton abandon, you can't, but if you put yourself in the right position at the right time and with the right frame of mind and preparation who knows what the man upstairs has in store for you.

Looking back on unquestionably the most amazing season in Manchester United's long and illustrious history, when could you point and say we are going to win this League, we are going to win the F A Cup, we are going to be Champions of Europe?

Only the most wishful thinking of people would have said we are destined to win the League after Beckham's last minute equaliser at home to Leicester on the first day of the season but who knows? In December a couple of

confidence shakers within a week, surrendering a two goal lead at Tottenham to only come away with a point and suffering the embarrassment of going 3 down at home to Boro. Maybe it wasn't to be.

Personally, my belief in destiny was awakened on Sunday, 24 January when we came back from an early Michael Owen goal to beat Liverpool 2 - 1 in the FA Cup 4th round, many people then said "United's name is on the cup this year". This is another phrase for the word destiny. It was further given credence to me when a week later Dwight Yorke scored in the last minute at Charlton to earn 3 valuable League points. I haven't mentioned the games in the Champions League but getting through the so called "Group of Death", undefeated and scoring a record 20 goals begins to give a hint of what I mean.

The 8 - 1 Away win at Forest made United look unstoppable but Arsenal almost dented United's hopes 11 days later when they took the lead at Old Trafford before Cole equalised late on. Dwight Yorke had also missed a first half penalty.

Next in the Champions League came Inter Milan at Old Trafford and two early goals from Yorke put United in command. The first real thought of destiny in the Champions League also come in this game when Schmeichel saved brilliantly from Zamaranos diving header and Inter left Old Trafford without an away goal. Again the brilliance of Yorke helped United ease through their 6th round FA Cup replay at Chelsea. Unstoppable.

United went to Milan for the return tie with Inter and despite having Ronaldo in the starting line up, taking the lead, hitting the post, United went through with a late Paul Scholes equaliser.

Back to the Premiership saw United ease past Everton and then slip up at Wimbledon. The games were soon forgotten as Juventus provided the opposition in the Champions League Semi Final 1st leg. They only took 25 minutes to do what Inter had failed to do in 90, when they took the lead through Conte for a valuable away goal. United thought they had equalised with a diving header from Sheringham only for the Referee's assistant to raise a flag for offside. In a frantic finale Ryan Giggs' half volley in the last minute brought United a glimmer of hope to take to Turin.

Two Semi Final clashes with Arsenal would leave nobody in any doubt that Manchester United were destined to win the F A Cup, robbed of a goal in the first tie when Keane scored, the teams were again back at Villa Park the following Wednesday. United took the lead with a superb shot by Beckham before Dennis Bergkamp equalised for Arsenal from distance. Late in the second half Roy Keane was sent off and Arsenal into overdrive. Anelka thought he had scored when he picked up a rebound from Schmeichel and side stepped him before rolling the ball into an empty net. The Referee's assistant saw differently - De Ja Vu! Arsenal should have won the game with a last minute penalty but Schmeichel saved brilliantly from Bergkamp, then came one of the goals of the decade in extra time as Giggs picked up a tired pass from Viera in his own half before going on a 60 yard dribbling run past 5 Arsenal defenders before lashing a left foot shot past the hapless Seaman. Destiny!! No offence Newcastle but don't even bother turning up at Wembley.

Another home win in the League over Sheff Wednesday saw United at the top of the League before some unfinished business with Juventus at The Stadio Delle Alpi in Turin. Juventus stormed into a 2 - o lead after only 11 minutes and even the most die hard Red must have thought it's not going to be this year. Keane and Co thought differently and were level by half time. Another late goal from Cole saw Manchester United cap one of the greatest comeback ever by an English team in Europe. Could anything prevent them from winning the European Champions League?

We could now concentrate on the League and with 6 games to go all was still to play for.

The League, in my opinion, was settled by United getting a point at Leeds whilst Arsenal didn't, irrespective of each teams last game of the season.

One down two to go was quickly followed by the inevitable at Wembley . Two down one to go.

My fourth visit to the Nou-Camp to watch United would turn out to be the finest. As a player the greatest Club honour would be to play in a European Cup Final and as a supporter the greatest thrill would be to be there and watch it. The game was no classic which was not helped by Bayern taking an early lead and sitting back on it quite content to let United come at them. In the last 10 minutes with United desperately attacking, the Germans hit the post and then the bar. My mate, "Chippy" next to me said "We are going to win this". I could only pray. With 90 minutes already on the clock and big Peter coming up for a corner Beckham swung the ball over. Panic followed in the German defence, Giggs mis-hit the ball, goal bound and Teddy steered it into the net. Absolute pandemonium broke out.

Two minutes later with extra time almost upon us Beckham swung another corner over, touched on by Teddy and Ole Gunnar Solskjaer flicked it into the net. Unbelievable, you could not have made an ending up like that if you had tried. I have tried to point to some games this season when the unnatural/unbelievable has happened not just once but on several occasions. If you don't believe in destiny it is unexplainable.

THE UNBELIEVABLE TRUTH
Barney Chilton

Barney, 28, saw his first United game in 1975 and has followed them all over the country ever since - seeing them play at over 65 English league grounds (he somewhat fraudulently though includes the friendlies where he's been too drunk to know what is going on and where he is) and a season ticket holder for the past 18 years. He loves travelling and, like so many others, the whole culture of United. It has been an absolute delight that he can mix the two - having followed United in over 20 countries, on journeys unlike any other. He has edited the first ever United fanzine, Red News, for its whole 13 year existence. With one of his three magic genie wishes now fulfilled on May 26th 1999 he is now waiting for that knock on the door from Winona Ryder and the relegation and disbandment of Liverpool Football Club in the year of the Millennium.

"What was it like?"
"How did it feel?"
"What did you do?"
"I was thinking of you Barney and what you'd be doing when that second went in"

And so, somewhat belatedly, I was back home in the midst of non believers but refusing to come back down to earth. Days passed, then weeks, then months, but forever part of me will refuse to acknowledge that my Groundhog Day - May 26th 1999 - has ended. You could tell the Reds - the real United fans - easily enough in those passing days after that win. There was a look, an aura which was just so unusual and so triumphant that you couldn't miss it. We'd won the ultimate - and were walking in a collective haze and daze that was just brimming with joy.

People got home and began watching the video, partly to witness it again and re-live it all but maybe more so to believe that it really did happen. Then it became something like a drug, watching over, and over again those fate-filled moments, wanting that high once more. The start, middle and most of the end became irrelevant to it all. Give me my feed of those last 5 minutes. And rightly so - perhaps there should be a competition to see how many times people have seen it. Hundreds for many and I bet someone has reached the thousand mark already. There is a shiver down the neck and spine when watching it and no matter what reality may give forth with in 'normal' life from here on in, that video brings back all the emotions of another world and time. It becomes even reminiscent of that old R-Whites lemonade video, sneaking down the stairs whilst everyone is asleep just to watch it 'one more time'.

So what it was like?

In looking back at that great night perhaps it's only natural to take a step back from it all and contemplate the journey we've all had - all so different - to get there. This book is full of various tales and exploits, a road to the Nou Camp that encapsulates so many different lives and eras. So varied the stories.

Some may call what we've just achieved the culmination of an impossible dream, the more I think about it I can only see it as a miracle. Dreams sometimes happen, miracles - well that's just mumbo jumbo land isn't it? Which is precisely what I would have told anyone if they'd have come up to me ten years ago and said what we would achieve under Alex Ferguson in the next decade, in a style of play incomparable to any English side over the past 30 years (just look at most of the rubbish Liverpool beat during their 'halcyon days' in Europe and see what I mean).

It's impossible to describe why United means so much to so many. I've tried and now given up. People who don't understand will never realise its importance. Although I wouldn't begrudge that the lengths some of us go to to see United play a game of football can border on the nutty it always has its purpose. They mean so much, and so much more than that. They're not a crux - although they are always there during good and bad times. You can see them once a season or go to every game but you'll be welcomed back whenever you want to. Akin to companionship I've grown up realising that if United are playing I want to be there. I may not attend some games, I may not be able to attend, but if I'm not there I feel there is something missing and although there are many great things to life alongside Manchester United, the times I have had supporting them ranks alongside the taste of any of life's greatest pleasures.

Even during the dark days which we so recently put up with there was always something, mainly then a kindred spirit on the terraces that provided the craic that we were missing on the pitch. Now we can admit it - we were really crap back then. Even as a kid when you'd appreciate anything served up, Sexton bored to tears and we only got excited about Atkinson's sides because we hadn't got that worked up for so bloody long. After the ten game opening winning run in 1985 and a capitulation of which Franny Lee would be proud I gave up the hope of ever thinking we'd remove the league albatross from our collective necks. If we couldn't do it that season what hope?

Those end of season home wins which personified the 80s where we thought 'this side will look tasty next season' even disappeared and I begrudgingly accepted that fate had cruelly destined it never to be. Seven years later I forgot all about the previous nonsense I had once spouted and I began entertaining the thoughts as April 1992 arrived that we'd finally do it. Imagine, Manchester United, winning the league again. It had been so long we simply had forgotten how. Tactical naivety and a bad Easter that ranked with the one 1992 years before saw it gone, summed up at Anfield where I was led away by the cops for sticking up for an old lady in the Utd end and put in the Kemlyn Road stands where I, the only Utd fan, enduring the worst day of my life with 12 Scousers spitting at me and singing that song.

I left there as low as I could ever sink. We would never win the league. 12 months later we somehow managed to snatch late two goals against Sheffield Wednesday, which at that time were the greatest moments ever, and finally we were at that promised land. I'd have sold myself to the devil for that one title and as a 1-0 defeat loomed at Old Trafford that day I remember making rash promises to myself, even praying for the first time since enforced assemblies at primary school, saying I'd return to church for the first time in 12 years and thank who ever you did in such circumstances if the course of that season were changed to enable us to win that game. But as with such ridiculous statements, in the passing weeks I passed a few churches and realised how silly it would be: "Er, Vic my old mate, Steve Bruce got a unbelievable brace and Kidd wet himself on the pitch. We all went loopy and ended a 26 year wait. Can you thank whoever". So instead I headed to my church - the Old Crown pub and praised the Lord of Mr Rolling Rock lager.

European travel suddenly arrived on the horizon just as the 1990s started - and forever remembering the classic tales of great low attended trips to Prague and the like I thought 'I'll have some of this'. After a season culminating at Rotterdam I made a promise that - no matter how skint, no matter what the situation - I would try to get wherever United were playing abroad. These trips are unique - and it's hard to imagine that only a few years ago we had just one European tie each season. But with title success came entry into the continually changed European Cup, and we were back playing with the big boys again. And boy did that feel good.

But as I once thought that we'd never win the league, a total and utter lesson taught by a great Barca in a 4-0 defeat at the mighty Nou Camp told me that we were once

again living in cloud cuckoo land if we thought we'd have a chance under those stupid UEFA regulations. But Eric was there and although it's a bit mad to realise we won the thing without him he was the catalyst for all that followed. Forever treasured he gave the team hope, even in his absence. He taught, they listened. May 26th was their exam.

But we're never allowed to see ahead and the defeat against Dortmund hurt - not as much as in 1992 but hard enough. We were that close in a competition where chances don't come that often. It was gone again and European away trips remained as they always were - a wild trip where the football was often secondary to the inebriation.

And so this season arrived. Some good signings but surely still two players short? Well it's still hard to fathom out just what happened and when it started to really clicked. We certainly and gratefully ditched the cautious away styled and played our natural attacking - and counter attack - game. But even after the group games and a bizarre end to the Munich home game ("let's be friends for the last 10 minutes") I was still so unsure. We'd played some cracking games and scored as if we were Dwight Yorke in one of his videos. But we still hadn't beaten either of Barcelona and Munich, only Brondby come the Milan game. Genie, what's it to be? All was soon to be revealed in spectacular fashion.

Milan and Juve came and went and with their elimination came the understanding that we had arrived. Now believing in miracles you look for signs and they were there. Berg's' clearances against Milan. Destiny? Gigg's last gasp equaliser against Juve? Destiny? Whatever, we knew what we had to do in Turin and boy did we do it. Things were beginning to change. Unlike most managers Fergie told his team to look way ahead and not worry about what the future had in store if they were prepared for it all. A master stroke.

One ABU said it all when he told me recently that he was envious of United not just for the trophies and who we are but for the fans, because "you all seem to know each other, you mix, you all act as though you're some sort of clan". Whatever, United fans are a cosmopolitan group and perhaps it's in the face of so much adversity and abuse that we do stand together and look at each other as one of us and other supporters' as one of them. Well, there can't be that many Reds who get on with that many ABUs. Likewise on Euro aways you get to know some of the many familiar faces and livers. Usually there is no stopping the 'clan' - the alcohol abuse is something to behold on these trips, and I speak from firsthand bitter hungover experience. But even those legendary few who have 'great pisshead' status bestowed on them - as the games became more important this year so the mass of Reds became less pissed than usual. The games were suddenly solely becoming the reason for the trips rather than vice versa which was a real and enjoyable novelty.

In Turin after a great stop-off in Nice I did it all the wrong way however. Despite approaching every game with a negative 'we're doomed' attitude the magnitude of this fixture still got to me. I decided to stay off my holy water and watched the proceedings sober. It was a nightmare. As the two goals went in for them not only did I realise that, perhaps for good, the Holy Grail dream was disappearing down the Swanee Po but just how much this defeat would hurt us. Not just in Europe but at home, during a crucial league campaign. There were tears around but I opted for cabbage mode and had a - it's hard to explain just how mad it got - full blown panic attack. I simply could not cope and, a bit like Davros the Dalek, skated round the back of our end watching the game from afar whilst seeing white spots appear before my eyes. Then it (what?) happened. Destiny? Certainly the greatest United performance of any generation and with that third goal the weight on my shoulders was lifted. United fans sang '41 years ago' and there was a look of disbelief on many. I could breathe, we were through to the European Cup Final, and my world was turning upside down. This can't have happened. What's the payback for all this? One league we said - now we've had five leagues, three Doubles and this. I couldn't - and still can't - believe it all.

Normal life in all but carrying out the motions went out of the window from there on in. In reality I went on to 'autopilot' doing everything I should but just thinking of one date, May 26th. Those of us in Turin were unlucky that some back home had nabbed the cheap flights straight after the Juve win whilst we were there - but whilst the non-believers smiled a smile and said 'how nice for you', showing no real sign of comprehension, the secret world that is the 'clan' spoke when together of nothing but plans of travel, tickets and a date with destiny...

And so as the most active ten days in our club's history arrived so the memories of a near lifetime's support came flooding in. As much about off field endeavours as on field (Eric's great moments, the team of '83, Barca in '84, 3-3 at Liverpool, Blackburn in '93) I couldn't get them out of my head. Certainly Europe has had its fair share - from that mental James Brown disco session during halftime ('get on up') in Dortmund (and the Munich PA playing the 'can can' after each goal - what's that all about!) to getting the whole of a packed bar in Nice for Monaco to sing 'What a friend" and their national anthem. In tribute, of course, of the man who dare not be forgotten.

It's been some journey - yet no matter how much fun, no matter what tales and stories, we all knew its purpose - and we were this close to achieving it. Some of those that had been fortunate enough 31 years earlier commented that they could now relax: "We'll enjoy this one because we were nervous like you last time", but no matter that first the league and then the FA Cup were on our minds, the Nou Camp was always there, whistling its tune in the back of our minds.

But don't get me wrong - I was desperate to reclaim our Championship and when I got into the ground at Wembley I realised just how much the FA Cup would always mean, yet in my eyes, the European Cup (as talk of the fact that we'd finished second and it wasn't right suddenly died down) was and is the one.

As an act of total irrationality I'd always had a picture in my head of how THE day would act out if we ever got to a European Cup Final. I didn't realise how close to reality it turned out to be in the end. For once the long held plans that for one Euro away all of our group would finally get off our arses and combine a holiday with a Euro away came true. It took all the flights being full to Barca to happen (plus the ridiculous charges of some of the tour operators - how much were they charging!) but come a late night celebrating yet another Double win (how weird does that sound?) we were all set for an early start to, of all

places, Magaluf.

The sheer volume of travelling United support meant that further afield had to be considered as a viable option and once it was confirmed with 30,000 phone calls that there were both planes and boats that ran from Mallorca to Barcelona daily, a cheap and nasty package deal was sorted - with the condition that no reps half our age would wake us up at 7am to suggest field activities for each day. Many more Reds were having the same line of thought as faces at the games leading up to the Final confirmed that Magaluf would be a tide, if not a sea, of Red. If Magaluf was fairly full of the Red Army I can't imagine what the other resorts would have been like. Mental. Great.

As is my way I got worried that the boat to Barca might a) capsize, b) break down, c) decide it wanted to go to nearby Minorca for the day instead of Barca and we opted for the reasonably priced flight with Iberia that would get us into Barca at midday. As a person who perhaps takes the attitude to have every possibility covered I think - and this is no joke - that arranging for an Arab friend of a friend of a friend of a friend who was over in Mallorca to have a boat ready to take us over just in case Iberia went bankrupt that morning is taking this all a bit too far. But even dedicated jibbers and relaxed Reds were a little bit tense until arrival in Barca was finally achieved.

All the lads together, in a cesspit, smelly apartment situated in a block with teenagers who talked a good story if nothing else was, I suppose, perfect foil and we made the most of it all. Just coming up to season some of the bars and clubs were decent but I found Magaluf nothing more than a wannabe Ibiza, forever living in its shadow and taking a quite bizarre pride in bars that said, on a stunning Spanish island, 'THIS BAR IS OWNED BY BRITS...BRIT FOOD ONLY'. You couldn't find any Spanish people let alone culture in Magaluf and apart from the main mad avenue of late night clubs and bars the town was full of would be Triggers watching episodes of Only Fools & Horses over and over again without leaving their hotel apartment block. But if the Cockney's forever trying to get you into their clubs with the most fucking annoying PR selling routine ever ("Where you from mate...sweet"), each night was superb. Made even better by the continual meets with fellow Reds and a bar war going on to impress the small numbers in town to drink themselves silly at two for the price of one. A few good sing-songs followed, a lot of pulling involving everyone on the trip bar me (no change there then - I'd now resigned myself to the fateful words 'if you don't pull here there is something wrong with you' and was wearing the 'something wrong with me' badge with pride) and some mental times in the late clubs. It was good fun and there were some faces from way back. Well when you hear the call.

But you could tell that the reason for the trip was playing at the back of people's minds. It was there- don't go too mental, don't do anything that might affect things - and I played the lightweight card on the Tuesday not wanting to be out of the game for the biggest day of my life. I didn't, however, plan to be spending my last night as a non-European Champion cleaning the sick out of a full sink after one of our number had, inexplicably, decided to use that as the destination for his vodka and red bull induced vomit. Welcome home - and the bizarre sight of the kitchen spatula being used to clear it out with. I can't imagine that this routine is being played out by anyone in the players' hotel - their minds presumably awash with nerves and anticipation rather than the bloody colour of discharged red bull.

We didn't need alarms to wake us - I doubt if I slept for more than half an hour - and after re-checking that I had my match ticket at least 6 million times we head off in taxis to the airport - the 'Red News Man Utd Drunks On Tour' flag which has been hanging over the hotel balcony safely packed after a night - because I'd been in the apartment early - where it had got so much abuse off the various ABUs walking past on the street that it made me feel good that at least there were some ABU twats around, rather than their ex-members who had given up membership so quickly after Turin and had suddenly declared how they wanted us to win the Cup 'for the whole of England'. However much ABUs do me in, I actually think I prefer the ones who stuck to their guns and didn't want us to win. So many had changed their tune (along with the tabloids) that I couldn't be doing with the people when we got back home who were saying how 'great' it was. Burn off.

There were a number of Iberia flights out to Barca, all ok and a massive relief to see on the flight board. The sea of Red has become a flood and everyone seems to have a form of Utd attire on them today. No Ralph's or Lacoste around. Even that crappy blue zig-zag shirt from the early 1990s is worn - and I would comment on the subject of bad taste but for the fact that my frequently washed (and looking haggard) first ever scarf from 1975 is bedecked around my neck after proudly being worn during the final ten games of the season.

Things take a turn however when we hear our flight has developed a fault in Madrid and is having urgent checks before it flies here. As every other flight departs we're not too worried until an hour delay turns into two and we discover that there is no changing on to any of the other flights. Where is that boat again? However slow the engineers in Madrid may have dealt with the problem, upon hearing that there were a good 100 football fans ready to commit mass murder in Palma Airport unless it's sorted soon got them to work and the delay was to be only that two hours. This hadn't done my manic state of nervousness and tension any good but even worse were the group of 20 Reds who had had their seats double booked by mistake and couldn't get on the next flights bar three of them. So those three with tickets took the available seats left but the sight of the rest of the Reds leaving unable to now get to Barca by any means was gutting.

A quick flight and we're on Barcelona soil - after watching a waiting row of planes (presumably Utd) packed in the air and waiting to land that was like something out of a battle scene in Independence Day. It felt good, everything was going to plan and, most importantly, we were here. We're that close to it all now. We are bizarrely informed that there is a complete blanket ban on any alcohol at the three Barcelona airports for the day to stop trouble - but we can head to the free-flowing booze in the centre. Oh right, and there we were planning to spend the whole day in the airport bar! Whoever thought that one up?

We catch up on news of United's stylish Concorde arrival the previous day, followed closely by Eric on an internal flight here to enjoy it as well and it's the bus into town. The visits in '94 and '98 show us where to go but you can now begin to feel the nerves of everyone, even if

there is the natural bravado to not show it. I'm surprised at how few Reds are active around town until we hear the driver announce 'Playa Catalunia'. It is nothing short of awesome. Reds everywhere and we depart to the Sports Bar nearby passing row after row of Red. This is what's it all about.

The bar is surprisingly empty - everyone is sunning it. As the imagining of what this day would be like first occurred as a kid (like it would have happened with Ashley Grimes!) the one thing I hadn't considered was alcohol. Where does that figure in the scheme of things? Do I go for the Brondby option - so legless I fell asleep - or the Turin panic attack? When you're a self-confessed 'cabbage' these are important things to consider and I veer to the middle ground, a few good cold beers to seek composure but avoid coma.

Not before a walk to take it all in. Sights of the city are for once discarded in this most stunning of places but a walk down La Ramblas is just that, stunning. You can't move for people - predominately United fans - on lamp posts, in bars, hanging out of windows, everywhere - and I can only compare it with being on Sir Matt Busby Way at quarter to three. It was that busy. I was amazed to keep bumping into people and each conversation was the same. How great it was, how great it felt but, Basil Fawltyish, don't mention the game. Perhaps funniest of all was seeing the many tourists who were staying in Barcelona - obviously clueless to just what was going on here today but treating the mass of Reds as if they were one of the sights to see and photograph. Yanks were perplexed, Japanese (Tokyo Reds apart!) amazed - what a club, nobody does it better.

Back to the bar and many of the people who weren't in a position to pay the tout charges seemed quite happy just to be amongst it all, part of it, and enjoy whatever was to be. The amount of Spanish students selling on (where did the tickets come from UEFA?) was amazing and one 'kid' had his only little area signposted in the bar, knocking them out for £200. Good that a student who agreed to sell on for £200 to a group of Reds, was given £40 by one and the Red then ran out of the bar with the ticket like Linford Christie on heat. The kid demanded to know where the Red was staying off of the remaining members of his group and showed his naivety through it all when they readily gave him the name and street of a hotel - perhaps he should have known that they were talking about Manchester and not Barca!

Too many games and too many problems previously made sure that we departed earlier for a game than I have ever, ever known - even going back to days of childhood and getting in to read the programme 50 times over at 1pm. By 6pm the metro was packed - and a cacophony of Stretford End classics. The system of policing when near the ground can best be described as absolutely clueless. They said 5,000 police were in attendance - with two hours to go you would have thought that they'd all buggered off for a siesta. The ends were segregated which involved a long march around the outskirts of the roads and around the ground to get to the Utd section. It was a sea of nervous energy, more Reds walking down the road to the checks than I can ever remember seeing in one place before. The corner of the road was full of the ticketless and those bloody students and as we approached a row of police and horses we could just tell what was going to happen.

It was so stupid and incompetent that I can only believe that they wanted it to happen. What else could explain a system whereby only a few could get in to three or four open spaces between a line of police and where bottlenecks were already developing as people moved to the gaps and the police closed them. This wasn't even the ticket check but horses were bolting in the midst of it all and already they couldn't cope. We dived to the side, slipped through and then watched in amazement as the police adopted an ad-hoc system of freeing the traffic. There was now an hour and a half to go and I began taking photos of it all.

The ticket check was to prove more ludicrous. Again the surge, again the police being too slow and senseless. A Scouser could have planned it better and it was no surprise to see us get through without having to show any trace of a ticket whatsoever whilst on the other side of the road the rise of a police baton could be seen regularly . There was yet more to come as the gates to allow you into the ground were filling up. We were in Gate 4, but the congestion outside Gate 5 was getting bad. I was amazed that only a third of the turnstiles into the ground were open - ridiculous - and to each there were only a few people manning them, slow and again, unable to cope. Top this that one gate remained reserved for 'VIPs & press' which nobody else could use and the tension began to turn to anger. Hardly anyone was getting through and four coppers outside couldn't have looked after themselves let alone organise 1,000 people to get in. We finally got through, before the first of many struggles between stewards and Reds wanting to get in. Every so often they would simply stop people getting in - for this game that is like holding a red flag to a bull. There were more people checking bags than there were police and stewards letting people in and so severe was the search that Paul was removed of an apple from his bag and ticked off for having it (?) and then walked into the ground with 6 other apples, a bottle of water and a bazuka gun still in there. For a ground that regularly holds over 100,000 - and a fantastic arena at that - I was amazed at the level of incompetence, delaying people getting in and a system that didn't stop but caused crushes.

Into the ground and to the top tier where we watched the goings on outside from the back of the terrace with growing incredulity. The telling sign was that so many of us viewing the chaos weren't surprised - and as more Reds unable to move surged forward the stewards manning the few open turnstiles would be pushed back, the Reds would scramble forward and then be batoned for their troubles. All they were doing was trying to get into their seats for the biggest game of their lives yet as people began to be dragged out of the crowd fainting (one lad batoned, collapsing to the ground and then not getting any sort of attention by medics or stewards for about 5 minutes) and it was barmy to think that Gate 5 down the road was even worse. By now we were 15 minutes from kick off and the 5,000 police had obviously woken from their doze as they arrived in force. They did what they should have done in the first place, helping to alleviate the crushing and directing people where to go, clearing Gate 4 in minutes. Yet where common sense was played out here, down at Gate 5, police horses adopted a different more hostile approach and went in gung-ho and

began to panic, pushing the crowd further back. Instead of directing people to a double flow between the now empty Gate 4 and there the police lined up to create a barricade. You could only feel sorry for the people who were going to miss as much as 15-20 minutes because of the clueless activities of others. And guess what? The police and UEFA, who for some reason had billed it as the "highest risk fixture" in Europe since Heysel, blamed the crushing all on ticketless fans and - in their words - had to hold back "an avalanche of several thousand United fans who tried to storm the entrance". Bollocks. This was the downside to May 26th 1999, together with the terrible stories of true hardcore Reds who were pickpocketed of their tickets on the day of the game or weren't allowed in because of a barcode system that your local newsagent wouldn't tolerate.

Watching all this meant that the pre-game shenanigans of Keith Fane trying to win a rap war with a barmy German were largely missed and it was just as the teams made their way into positions that we found ourselves actually in our exact seat. Too big a game to congregate all over the place and a bit of a relief, he says adopting a normal tone!

The Zidane like scam of Beckham wearing a bandage on his leg in training the day before was another Fergie 1999 psychology lesson and the game began in a crescendo of noise and colour. United fans were everywhere - way into the VIP section and more than half way around the ground the other side. There were also a number of Red flags right in their section on all three tiers and I'd put it at a 65,000 turn out,

In daylight, so high up (stairs that made the North Stand at Old Trafford look like a tiny trek) it was a magnificent sight. This was where all journeys led to. A European Cup Final, able to see the whole of the city, sharing it with the people that have been through so much with you and eager for what was to come. But could we do it?

Perhaps I wasn't the best to ask as this was the year when at the start of the season I usually have a five tiered £5 accumulator, and this time I had written out Manchester United - League and European Cup, Sunderland - First Division, Fulham - Second Division and Brentford - Third Division. My mate Tony told me to put it on as intended, instead I opted for two pints of lager and a massive regret. The thought that Brentford weren't top the whole season kept me going but then,to my devastation, they jumped to the top on the last week of the season. With all three other non-Utd bets coming up Tony and I convinced ourselves that the omens were on - and the only way I can console myself that I didn't pick up the massive winnings is that it was the price to pay for the glory. Yeah, right.

After Berg in Milan, Giggs in Juve, the Arsenal semi, my accumulator and the fact that aliens hadn't landed on earth all gave me the feeling as I made my way into the ground that this would be the year. Until I got into the ground of course and I shat myself and muttered to myself "we'll never do it".

But as the game seemed to pass as quickly as one of those computer games you sometimes play, I was amazed at just a few of the people around me. I couldn't believe some of the abuse that was levelled at Utd players. Yeah we didn't play well at the start but losing against Norwich in a midweek farce ten years ago was the opportunity to let them know what was going wrong - but here? It was only a few but I was dumbstruck that instead of giving their all, like the team were doing, this crucial time was being used for negativity.

Maybe it was just the circumstances and the ground - and so many Reds together in the unusual surroundings of being outside Old Trafford - but for much of the first-half the atmosphere was pretty poor, with most sitting down during crucial stages. The suits aren't here you know (well they were but all nicely putting themselves into the front row behind the goal to watch the game)! Half-time came and the hardcore began to take the initiative, geeing up the Calypso and the second half saw all things improve. Still the game went so quickly - the amount of matches that have seemed like years and this one, the one you never want to forget anything about, went by like a cannon.

And then it happened. No, not the goal. Not that, just yet. But as the clock began its desperate decline and the emotions of the Utd fans began to get overwhelming I began to feel something. I know I'm beginning to sound a bit like David Icke during his worst turquoise ramblings here but bear with me. There could have been no more than 5 or 6 minutes left - I could barely talk such was the anguish and I looked around me to see my mother crying, perhaps thinking that she'd never see the cherished win, and the faces of the crowd, torn. You can't even describe what this felt like to be so close to the dream but staring defeat in the face, let alone the senses felt in victory.

I managed just a few words between then and the divine moments that followed. I didn't think that we were out of it yet but I turned to Paul as 5 minutes edged towards four and said: "You know if we don't do this tonight - I know now we'll be back to win it. Not in years but next year. We're going to win it, and if it's not tonight they'll be back next year". Maybe I was just trying to null the pain early, or convince myself but I don't think so. We would have been back.

Then 240 seconds passes I don't know where. It is here where people begin to 'see' the moments or acts that changed the course of history. A 'what if that hadn't have happened' sort of scenario. Later that night I was to hear a clued up lad tell me that there was no doubt that Sir Matt had looked down at the whole game, and thought that as it's United and that's the way we do things it may be fun to make it go to the wire but just at the end say 'right lads, it's time now' as Schmeichel went forward.

Another told me that the bloke who caught an earful off of all the Reds around him when he caught the ball just before the corner when we scored and kissed it with bare seconds left was the catalyst. He had wished it luck and that was the defining moment. Now it may sound like nonsense, and there were many more observations like that throughout the night. All I know is that what we witnessed that night, if it wasn't some kind of divine intervention, then it was certainly Lady Fortuna and her wheel of fate playing the winning card. Or perhaps just because we have a team who do not know how to give in!

But the awesome Beckham twists and turns, desperate to get a cross in and the ball is out of play. Is it seconds or minutes later. I don't know. We have a corner. I then see Schmeichel head up field which for some bizarre reason always make me feel a little safer (as if, it's only worked twice and one of those was disallowed) and I

again turn to Paul. "You know what, the way this season has gone, we'll score here, we're going to score here. It's this season. It's mad". I have to delete the following sentence which is the sexual act I'd do if we did score as I watch - is it played out in slow motion or is that my memory? - the ball goes in the net. I'm fucked. I think Schmeichel has headed it to Sheringham but that's not what happened at all - both goals being totally different in reality to how I imagined them at the time.

My precarious emotional state disintegrates and there are incredible scenes. The third tier is literally shaking like some prop out of a dodgy Hollywood disaster movie - what a way to go I think - and the next thought I know is of perfect clarity. Everyone later tells me that they now knew we'd won it but I'm not so sure. This defeat would be so much worse now surely and I can't get the words 'oh no, golden goal' out of my head. It doesn't stay there long. There is another corner - I grab Paul forcefully by the arm now and tell him the disgusting sexual act that I've just promised, he has to do as well if we score from this one. It's in. What wonderful, concise words. Ole's done it and I still don't know how. And like my non-existent church visit after Sheffield Wednesday, we don't carry out the sexual promise, of which the goats of Magaluf outside our apartments should be extremely grateful that we got the glory before we had to pay the forfeit!

Immediately the magnitude hits me and I can't breathe - I'm gasping for breath and in doing so
become detached again from all that is going on from me. Paul tells me as we drink our umpteenth European Cup winning drink later that he thought I was about to collapse but whatever this dizzy 'feeling' was, I was able to watch the scenes going on around me as if away from it all. I have never seen anything like it and never will again. Wild abandon. Not a good enough word. Bedlam. Perhaps. Mental. Nowhere near. There perhaps isn't one - because what word would count when we can instantly recall it in our minds.

65,000 people going mad - I didn't know what was going on on the pitch but it was that many people on the terraces hearing the best news in the world ever, all at the same moment. I know now that not one of us present that night will ever win the lottery. We had our perfect moment there and then. We had our once in a million chance in life. And play a million European Cup Finals again and not one will end like that.

For once even the ITV (and if you want to know why they cut to commercials so quickly after the game the £185,000 per advert fee may have something to do with it) commentary (well done Clive!) gets it right. Do you mind if I remind you - after all, it seems so fitting.

"Is it going to happen?...They need more...Is there a hero in Red out there waiting to be revered?...They're now creating chances for fun...We're in the last of the ninety minutes....what we need now is the fourth official to hold up a board with about 20 in it...it's not over until it's over...the last final assault...Deflected. Time for a corner. Can Manchester United score? They always score. Peter Schmeichel is forward. Beckham in towards Schmeichel, it's come for Dwight Yorke, cleared, Giggs, with a shot. SHERINGHAM! (PAUSE) Name on the trophy. Teddy Sheringham with 30 seconds of added time played has equalised. They are still in the European Cup. Oh Teddy, Teddy. Extraordinary climax in the Nou Camp stadium...as things stand we will go into extra time with the golden goal hanging like a massive shadow over this final. Unless Ole Solskjaer can conjure up another. You have to feel this is their year. Is this their moment? Beckham, into Sheringham and Solskjaer has won it! MANCHESTER UNITED HAVE REACHED THE PROMISED LAND...and the treble looms large. We've needed a good European Cup Final for a while...What must Matthaus be thinking. With the greatest respect - who cares? Now is that it - or is there something more?...history is made. Manchester United are the Champions of Europe again and nobody will ever win a European Cup Final more dramatically than this. Champions of Europe, Champions of England, winners of the FA Cup, everything their hearts desired. Down and out. Not a bit of it. They are never out. Memories are made of this for ever and a day. United fans will ask 'where did you watch the 1999 European Cup Final. Where did you see Ole Gunnar Solskjaer win it with virtually the last kick of the final. And 50,000 or so will be able to say - I WAS THERE. What a party...".

And then the heavens open. Watching it with a sense of magic, the game on TV is different to the one I saw that night. We certainly weren't as out of it as I thought and did deserve the win. By the end we were creating so many chances that perhaps it wasn't that old docile Lady Fortuna but just constant Utd bombardment. But looking at the scenes of joy played out on the Utd faces captured by ITV in the few seconds between goals, everyone looks as though they knew we'd won it before the second went in. That word destiny again.

But back at the ground, the detachment started to leave me and I rejoined my body (bizarre!). The dizzy spell ended and I lost it. Readily admit it. Many were crying around me but I couldn't stop repeating myself: "We've done it". I must have said it clasping anyone I could at least 500 times. The players were going mental and their celebrations all night showed how United they were and what it meant to them. I could not believe it. Had it happened? Surely not. This is some convincing dream. Pinch myself. Feel it. What's going on? We've done it! As time slowly lapsed I began grabbing all of my mates - not knowing just how violently - and just shouting in their faces: "Remember this now. Take this in. Soak it up. Now. Here. Remember this. It will never get any better. It will never get any better".

My dreams as a kid and view as an adult were now merging. This was even better than I'd pictured it. Our European record, year after year, had got better over the years and finally we had taken the step up in grade . American babbling sports psychologists talk of the 'zone', the area or moment when you are totally focussed and unable to take in anything but that of your task and reaching perfection. I'd say from the 80th minute onwards we were in that zone on May 26th 1999.

The celebrations were awesome - in spite of and not because of the now predictable Keith Fane ensemble - and as that holy trophy was lifted it reached a peak when the players sat down and began taking it in shushed tones to celebrate with the trophy individually. Roy Keane and Scholes getting the sword of honour was a nice touch as my thoughts drifted to all those Reds we knew who are no longer with us - sorely missed people - but there tonight in spirit.

On and on the cheers went - each time the players approached our bit I just bowed down and thanked them, presumably thinking that they could hear through 30 odd thousand people and three tiers - and not really taking in that I'd ripped off my shirt as soon as the second had gone in, swinging it round my head like a demented Leeds fan.

Finally, after two trips round the pitch, the players left, Schmeichel lapping it up deservedly until the last and the only disappointment that Fergie didn't take his own individual bow that we clamoured for. It was now imperative that we stayed until the last possible moment - for that had been how I'd pictured it. It was just heaven. Sitting as the stadium became all but empty and just beginning to take in what had happened, and knowing that it could take years even to sink in. With about 200 Reds left with the same notion of staying until next morning if so be it, the police moved in, looking bemused, especially as the song from all sections between the 200 became "We're not going home" and then a poignant "Happy Birthday Matt Busby".

Next was to regress by about 20 years and see if we could see the players' off. This became easier said than done as the whole ground was being emptied - now nearing 1am - and the gates where we were pushed through were as interesting as a Man City home game - even if we did have that big bloody trophy somewhere nearby. An out of sorts Jordi was nearby (how did he feel about it - he could have been a sub presumably?) and then a host of Utd faces came by. Paddy Crerand. Wilf McGuinnes. And Steve Bruce and Bryan Robson among a number of top Reds - the latter going on for some wild celebrations apparently. Does any other club have players who stay Red - fans just like us - after they've left? No chance of jibbing into the players' do - although one Red managed the dressing room! Time for a toast.

The night ended like no other - because it didn't end. Thankfully the metro was running again and took us back into a joyous city. We end up in the Velvet club, an old haunt that plays host to 100 odd mates. It is perfect. It all means the same to one and all, and there is a collective barmyness in sight as everyone goes ballistic, drunk on emotion, then alcohol and then reaching some sort of nirvana. All the songs are out by the DJ, culminating in all of us collapsing on the floor to SIT DOWN and I don't want this day to end. It's unbelievable and perfect - but I savour it knowing that it will never be like this again. Simply the day was one which could not have been any better, everything about it just right.

But even though this trip is one made on the pitch, the surreality that is a Euro away was never far away. Amidst the hordes of ecstatic Reds in the Velvet there were a number of locals doing perhaps what we may do finding ourselves in similar circumstances. Joining in. Amongst these are three businessmen, so off their heads that they are swinging their briefcases around their heads and eager to tell us all that they are now going to go straight to work in 30 minutes. Now how do you explain that to the boss! Bizarre is never far away and as we depart one joins us in the usual impromptu 'trousers round the ankles' walking tournament amongst Reds taking place. This slaughtered Spanish executive then strips naked and walks down off towards La Ramblas with his briefcase in his hands and his clothes in the other. Amazing!

At 7am we have to leave for the airport, passing the Playa Catalunia which now hosts more United prone sleeping bodies than any hotel that night in Barcelona could possibly have. The airport gives just a few hours sleep but even that bounces by and I wake up wanting to tell people what's just happened. Thankfully they all seem to know as there are more Reds here than City have all season. Back to Magaluf and the celebrations that Thursday night are nothing short of George Best standards.

There are many stories - a well known Red so tired without any hotel bed in Barca after two nights that he just slept on a round-about as the cars honked him and a near 50 year old Red who should know better deciding that it would be fun on the Friday to start the annual 'throw stones at Spanish cars' competition with the prize being a night in the cells. But I'll end tales of the trip on the Thursday - although the celebrations and the piss-taking in Magaluf lasted until the Sunday. And some...

We all knew where to head, and by the early hours one of the bigger Magaluf 'topspots' (sic) was full with 150 Reds out of the 500 crowd. Well choreographed we headed to the stage - and set the scene for THE celebration of the summer played out by possibly every Red wherever they were - each taking it in turns to shush the crowd as they sit on the floor and then one lifts a bottle of Bud as if it were that cherished trophy. This lasted for some time and, for once, had the girls flocking. It was pure magic and as the DJ played Sit Down we all dropped to the floor and started singing 'Champions of Europe'. Could things get any better? Yes! A Liverpool fan comes up to me. He is sticking two fingers up and clearly fuming. I go up to him and say: "No, you've got it all wrong, but good try. It's three trophies we won". With that he turns into the typical bitter 'living in the past mode' and starts talking about Scouse successes 20 odd years ago. "Please go away, you're making me laugh too much...you are just the perfect icing on the cake", and as we piss ourselves he heads off to probably beat up the person who booked him a holiday in Spain the very week that we were to secure glory there! Destiny, irony, it's all here now!

So was it destiny, a great team or both? Well, let's go with both of them because the finest United side I've ever seen did do it all on their own but the way they achieved it has to leave you talking about fate, destiny and bumps in the night. Whatever you think, when it's time to push the play button, those last few minutes are unbelievable. It could only have happened to Manchester United.

So how do I explain it all to non-believers? I can't. But there has not been an experience, a moment, a taste, a book, a piece of music, a food, a sexual moment (but I'll keep trying so don't worry Winona!), a country, a sight, a person, a moment or a sensation that could ever compete with those after the clock had ticked to 90 minutes in Barcelona. On the 26th May 1999.

Some say it might not get any better. Possibly. But as this personal journey of fulfilment has ended so another one can begin - one where we start back on top. And you never know, it might even be bettered. I can't think how, but 3 goals in the dying minutes against a 2-0 up Scouse team would be a start! Perhaps I'll just go mad trying to work out all this fate lark, but if, and just if, there was a Red heavenly body up there or wherever giving a helping hand in Barca I'd like to put in an official request for the 65,000 present to have their Groundhog Day repeated soon so that we can just, if only once more in our lives, be inside the Nou Camp again, with 90 minutes up, about to savour the sweet taste of mayhem once more.

But for now I'm off to watch the game again, wondering just what the wheel of fate and Manchester United have in store for us next.

CHAMPIONS OF EUROPE
WE WERE THERE!
SUBSCRIBERS LIST

CHARLOTTE GRIST
ROGER PURDUE
ALEX COLMAN
ROBERT BRIMICOMBE
ALAN STEPHENS BSc
LYNDON LOMAX
MICHAEL BAILEY
SIMON COOK
ROBIN BAINES
JIM CONNOLLY
DANIELLA CONNOLLY
ROB JONES
"FOR THE BOYS OF '58" D.J.WRIGHT
PADDY McANEA
DAVE WARD FEVRED CLIVE SAFFERY
DARREN HARRIS
SCOTT KERR
TUNA
LEO AUTIO
SHAUN BROMLEY
CHARLES LEDIGO
DEREK CLARKE
DAVID 'DIA' REDFEARN
ALAN APPLEBY
ROB UNDERWOOD
PAUL DANIELSON
STEVE LYNCH
STEVE BELCHER
SEAN FINLAY
PETE, ALNWICK
RUSSELL GIBBS
MIKE BETTNEY (HULL RED)
PAUL SHAVE
PETER QUICK
STUART HENSON
MARK ROBERTS
PAUL SCULLY
LEE PRICE KEVIN
FERRIN
PETER WINKWORTH
PHIL LUFFMAN - BERKSHIRE RED
EDDY SNAPE
NORMY, FROM NORMANTON
JOHN BIRD
GERRY MILLAR
STEVE BUSBY
DAVID AINSCOUGH
PEBBLE
MICHAEL GEOGHEGAN
TERRY AND KAREN PATTEN
MARK PARSONS
PAUL 'LEGS' LEAGAS
GARRY 'GAZZA' SMITH (AUSTRALIA)
MARKUS LEIS
ERIC FAIRCLOUGH
ANNA JONES
DAREN COUNSEL
DEAN GREENBURY
GARY STILL
BRIAN BUTTERWORTH
MICHAEL BUTTERWORTH
ANDREW BUTTERWORTH
A & A.K. BUTTERWORTH
JONAH (HOWARD JONES)

KEVIN (NOSH) BURSTON
CARLY JOANNE BURSTON
SEAMUS McENEANEY
STEVE FISHER (FISH)
CANADA REDS
SHAUN M.FORREST
SIMON RUMSEY
LEE BARNARD
MAGDI SEFARI
IAN CLARK (WIGAN RED)
COLIN CLARK (WIGAN RED) LEAH
CLARK (WIGAN RED)
DAVID HILL (WIGAN RED)
BELSTONE FOX
CARMEN PRITCHARD
JADE PRITCHARD
ALISON CARRUTHERS
JOHANNES SCHNAPP
RALF ENGEL
STUART DYKES
ANDY MARSH
MICK MEADE
JACKIE SMITH
WOODRUSH R.F.C. AND BRUCE
SPRINGSTEEN (THE LAND OF HOPE
& DREAMS)
ALAN JACKSON
STEVE PAGNAM
PAUL NICHOLAS
ANDY FLACK
ROCHELLE LIBSON
CHRISTOPHER CATLEY
PHIL "SNAPPER" SMITH
ANDY DAY (FACE)
STEPHEN BARLOW
TREVOR COOKE
DAVE TULLY
PAUL COOPER
TIM WILLIAMS
FROSTY
KEVIN CHERRY
PAUL DUFF
SHANE MATTHEWS
GARY BRAMWELL
PAUL ATKIN
MICK WOOD
JASON 'OUR KID' CARTER
JOHN SMALES
HANNAH & AMY TAYLOR
IAN STONE
ANDY MOONEY
STEVE HEALEY
GARY LEWIS
MARY WORKMAN
TONY DEVANEY
LEE PARKER
MIKE AND TOM BIRD
PETER ROGERS
PAUL WHEELER
RICK HOLLAND
THE BRANDY FAIRY
BILLY NO MATES
KENNY ROGERS
PHIL DANIELS
GARRY DANIELS
PHIL "HOW MANY MAN.UTD. KITS?"
COVEY
STEFAN SADNICKI
ALEKS SUDAR
CHRIS KARAISKOS
JOE & BRIAN METCALFE
ANDY PHIPPS (BRUM)
KATHRYN

BARRIE PURDUE
FRANK APPLEBY
STUART CAWTHRAY
DUTT
PAUL O'HARE
DAVID CRABTREE
DUNCAN QUINTON
PHIL MALKIN
DERMOT McPARTLAND
PAUL "I'D RATHER BE A BEAVER
THAN A BADGER" BEAVER
SEAN GILMARTIN
EDDIE COLLINS
DOUG SIMPSON
LOUISE DODD
MARK "SNOBBY" HOBSON
JACQUES STAMBOULI
MIKE DEAN
ERIK FROM ROTTERDAM
SEAN HENNESSEY
TOM WINDRIDGE
JOHN WILLISCROFT
STEVE GAFFNEY
KATHRINE BLACKBURN
CARL GUNARATNAM
WILLIAM B.KILMURRAY
MIKE LOWE
IAN DE WAL
DAVE TAYLOR
SEAN REILLY
JASON TAYLOR,
MARIO GEORGIOU (MAZ)
MARGATE RED
ALISON WATT
ROB FERRARI
RICHARD CONNOLLY, "CONNO"
HOWARD COOMBER
PETER HARGREAVES
RAY EVANS
PAUL WINDRIDGE
ANDREW LINDSAY
PETE BOYLE
PHIL WILLIAMS
PETER SHAW
WAYNE IBALL
KERRY DAVIES
MARTIN DAY
JP
ROB PATTINSON
NIGEL APPLETON
PHIL HOLT
TERESA MCDONALD
ANDY MITTEN
EUGENE WEBER
CHARLES BOGLE
TED NESPRI
DR.EDWARD MARTINS
KEVIN JONES
LINDA HARVEY
TONY SMITH
GUY PARSONS
SUE SIMPSON
ROGER BRIERLEY
SID THE ******
STEPHEN RYAN
MARK SOUTHEE
EMMA DODD
RICKY
JULIAN SMITH
MICK BURGESS
BARNEY CHILTON
TONY MYERS